PROHIBITION IN MARYLAND:

A COLLECTION OF DOCUMENTS

Edited by George W. Liebmann

Calvert Institute for Policy Research
Baltimore

All rights reserved.

Published in the United States by the Calvert Institute for Policy Research, Inc., 8 West Hamilton Street, Baltimore, Maryland 21201, tel (410) 752 5887, fax (410) 539 3973, info@calvertinstitute.org

"Mencken, Ritchie, and Prohibition" by Marion Elizabeth Rodgers. Copyright © 2011 by Marion Elizabeth Rodgers. Reprinted by permission of Marion Elizabeth Rodgers.

www.calvertinstitute.org

Library of Congress Cataloging-in-Publication Data available upon request

ISBN 978-0-578-07992-9

Printed in the United States of America

February 2011

PROHIBITION IN MARYLAND: A COLLECTION OF DOCUMENTS

These writings provide a text for our time. They show what a determined state governor can do to change national policy. Albert Ritchie was the only state governor and Maryland the only state that refused to enforce national alcohol prohibition and that refused to enact a "little Volstead Act.". He did so notwithstanding the Eighteenth Amendment's reference to "concurrent enforcement" of prohibition. For five years Ritchie stood alone, until in 1926 Maryland's example was followed by Al Smith's New York and by several other states. By then, the disastrous consequences of prohibition, outlined in Senator William Cabell Bruce's speech in this collection, were manifest. Even so, 'respectable' opinion shrank from the consequences of repeal. All the members of the Wickersham Commission save for the New Orleans lawyer Monte Lemann signed its 1931 report opposing repeal, though the signers all equivocated. Lemann's 'radical' recommendation, that alcohol regulation be returned to the states, was embraced by the Roosevelt administration. Within a month of Roosevelt's inauguration, the Beer and Wine Tax Act was enacted, "interpreting" the 18th Amendment to allow the sale of 3.2% beer and taxing it; within a year, the 18th Amendment was repealed and the sale of alcohol was federally regulated first by the N.R.A. Codes and then by the Federal Alcohol Administration Act of 1935, in effect to this day. In Maryland, true to his de-centralist convictions, Ritchie secured legislation providing for county-level control of alcohol sales, a design still in effect.

Far from rendering him a political pariah, Ritchie's stand secured him three re-elections as Governor, a tremendous ovation at the 1932 Democratic Convention, and an offer of the Vice Presidency from Franklin Roosevelt.

Contrast this with the record of today's national and Maryland politicians on the much-vexed issue of marijuana prohibition. In 1970 the national government, without benefit of a constitutional amendment, asserted plenary jurisdiction over marijuana sales; indeed, it rendered mere possession a federal crime, something that had never been done by the Volstead Act. It was immediately apparent that a large portion of the population was prepared to defy the prohibition. Throughout the ensuing forty years, between 15% and 25% of persons in the 16 to 25 age group report having used marijuana within the preceding 30 days; arrests have averaged 750,000 per year; millions of Americans have been given criminal arrest records; the murder rate in large cities has come to far surpass that during prohibition; a state of near anarchy prevails on our nation's southern border; and proposals for a military role in law enforcement have gained favor in two nations that have hitherto forsworn such intervention. While drugs other than marijuana cause problems, marijuana accounts for the major share by volume and value of illicit drug sales and imports; no other drug is used by more than about 2% of the population. Reliance on the criminal law, with its privileges against search and seizure and self incrimination and its requirement of proof beyond a reasonable doubt has been ineffective. Reliance on it has caused other methods of control to wither; schools, colleges and parents do not test or screen or even question students for fear of incriminating them.

In 1997, there were 13,500 marijuana arrests in Maryland; about one-fourth of those arrested spent at least one night in jail; of those jailed, the mean time served before and after trial was seven days. Four per cent of young black males were arrested on marijuana charges in a single year. P. Reuter, *Assessing the Crackdown on Marijuana in Maryland* (Abell Foundation, 2001). The number of persons jailed was twice the number entering treatment programs. Although marijuana use gives rise to some emergency room visits, some accidents, mild dependence in about 10% of users, and de-motivation of many young people during student years, forty years of experience suggest that the criminal law does not supply the answer to these evils. Three conservative former Latin American presidents, Gavrilia of Colombia, Zedillo of Mexico and Cardoso of Brazil together with the *Report of the Latin American Commission on Drugs and Democracy* have urged the United States to de-criminalize marijuana and institute instead the more effective control strategies taken with tobacco and alcohol.

The present federal legislation provides wide latitude for gradual de-criminalization without the need for an immediate act of Congress. Reclassifying marijuana as a Class III, IV, or V rather than Class I drug is supported by the available science and would allow users to obtain prescriptions on the same basis as drugs like valium; this would allow the consequences of controlled legalization to be assessed. Complete de-classification of the more benign strains of cannabis would remove fear of self-incrimination in those states adopting the same policy and would revive the effectiveness of the Marijuana Tax Act of 1937 in those states, again without need for an act of Congress.

There has been more than an alphabetical declension in American political leadership from the age of Ritchie and Roosevelt to that of O'Malley and Obama. These documents show how true political leaders function, and provide instruction in sound principles of government.

The assistance of The Abell Foundation in funding publication of this work is gratefully acknowledged.

GEORGE W. LIEBMANN

Baltimore, March 16, 2011

The SMART SET

NOVEMBER, 1920

A Litany for Bibuli

By Major Owen Hatteras [H. L. Mencken]

FROM bad gin at $95 a case and from bootleggers who promise to dig up some genuine Rhine wine and are then never heard of again; from home-brewed ale with a faint, cyanotic flavour of dishwater and from home-brewed ale with so much steam in it that it squirts all over the ceiling when the bottle is opened; from old family brandy that has been lying in the wood since 1867 and that now tastes like coffin-varnish or Jap-a-lac and from vermin who invite one to dinner parties in remote suburbs, promising leeringly to get one stewed, and then turn out to have nothing on tap save a quart of drug-store rye whiskey and two bottles of American curaçao; from fat hostesses who insist upon mixing the cocktails and manage to get at least 75% of melted ice into every one; from louts who call one up by telephone at midnight to report that 20 cases of vermouth have just been smuggled ashore from an Italian ship, and who report the next morning that the captain has been jailed and the vermouth seized by revenue agents who demand $6 a bottle for it; from liars who circulate the false news that Scranton, Pa., is still as wet as Hoboken ever was, and who thus tout for the hotels of the town, and break many a trusting heart; from bores who have just returned from Havana, and complain that they drank so much Scotch at 30 cents a drink that they have now been ordered on the water-wagon by the life insurance companies; from idiots who know where authentic Lacrimae Christi is to be had down in Greenwich Village at $1.25 a quart, and who discover, after hauling one about in a taxicab for three hours, that the place closes at 6 P.M.; from home-made wines made of dandelions, elderberries and other such garbage, recommended for the stomach by grandmothers too respectable to be handed over to the police; from barbarians who invite one to dinner and then serve only *one* cocktail; from Presidential candidates who run as wets in New York and as drys in Elyria, Ohio; from police sergeants in small towns who volunteer to show one where to get a safe drink at $7 a pint, and then guzzle half the bottle in lieu of a *pourboir;* from members of the Elks who manage to get beautifully snooted every night, but always keep sober enough to avoid telling one where they get it; from cuties who go with one to studio parties, and horn into the gin with such voracity that the host gets cold feet and begins to hide his reserve stock; from old friends who betray the confidence of years and shame the Christian religion by trying to deceive one with grape-juice reinforced with 6% of denatured alcohol; from Herbert Kaufman, who lets it be whispered that he has 3,000 bottles of Culmbacher cachéd in Tarrytown, and then never invites one out to see his collection of Cézannes; from the kind of Scotch bootlegged by one of the embassies in Washington, and from San Francisco grappo; from moonshine corn whiskey, two days old, at $30 a gallon, and from Prohibition spies who agree to get one a case of genuine Chambertin for $27, and then try to palm off a case of corked California Barbera; from non-alcoholic vermouth and from synthetic Dubonnet; from near-beer reinforced by the addition of a cake of yeast to every *Achtel;* from hard cider that turns out to be full of salicylic acid and from absinthe in bottles showing the coat-of-arms of the Glassblowers' Union of Allentown, Pa.—good Lord, deliver us!

* * *

GOVERNOR ALBERT RITCHIE
SECOND INAUGURAL ADDRESS
JANUARY 9, 1921

One of the contributory causes of this Federal invasion of the pocket-books of the people, is the maintenance of an enormous and growing overhead of bureaus and commissions, of which some are not needed, others should be curtailed and still others do work and spend money for purposes which should be turned back to the States, because they belong to the realm of State Government.

The most outstanding illustration today of the latter class relates to the enforcement of the 18th Amendment. For this purpose the Federal Government has already appropriated $9,379,770 for the next fiscal year and the Federal Budget Bureau has just approved $28,500,000 more.

The people of Maryland must, of course, pay their proportionate share of this vast sum of $38,000,000. In addition, you will be asked to enact the Volstead Law in Maryland, and place upon our people a further direct State charge which would impose a burden of millions upon them.

It is not my purpose in this connection today to complain of an unwarranted invasion by the Federal Government of the liberties of the Maryland people. It is not my purpose now to contend that this vast burden of taxation must in no event be imposed. It is not even my purpose to contend that under no circumstances must Maryland join in what so large a part of her citizenship honestly believe to be a denial of their guaranteed rights.

But it is my purpose to ask that you do not do this thing unless and until Maryland has had her day in court, and her people have had the opportunity to decide for themselves, as free Americans at the polls, whether they want this restriction on their liberties or whether they do not.

Prohibition enforcement is only one instance of the encroachment of Federal power upon the functions of the States. Just now it holds the stage and holds it so prominently as to obscure the fact that after all it is simply one phase of the only question of principle upon which the American people can with consistency divide politically today. That is the wisdom of a score of Federal encroachments upon the rights of the State, of which prohibition enforcement is only one.

Take the Federal appropriations for the support of all sorts of social, economic and educational undertakings, which are by nature local, and the alarming increase in the demands for more.

These are perhaps most familiar to us as grants of Federal Aid for specific subjects, provided the State matches the grant with a like amount. Of these Maryland receives from the Federal Government three-quarters of a million dollars for roads, several hundred thousand dollars for agriculture, and lesser amounts for health and vocational education.

So long as the practice continues to exist, and other States take advantage of it, there is no reason, of course, why Maryland should penalize herself by refusing to accept her share.

But could not Maryland do all these things just as well herself without Federal help? Does anyone think, for instance, that our road system would be less notable if we had built it all with our own resources? Or that our public health work, which has been directed and developed by some of the great physicians of the country, who make Maryland a medical center of the world, would be any less advanced if we had paid for it all ourselves?

Might it not, in fact, have all been even better done, had we relied exclusively on our own resources and self help? Private business and private interests are sure to suffer both in initiative and in effort if they succeed in persuading the Federal Government to give them all the grants and credit and aid of various sorts which they are demanding at the hands of Congress. Why do not public interests suffer in the same way from the same cause?

The original purpose was, of course, a worthy one. It was a method whereby the Federal Government encouraged agriculture and mechanical education in States which did not have the resources and could not reasonably provide them for themselves, and also, perhaps, a reward from the Federal Government for State efforts along these lines.

But surely in all the States the need for this has passed. It tends directly now to encourage political manipulation and trading for special favors to special localities and to special interests, which is in no way helpful to the National good.

The granting of Federal Aid generally means the taking of Federal control in a manner which could not be done directly under the Constitution. The Federal Government always demands the right of supervision. It can withdraw its appropriation at any time if its directions are not observed by the State. It is really a trade in which the State gives the Federal Government the right to superintend activities which primarily belong to the State in exchange for the payment by the Federal Government of one-half the expenses of administration. And after all, it simply means taking money out of one pocket and putting it in another.

Then comes increased expense. Then the everlasting annoyance of Federal inspectors and investigators and agents, often irresponsible and incompetent, prying into business which ought to be private and into affairs which ought to be personal, and exercising supervision and demanding reports and audits of almost every conceivable kind. Then an inevitable impatience, and finally a lack of respect for law itself.

Who knows, for instance, to what length the Federal Government might sometime go if some of the proposals for Federal Aid to education should be adopted? Education is a local function. It should not be centralized. It is inherently the State's right to see to the education of its own boys and girls, uncontrolled and untrammeled by outside influences.

Just as it is the State's duty to provide a competent public school system for its children of all creeds and denominations, so when recognized creeds or denominations maintain competent schools of their own, such, for example, as the parochial schools in Maryland, it is the State's duty not only to leave them alone, but to protect them too, so that freedom of religion and freedom of education may be inviolately maintained.

A great, a fundamental, an enduring principle is at stake. No question of sectional advantage, of group gain, of party benefit or of class. But a principle which reaches back through the ages, past the industrial and economic eras and the mighty wars which have made our country great, straight into the very heart of our institutions.

That principle calls for an end to centralization. It is no the call of class or of party or of creed. It is the call at las of principle. It is the call of the people of this country, fron city and hamlet and farm, to be allowed to lead their lives in freedom and in liberty, so long as they live them cleanly an(honestly, and do not hurt their neighbors or injure society. I is the call to resist unwarranted encroachment of every kind by the Federal Government upon the sovereign rights of out State and the guaranteed liberties of our people; and, with head held high and standing erect, no matter if we stand alone to proclaim once more that Maryland, relying on the integrit of a native manhood and womanhood which has never failed demands that every question which concerns her people alone shall be decided as her people will.

ADDRESS BY H. H. WALKER LEWIS

THE BATTLE OF FRANKLIN FARMS

1 F.,2d 954 (1924)

In the 1920's, when this brief history opens, 3 West Franklin Street, Baltimore, was a three story town house squeezed in between the Rochambeau Apartments on its East and a solid row of nondescript brick buildings on its West. Built in about 1840, its pleasing proportions stemmed back to the classic simplicity of the Georgian period. Its oversize windows had a cheery, open look. Its massive mahogany front door and brass knocker glowed with hospitality.

In the more stately era of its birth, the location had been on the outskirts of Baltimore and at one time had been known as "Howard's Woods". Rochambeau's troops had camped there in 1782 after the great victory at Yorktown. In the early 1800's the area gained further distinction when part of the block became the site of the Roman Catholic Cathedral.

For a time there had been lawn, trees, a carriage house, and even a view of the Washington Monument. Now, 3 West Franklin Street seemed smothered by its neighbors. The only breathing space that remained was a little courtyard, dark and undistinguished. Undistinguished, that is, except for one thing, the lively imagination of Congressman John Philip Hill, whose wife had inherited the property from her mother.

John Boynton Philip Clayton Hill, later self-simplified into just John Philip Hill, was born in Annapolis, Maryland, in 1879. His place of birth, it seems, was a whim of fate. Years later when drumming up votes in the Third Congressional District, he marched into an East Baltimore home, stopped an astonished housewife in the midst of her sweeping, and declared with a grandiloquent gesture, "Madame, I might have been born in this house if my mother had not been away visiting at the time." It is said that he managed to find more Third District homes to be almost born in than there were beds for George Washington.

In 1900 he tied for top honors at Johns Hopkins and in 1903 graduated from Harvard Law School with such eclat that he was asked to teach government at Harvard, which' he did. After a year he came to Baltimore and in 1910 was appointed United States Attorney for Maryland, an office which he held until 1915, when he left with the National Guard for service on the Mexican border. He had turned his talents to'many things besides law, including politics, military activities, and, last but not least, lectures on government at Johns Hopkins, Goucher, and The University of Virginia, the substance of which were published in 1916 in an excellent little book entitled "The Federal Executive".

After World War I, from which he emerged as a lieutenant colonel, politics absorbed him. In 1920 he was elected to Congress as a Republican from the normally-Democratic Third Maryland District. In this period, the most inflammatory of all political issues was prohibition. The fact that Maryland was one of the few states that rejected a local enforcement law showed the temper of a majority of its citizens. On this issue John Philip Hill could hardly have been a more loyal son of his own State. He was a wholehearted, dyed-in-the-wool, 100% anti-prohibitionist.

Prohibition was the most philanthropic political phenomenon that we have ever experienced. Its sole motivation was the alleged benefit of others. No one wanted prohibition for himself, it was always for the good of someone else.

The backbone of Prohibition was in the rural areas, but it was designed for the salvation of city people. Righteousness demanded that city dwellers be parched dry for their own good, even though farmers were to remain free to convert their apples and fruit juices into time-honored beverages.

Section 1 of the Volstead Act defined "intoxicating liquor" as any beverage containing more than $\frac{1}{2}$ of 1% alcohol, but a neat little amendment was tacked onto the punishment section stating that:

> "The penalties provided in this Act against the manufacture of liquor without a permit shall not apply to a person for manufacturing nonintoxicating cider and fruit juices exclusively for use in his home. . . ."

The avowed purpose of this amendment was to spare farmers from a pitiable plight. Representative John A. Moon, of Tennessee, pointed out that:

11

"If a farmer should permit a keg of sweet cider to ferment and contain more than ½ of 1% of alcohol and did not throw it away immediately on knowledge thereof, he would have to pay fines or have to go to jail and probably lose his farm."

Farm-lovers all over Congress suddenly discovered that the making of cider from non-salable apples was essential to the national economy. And in the general spirit of thinking of the other guy, a tearful plea was made for citizens of Italian and Greek birth, "whose custom it is to make a small quantity of wine for consumption in their homes".

Thus were cider and fruit juices exempted from penalty if made in the home for domestic consumption, provided only that they were nonintoxicating in fact, whatever that might mean. Unlike other potations, they were not arbitrarily limited to ½ of 1%. Nor did it seem likely that revenue agents would be able to get into people's homes to see if their cider and fruit juices proved intoxicating when imbibed.

Some people liked to think that this exception showed proper respect for God. After all, it was not the farmer who made fruit juice ferment. But whether or not it exemplified reverence, the exception had broad support from the agricultural areas. In fact, it has been authoritatively stated that the Volstead Act could not have been passed if it had outlawed the pious enthusiasm with which farmers salvaged their bruised apples and other fruit. On the other hand, righteous regard for the souls of city dwellers required that beer and other urban beverages be kept strictly below ½ of 1%.

From the very first John Philip Hill's heart bled for the city dwellers. In addition, it bled for John Philip Hill, and no one was quicker than he to sense the campaign possibilities. From his first moment in Congress he became a thorn in the flesh of the Drys. He challenged Wayne B. Wheeler to debate. He kept up a stream of needling correspondence with Prohibition Commissioner Roy A. Haynes. He denounced the minions of the Anti-Saloon League. At every opportunity he pilloried the outrageous discrimination in favor of the farmers.

From a political standpoint it paid off magnificiently. In January, 1923, a debate in New York with Wayne B. Wheeler, General Counsel of the Anti-Saloon League, drew not only a capacity house but also headlines. In April, a mass meeting turned out in Cumberland for his denunciation of George W. Crabbe and the local Drys. In July, more headlines heralded his attacks on Roy A. Haynes. It was heady stuff but, thus far, past was merely prologue. It was not until the autumn, that he really hit his stride.

In the format of the Baltimore *Sunpapers,* the back page customarily carries the most important local news. It is here that readers look for hometown headlines. In fact, the true Baltimorean normally starts here, knowing that he will be rewarded with things that matter, unencumbered by items about the doings of Congress, the President, and other outsiders. For a time John Philip Hill made the back page his home.

On Wednesday, August 22, 1923, it sported a large picture of him with the following story:

"Congressman John Philip Hill today served formal and solemn notice on the Probation Commissioner and the Collector of Internal Revenue for Maryland that on or about noon, September 7, he will begin producing non-intoxicating fruit juices for use in his home. His intention is to get from the prohibition department a definition of 'non-intoxicating' as used in the Volstead Act.

"When the new regulations concerning the manufacture for home use of cider and similar fruit juices were issued; he said, 'I expect to find the definition in them. But after reading them carefully I find that 'non-intoxicating' is defined simply as 'non-intoxicating'.

"So I'm going up in the country and get some grapes and go down on Baltimore Street and get a press, and I'm going to start making grape juice. I have written the Prohibition Commissioner to ask him just when I should stop fermentation. In his answer I expect to learn after two years of inquiry just when a beverage ceases to be non-intoxicating and becomes intoxicating."

Reporters were prompt to interview local officialdom.

"Before I can do anything", said Edmund Budnitz, Director of Prohibition in Maryland, "I'll have to look up the regulations."

"The question will require elucidation", said William H. Pohler, his chief clerk.

"Politics!" sniffed George W. Crabbe, Superintendent of the Maryland Anti-Saloon League.

On Wednesday, September 5, the paper carried a back page picture of John Philip embarking on a hydrometer hunt, in the capacity of "private citizen and seeker for truth".

On Thursday, another picture showed him with baskets of Anne Arundel County grapes. "In making my grape juice", he said, "I will follow the directions of the Department of Agriculture." There was, however, a cloud on the horizon. He could find no hydrometer that would register the alcoholic content of fruit juice. The Bureau of Standards in Washington advised him to distill and measure a known

13

amount, but this was against the law. He had been told that an ebulliometer would do it. This was a costly instrument, however, and the Prohibition Enforcement Unit had the only one available. "What's a poor man to do?" he demanded.

On September 7, the paper reported that the great experiment to learn the truth about prohibition had begun. With his staunch ally in science, Captain W. H. Stayton of the Association against the Prohibition Amendment, Hill had waited fifteen minutes for government agents to show up and when none arrived he proceeded to squeeze his grapes, amid photographers' flashes in his cellar.

"Tomorrow" said John Philip, "I'm going to take samples of my stuff and ask the Prohibition Department for an analysis. Then after ten days I'm going to ask another test and so on until I am ordered to stop fermentation. In ninety days I'm going to bring over the Judicial Committee of the House and ask them to sample my nonintoxicating fruit juices."

On September 8, the headline read, "HILL'S GRAPES BUBBLING AND HE AWAITS RESULTS."

On September 10, Congressman Hill was reported in Southhampton, Long Island. "But" said the paper, "His Spirits go Marching On."

On September 18, it was reported that samples tested by Penniman & Browne, Chemists, registered a high of 6.31%. John Philip so advised Prohibition Director Haynes and penned a further appeal:

"My grape juice is still fermenting and the alcoholic content is daily becoming greater. I therefore request an immediate answer."

Haynes and his minions purported to remain stonily aloof. But on September 27, just after an official pronouncement that the Prohibition Unit would have no part in Hill's shenanigans two agents arrived at his home with an ebulliometer. John Philip greeted them as long lost friends and enthused over their miraculous contraption. "The first ebulliometer ever seen in Maryland," it was reported. It was a device for measuring boiling point, but after John Philip had helped the agents do this with every sample in the cellar, it was discovered that they did not have the chart needed to translate boiling point into alcoholic content. The agents retired to Washington, while John Philip retired to the privacy of his parlor, already filled with representatives of the press.

On September 28, the back page headlined that Haynes was awaiting a report on Hill's wine. But it seemed that the Congressman had amount, but this was against the law. He had been told that an ebulliometer would do it. This was a costly instrument, however, and the Prohibition Enforcement Unit had the only one available. "What's a poor man to do?" he demanded.

On September 7, the paper reported that the great experiment to learn the truth about prohibition had begun. With his staunch ally in science, Captain W. H. Stayton of the Association against the Prohibition Amendment, Hill had waited fifteen minutes for government agents to show up and when none arrived he proceeded to squeeze his grapes, amid photographers' flashes in his cellar.

"Tomorrow" said John Philip, "I'm going to take samples of my stuff and ask the Prohibition Department for an analysis. Then after ten days I'm going to ask another test and so on until I am ordered to stop fermentation. In ninety days I'm going to bring over the Judicial Committee of the House and ask them to sample my non-intoxicating fruit juices."

On September 8, the headline read, "HILL's GRAPES BUBBLING AND HE AWAITS RESULTS."

On September 10, Congressman Hill was reported in Southhampton, Long Island. "But" said the paper, "His Spirits go Marching On."

On September 18, it was reported that samples tested by Penniman & Browne, Chemists, registered a high of 6.31%. John Philip so advised Prohibition Director Haynes and penned a further appeal:

"My grape juice is still fermenting and the alcoholic content is daily becoming greater. I therefore request an immediate answer."

Haynes and his minions purported to remain stonily aloof. But on September 27, just after an official pronouncement that the Prohibition Unit would have no part in Hill's shenanigans two agents arrived at his home with an ebulliometer. John Philip greeted them as long lost friends and enthused over their miraculous contraption. "The first ebulliometer ever seen in Maryland," it was reported. It was a device for measuring boiling point, but after John Philip had helped the agents do this with every sample in the cellar, it was discovered that they did not have the chart needed to translate boiling point into alcoholic content. The agents retired to Washington, while John Philip retired to the privacy of his parlor, already filled with representatives of the press.

On September 28, the back page headlined that Haynes was awaiting a report on Hill's wine. But it seemed that the Congressman had

15

already gotten inside information. There was said to be 11% in one sample and John Philip was loudly proclaiming 12% as the permissible limit. He wrote Attorney General Daugherty. He laid the matter before the Council of Governors. He placed a call for President Coolidge.

It was a woman who decided that matters had gone far enough. Mabel Walker Willebrandt, Assistant U. S. Attorney General in charge of prohibition enforcement, directed the District Attorney for Maryland to take action. At first, U. S. Attorney Amos W. W. Woodcock demurred. He and John Philip Hill had been brother officers in the Maryland National Guard, and he knew that Hill hoped for the publicity of an indictment. But orders were orders and on October 4, the *Evening Sun* reported that the matter would be submitted to the Grand Jury.

The Congressman's reaction was prompt and characteristic. The U. S. Attorney and the members of the jury received the following formal invitation:

JOHN PHILIP HILL, M. C.

Requests the Pleasure of the Presence

of

THE FEDERAL GRAND JURY

At an Informal Inspection of his Home, 3 West Franklin Street

Thursday, October 11, at ten o'clock

Refreshments

Pre-War and Otherwise

The climax came quickly. Col. Woodcock did not seek an indictment but instead obtained a court order padlocking John Philip's cellar. It was the first such proceeding known to have been taken against a private dwelling, although it was standard practice to padlock speakeasies under the nuisance provisions of the Volstead Act. In keeping with this procedure, an order for a temporary injunction was signed by U. S. District Judge Morris A. Soper.

This was on Thursday, October 11, and on that afternoon the back page of the *Evening Sun* carried a picture of John Philip Hill applying red, white, and blue seals to his cellar door, each bearing a profile of President Abraham Lincoln. The same afternoon an order came through from the War Department promoting the Congressman from Lt. Col. to Colonel in the Reserve. "This is my lucky day", he said.

The day may have been lucky, but the ensuing period was one of discouragement. For more than a month few, if any, newspapers had gone on the streets of Baltimore without John Philip Hill's name or picture on the back page. But there was reticence about matters pending before the courts and the publicity dried up. There were occasional headlines, such as, "Arthur W. Machen, Jr., President of Maryland Branch of Assn. Opposed to the Prohibition Amendment will represent Congressman Hill" and "Hill Answer Denies Volstead Law Infraction", but for a public man with his hunger for print this was a starvation diet.

Besides, the injunction proceeding seemed to have been put on ice. The Court was reluctant to·be used as a stepping stone in Hill's progress towards re-election, and the District Attorney could think of hundreds of things he would rather do than try the case. It was argued that since Hill had not been arrested he should be willing to give way to those who were in jail waiting trial, and the Prohibition Unit obligingly went on nabbing offenders faster than they could be tried.

Hill's attorney, Arthur W. Machen, Jr., was one of the most astute and forceful lawyers of his day. But strain and struggle as he might, he never could get a date set for a full scale trial. Either the Court or the U. S. Attorney or both always had weighty reasons why some other time would be better.

And so the wine experiment was left, temporarily, in a stalemate. To one of John Philip Hill's temperament, this was galling. But even aside from all the publicity, he had gained at least one victory. On September 7, 1923, Roy A. Haynes, goaded beyond endurance, had answered a letter of Hill's in a way that made the front page in Baltimore and many other cities, summarized by the *Evening Sun* of September 18, in the following headlines:

HAYNES ADMITS DRY LAW DISCRIMINATES
IN FAVOR OF FARMERS.

SAYS IN REPLY TO HILL'S QUERY MEASURE WAS NEVER
INTENDED TO CHECK THEIR ALCOHOLIC RIGHTS.
VAGUENESS OF RULE INTENTIONAL TO ALLOW
MAKING WINES AND CIDER.

MUST BE FARMER TO ENJOY THIS PRIVILEGE, IS INFERENCE,
AND CITY DWELLER WHO USURPS IT IS LIABLE
TO ARREST.

This of course, is just what John Philip had been claiming all along.

Any other person might have been content to rest on his laurels at this point. But not Hill. He was all bounce and brass and he had an election coming up in November.

In June, 1924, he sailed for England to address the anti-prohibition conference in London. After his return it was apparent that the ocean voyage had exerted a benign influence. "He had", he said "decided to become a dirt farmer and raise apples in the backyard of Franklin Farms."

Under the Volstead Act, cider was in a preferred position. It was not covered by the ½ of 1% limitation and was not illegal unless in fact intoxicating. At what point would cider be considered intoxicating? No one, of course, knew, but John Philip had by this time managed to worm out of Prohibition Commissioner Haynes that farmers were not molested if their cider stayed under 2.75%. This, of course, was only farmers. City slickers who bought apples for beverage purposes were outside the pale of the law according to Haynes.

This was all the encouragement that John Philip Hill needed. "I am delighted to be at home", he said. "It is a most auspicious time to be in Maryland. The cider season is approaching and throughout the State farmers are getting ready to press the legal juice from the Maryland apple.

"I shall go to work at once to convert the land adjoining my home in Franklin Street into a small farm and make for myself a press in accordance with the recommendations of the Department of Agriculture.

"On September 8, next, at noon, I shall press the legal juice of the Maryland apple into the cask. Of course, I shall request Federal Prohibition Commissioner Haynes to advise me at which point I must stop developments if, by chance, the apple juice shall enter upon the various stages of fermentation, since I desire to obey all laws, in accordance with the platforms of the Republican, Democratic, and Progressive Parties."

The so-called "land adjoining my home" was a small brick-paved courtyard, inhabited only by stink-wood trees and trash. Except for an entrance-way leading in from the sidewalk, it was completely enclosed on two sides by Mr. Hill's house, on a third by the frowning battlements of a seven-story apartment building, and in the back by a high brick wall.

But now, under the aegis of John Philip's green thumb, it was transformed. The stink-woods had miraculously become apple, their boughs laden with forbidden fruit tied on with string. Here and there in tubs stood smaller trees which had been apple from birth. An old fashioned cider press occupied the center of the stage and in the background loomed a freshly painted barn through whose windows

18

peered contented cows. It was the look of these gentle ruminants that was most arresting. Although convincingly bovine, one wore horn-rimmed spectacles and the other sported a large cigar.

Hill's agricultural miracle drew admirers like a magnet. The great Henry L. Mencken, himself no lover of prohibition, was an early visitor and inspired, if he did not write, the following tribute in the *Evening Sun:*

> "Under the spreading apple tree Congressman John Philip Hill stood today and watched the birth of Franklin Farms.

> "As proof of Mr. Hill's wizardry in enticing trees to grow, there stands this afternoon an orchard of seven healthy trees, their branches drooping beneath the weight of cider apples. The brick wall in the rear has become a red and white striped barn and over the door is the legend 'Franklin Farms'.

> "Mr. Hill's painstaking fidelity to nature has gone even further. On either side of the barn door is a window and from each window leans a fragrant breathed cow, so lifelike that one expects a contralto 'Moo' at any moment. By some freak of nature they resemble George W. Crabbe, Superintendent of the Maryland Anti-Saloon League, and Prohibition Commissioner Roy A. Haynes. When Mr. Hill's attention was called to this he evidenced a surprise which was equaled only by his profound interest in the phenomenon."

To a casual observer, the cows seemed to have been sired by the cartoonist of the Baltimore *Sun,* but this was indignantly denied. "Nature's ways are wondrous to behold", said Mr. Hill.

On September 8, Franklin Farms was formally dedicated, amid musical renditions of "Down on the Farm" and "In the Shade of the Old Apple Tree". On September 9, farmer Hill, in overalls, started making cider. After a decent interval, on September 16, the *Evening Sun* reported:

> "HILL WILL STAGE PARTY TO FORCE HAND OF HAYNES. PLANS TO INVITE FRIENDS TO DRINK 2.75% CIDER.

> "Mr. Hill estimates that tomorrow at noon his cider will contain 2.75% alcohol. He will then pasteurize it to stop fermentation and on Saturday night will invited in his friends to drink."

On Wednesday, the paper explained how Hill planned to pasteurize his cider, by immersing jugs of it in 140 degree water, and on Thursday reported:

"CONGRESSMAN WORKS ALL NIGHT TO KEEP
APPLE JUICE IN BOUNDS.

" 'Anybody who wants to help me force Probation Commissioner Haynes to testify for 2.75% beer and is willing to take a chance of arrest is invited to my party Saturday', Hill said.

" 'The cider will be labeled "2.75% cider, legal for the farmer". There will also be some beer marked, "Less than ½ of 1% beer, legal for the city man".' "

Each day the headlines grew and by Saturday everyone in town was Hill's friend, eager to taste his cider. Sixty-five gallons disappeared in about as many minutes, along with a few swigs of near-beer and mountains of doughnuts.

In spite of rain, the turn-out had been so enormous and so highly publicized that it could not be ignored. Not by Haynes; not by Wheeler; not even by Coolidge. On Tuesday, September 23, the headlines ran:

WOODCOCK TOLD TO TAKE ACTION ON HILL PARTY.
MRS. WILLEBRANDT, ASSISTANT ATTORNEY GENERAL
ORDERS INVESTIGATION.

There was no dilly-dallying this time. On September 24, Hill was indicted by the grand jury, and on September 30, he was arraigned. He pleaded not guilty and his lawyers, Arthur W. Machen, Jr., and Shirley Carter, asked for an immediate trial, but Judge Soper wanted no campaigning in his courtroom and set the case for November 10, after the election.

Franklin Farms proved as fruitful of votes as of apples. On November 4, Hill swamped his Democratic opponent, Dr. George Heller, by almost two to one.

On Monday, November 10, the trial got underway in the very court in which for five years Hill had himself been the chief prosecuting officer. Presiding was Federal Judge Morris A. Soper who had been appointed to the U. S. District Court in 1923. Before that he had been for seven years Chief Judge of the Supreme Bench of Baltimore City; later, in 1931 he was to be elevated to the Circuit Court of Appeals for the Fourth Circuit. There has been no better beloved and more respected judge in Maryland. On the occasion of his eightieth birthday, on January 24, 1953, the *Sun* was to refer to him as the youngest octogenarian ever to adorn the State, a man so jaunty, so well-adjusted, and so lovable that it makes us all feel happy just to see him.

Judge Soper was regarded as a bulwark of Prohibition. But no one could have handled a trial with greater dignity and impartiality.

20

Hill had been indicted for manufacturing and possessing intoxicating wine and cider, and for maintaining a public nuisance at his home at 3 West Franklin Street. Judge Soper was to find the nuisance charge unsupported by the evidence, and even at the outset it was apparent that the crucial issue was whether Hill's wine and cider were intoxicating. On this Judge Soper held that the ½ of 1% limitation was not applicable, and that the wine and cider were not illegal unless they were intoxicating in fact.

At the time, Judge Soper's ruling was of great legal significance. Notwithstanding the language and the background of Section 29 of the Volstead Act, the Prohibition Enforcement Unit claimed, as against city dwellers, that any beverage was legally intoxicating which contained more than ½ of 1% of alcohol by volume. There was powerful backing for this view and it was strongly urged upon the court by U. S. Attorney Amos W. W. Woodcock and his talented assistant, James Treat Carter. The Court's ruling to the contrary was a landmark.

What then was in fact intoxicating? Hill's witnesses described prodigious feats of drinking without intoxication. Anthony Dimarco, who said he had once had the honor to be defeated for Congress by Mr. Hill, testified that he had drunk quantities of Franklin Farms cider without adverse effect.

"Perhaps you do not know when you are drunk", said Mr. Woodcock.

"Oh yes I do!" retorted Mr. Dimarco.

The Government, on the other hand, produced people who tottered at the mere mention of alcohol. One was the eminent and respected Dr. Howard A. Kelly, of Johns Hopkins fame. He testified that anything over ½ of 1% was intoxicating. This was just what the prosecution wanted, but on cross examination Dr. Kelly said that even the minutest drop must be considered intoxicating.

In a sense, also, Dr. Kelly was trapped by his own eminence. Medical confreres who differed with him about prohibition longed to see the great man stumble and spent hours combing through his mountainous writings. With their help, Hill's attorneys led him gently out onto a limb, later described by a spectator as follows:

"Dr. Kelly", asked Shirley Carter, "have you always opposed the use of alcohol?"

"Always", said the good Doctor.

"Have you never recommended its use?"

21

"Certainly not! It is a poison."

"Dr. Kelly, have you contributed to the medical literature on operative gynecology?"

"Perhaps", said the Doctor, who had written more than most individuals read.

"Perhaps in this book?" said Mr. Carter, producing a medical tome of inspiring proportions. "And would you kindly read the passage which I have marked."

And there, for all to see, the great Dr. Kelly had in 1898 extolled the virtues of whiskey eggnog and recommended it for both nutrition and stimulation.

Another government witness, Dr. Harvey W. Wiley, also testified that any alcohol is intoxicating, even the least quantity. He had been Chief Chemist of the Department of Agriculture for thirty years and, in puffing up his professional qualifications for the benefit of court and jury, the District Attorney brought out that he held a degree from the University of Berlin. This was all the lead that Mr. Machen required. Soon he had Dr. Wiley reminiscing happily about beer parties as a feature of German student life. He had often drunk beer all night, he said, without missing any classes next day. And, he recalled with special pride winning a prize by walking a straight line after thirteen quarts of beer. After these revelations even the hardiest of Hill's witnesses seemed to hang their heads in shame.

It was clear that the element of time had also to be considered, since the wallop of an alcoholic beverage depends on how fast you drink it. To the defense, the appropriate pace was that of a Kentucky colonel contentedly sipping a julep on his wisteria covered veranda; to the prosecution, it was a question of whether one would drown before becoming inebriated. The choice was between the parlor and the pig sty.

On this issue, Judge Soper was something less than helpful to the defense. He instructed the jury that:

"Intoxicating liquor is liquor which contains such a proportion of alcohol that it will produce intoxication when imbibed in such quantities as it is practically possible for a man to drink."

This definition would make it difficult to wink at the intoxicating qualities of 11% wine.

At times it was puzzling to know just who was being tried. Mr. Hill's admirers had presented him with a huge basket of pink and yellow chrysanthemums and he looked more like an honored guest than a prisoner in the dock. Also, his lawyers were not only corporation counsel of great eminence, serving without fee, but whenever possible, they took the offensive. They demanded the introduction of the Hill-Haynes correspondence, and they kept offering in evidence bulletins of the Department of Agriculture on the fermentation of cider, the processing of grapes, etc. The government had to struggle fiercely to have such embarassments excluded.

Mr. Machen told the jury, "What is on trial before you is not John Philip Hill but the last vestige of American liberty."

"I object", said District Attorney Woodcock.

"Mr. Machen", said Judge Soper, "If you desire to practice in this court you must conform to the rules. This is no place to make a speech for or against prohibition. You may feel that the law robs you of your liberties, but it is not for you to say it here."

As befitted a pillar of the Church, Judge Soper approached the question of intoxication on an intellectual plane. In instructing the jury on how to gauge the power of John Philip's wine, he said:

"* * * You were shown by ocular demonstration the amount of brandy which would contain a like amount of alcohol as a quart of the cider which was manufactured by the defendant. Now the wine which we are now discussing contained, some of it, approximately four times as much alcohol as the cider. If you can visualize the amount of brandy pictorially represented by Dr. Kelly as containing as much alcohol as was in a quart of the cider, and multiply that by four times, you get an idea of the brandy equivalent of a quart of the wine which contained the highest alcoholic content. Now, then, if you believe it was practically possible for a man to drink two, three, or four quarts of that liquid, you would be able to figure out how much would be represented by an equivalent of brandy. Matters of that sort may assist you in determining this question."

Finally, the shouting and the tumult died, and at 1:47 p.m. on Wednesday, November 12, John Philip's fate was entrusted to the jury.

For a time the crowd in the courtroom lingered, expecting a prompt verdict. When the jury failed to return, the spectators drifted away and the participants grew tense. John Philip fingered a copy of "Pilgrim's Progress", which, he said, gave him great consolation. Soon he seemed to lose interest. Possibly he remembered that John Bunyan had written it while in jail.

Night came and still no verdict. It would be a close thing and for the first time, perhaps, John Philip saw yawning before him an abyss which the excitement of the prior proceedings had tended to obscure. A conviction would almost certainly mean his expulsion from the House of Representatives.

Prohibitionists possessed more hate than humor. Hill's persistent needling and ridicule had infuriated every Dry in Congress. During the earlier wine episode there had been an organized movement to censure or impeach him for deliberate violation of the Prohibition law. It failed chiefly because his padlocking had left the issue of guilt in suspense. If he were now convicted, it was easy to foresee the result. The Drys had the votes and it was only a question of how they would go about it.

When Judge Soper went home for the night he left word that if the jury came to an agreement it should leave a sealed verdict. The night wore on without it. Finally, after seventeen hours, the jury left a paper with the clerk and went out for breakfast. Apparently, it was the tantalizing smell of bacon from a restaurant across the street that got the wheels of justice off dead center. At 10:00 a.m. the Court reassembled and the verdict was opened. It read, "Not guilty of the matters in which he stands indicted."

Congratulations poured in from all sides.

"Wish we had you in Georgia", telegraphed William E. Bush of Augusta.

"Hail to the tribune of the people", wired George Stewart Brown from New York.

"Politics, pure and simple", said Andrew J. Volstead in Granite Falls, Minnesota, while Roy A. Haynes declared himself "Unmoved", and President Coolidge made no comment.

There was even a poem for the occasion, entitled "Johnfillup's Victory", which ended:

"Twelve honest men and true the court did choose
   To try Johnfillup for his jest with booze,
Twelve honest men heard learned doctors say
   A single drop of wine will make you gay.

Twelve honest men discussed for weary hours
   The arrant nonsense of the Volstead powers.
Twelve honest men who knew the strength of thirst,
   Gave their opinion and were then dispersed.

They ruled a townsman, and a farmer, too,
   Were not intoxicated by home brew,
A simple wine, of merely ten per cent,
   Was just and fair and was the law's intent.

"My flat is tiny, there's no home brew space,
But if some friend will send to me a case,
An ancient beaker to the brim I'll fill
And drink the glory of Johnfillup Hill."

What passes for progress has long since reduced the house to rubble and converted Franklin Farms into a parking lot. The roar of traffic has replaced the squeak of the cider press. But to the initiated, a special aura still lingers. Such a one need only stand there in the autumn moonlight and the passing rumble will conjure up the deep-throated laugh of John Philip Hill sampling his vintage.

THE NATIONAL PROHIBITION LAW

HEARINGS before the SUBCOMMITTEE OF THE COMMITTEE ON THE JUDICIARY UNITED STATES SENATE - SIXTY-NINTH CONGRESS

April 5 to 24, 1926

STATEMENT BY HON. WILLIAM CABELL BRUCE, A SENATOR IN THE CONGRESS OF THE UNITED STATES FROM THE STATE OF MARYLAND

Senator BRUCE. Begot by, the abuses of the old saloon, and hastened to maturity by the economic necessities and uncalculating enthusiasm of the World War, and by the lavish use of money and political threats by the Anti-Saloon League, national prohibition went into legal effect upward of six years ago, but it can be truly said that, except to a highly qualified extent, it has never gone into practical effect at all. The appetite for drink, which has been one of the primal impulses of the great mass of human beings ever since Jesus at Cana manifested forth His glory, to use the words of St. John, by converting the water in six water pots into wine, has, In its struggle with the vast repressive agencies set in motion by the eighteenth amendment and the Volstead Act, furnished another illustration of the truth, which neither moralist nor statesman should ever forget, even in his most fervid moments of disinterested or generous feeling, that man is a creature who can be regulated and bettered, but can not be made over. Once, during the agitation for the abolition of human slavery, Henry Brougham decried what he termed "the wild and guilty fantasy that man can hold property in man." As wild and guilty is the fantasy that even the power of the Federal Government can totally divest man of his warm garment of animal sensations, desires, and appetites. Ever since the eighteenth amendment and the Volstead Act became parts of the legislation of our land the human instinct of personal liberty, guided by a correct sense of the limits within which natural law can be controlled by municipal ordinances, has maintained an unbroken resistance to them; and nothing can be more unwarranted than the statement often heard that this resistance is limited to a single self-indulgent social class.

It is not kept up more stoutly by what the prohibitionists, vainly seek to excite social disaffection and jealousy, call the smart social set, than it is by the members of the American Federation of Labor. It is not limited to any social class or sect. It has brought about close working relations between the bootlegger and thousands of the most intelligent and virtuous members of American society who feel no more compunction about violating the Volstead Act than the Free Soiler did about violating the fugitive slave law, or the southern white did about nullifying ignorant negro, suffrage, the Federal Constitution in each instance to the contrary notwithstanding And the ever mounting record of arrests for drunkenness in all of our American cities since the enactment of the Volstead Act indicates only too significantly that the humbler and less fortunate members of society have their illicit purveyors of drink too. The recent utterances of Jewish rabbis, Protestant bishops and ministers, and of Catholic prelates like Cardinals O'Connell and Hayes, demonstrate the existence of a growing feeling, even among the American clergy, that absolute prohibition is not the ally but the enemy of human morality.

General Lincoln C. Andrews, the head of the Prohibition Unit, said what can not be gainsaid when he declared last year that the bootleg industry is coextensive with our entire national territory.

From the extent to which prohibition monopolizes private conversation everywhere in the United States without or within doors from the amount of space that is given to its merits and demerits in the editorial, reportorial and news columns of our newspapers, and from the innumerable polls that are now being taken for the purpose of testing public opinion with respect to it, one might well imagine, at the present time, that the eighteenth amendment and the Volstead Act, instead of having been technically in force for more than six years, had never passed beyond the ordinary stages of popular agitation.

The explanation of this state of things is to be found, of course, in the fact that prohibition in the United States, under the provisions of that amendment and that act, has proved a disastrous, tragic failure, and aside from precipitating the end of the old saloon, which would have gone in time anyhow, with the steady increase of temperance that was under way when the eighteenth amendment was adopted, has had no effect, on the whole, except that of blighting human happiness, debasing human morals, and discrediting human laws. Once there was a time when it was commonly said that whether the States or their cities failed to enforce their penal laws or ordinances, or not, the Federal Government never failed to enforce its penal laws; and that was true, but it is true no longer, for the fact has been established by irrefutable proofs that during the last six years the Federal Government, effective as may be the ordinary course of its judicial procedure, is powerless to enforce a statute, or even a constitutional provision that attempts to make some thing criminal at all times, and places, and under all circumstances, that is not essentially criminal per se, and therefore has no true moral sanction back of it.

The vast majority of the people in the United States can use spirits, wine, or beer without the slightest injury either to themselves or to others; indeed, with nothing but a perfectly legitimate enhancement of the joy of agreeable and rational living, and to say that even as to drink must be totally abolished, no matter how carefully safeguarded by proper municipal regulations, is about as just and sensible as it would be to say that motor cars are no longer to be used for pleasure purposes because they are often made the instruments of lewdness, robbery, or murder; or that we are no longer to warm our hands before a cheerful fire in a fireplace because it might escape from its confinement and work untold havoc and ruin.

Like cancer, which, in its last stages, seems actually to thrive upon the knife, violations of the Volstead Act may almost be said to have thriven upon the enforcement of that act. During the first 12 months after it took effect it looked as if it might work. The general disposition of every respectable man to obey the law, and the time that necessarily had to elapse before the opponents of national prohibition could recover from the dejection of defeat, the arts of home distillation and fermentation could be acquired and the establishment of a vast trans- and cis-Atlantic organization for the illicit distribution of drink could be perfected, all conspired to produce that result. But in an incredibly short period an entire underworld for the manufacture, sale, and distribution of drink was called into being, and with the patronage of the inextinguishable human want that it was created to serve has baffled every effort to subdue it. This fact can be convincingly illustrated by just a few figures:

Arrests for violations of the national prohibition act made by Federal prohibition officers since the effective date of that act have increased from 34,175 in 1921 to 62,747 in 1925. Convictions under the national prohibition act have increased from 17,962 in 1921 to 38,498 in 1925. Seizures of illicit stills, still worms, and fermenters have increased from 95,933 in 1921 to 172,537 in 1925. It may be added that 70 per cent of these illicit plants and agencies were seized in the conventionally dry States of Alabama, Arkansas, Florida, Georgia, Louisiana, Mississippi, North Carolina, South Carolina, Tennessee, Texas, and Virginia. In his report for 1925, the Attorney General states that out of 8,039 civil cases begun in the district courts of the United States, 7,271, or 90.4 per cent, were brought under the Volstead act, and that of the 58,128 criminal cases begun in those courts, 50,743, or 87.2 per cent, were brought under that act.

What the burden of enforcing the Volstead Act, since its enactment, has been to the Federal district courts, may be inferred from certain letters, written by the judges of some of those courts, to Senator McKellar of Tennessee, during March of the present year, and published in the Congressional Record of March 13, 1926.

In one of these letters, the Hon. George W. McClintick, the Federal judge for the southern district of West Virginia, says that during his four years and a half of service, he had had before him about eight thousand persons charged with crime, of which about 80 per cent were for liquor violations.

In another letter, the Hon. C. M. Hicks, the Federal judge for the eastern district of Tennessee, states that about 90 per cent of the criminal cases that he had handled since his appointment in March, 1923, were prohibition cases.

In another letter, the Hon. Morris A. Soper, the Federal judge for the district of Maryland, states that in his district at least one-half the time of one judge could be continuously employed in the trial of liquor cases, and that a bill was then pending in Congress, authorizing the appointment of 10 additional district judges, one of whom would be appointed for the district of Maryland. The district of Maryland is justly entitled to this judge, for while only 409 persons were convicted of violations of the Volstead Act in Maryland in 1922, in the year ending June 30, 1925, the number was 1,065.

In another letter, the Hon. John B. Sanborn, the Federal judge for the district of Minnesota, says that in his opinion, if he had to try in his court all of the violators of the national prohibition act who were apprehended in the cities of Minneapolis, St. Paul, and Duluth, as well as in the country districts, they would have to go out of business as a civil court altogether and devote themselves entirely to that work.

On February 15, 1925, Judge John F. McGee, a Federal judge for the district of Minnesota, committed suicide, leaving a statement on his desk which read as follows:

The fact is that the United States district court has become a police court for the trial of whisky and narcotic cases which the State courts should look after. These cases occupy 80 per cent of the court's time and are exciting and trying on the nerves, with the end not in sight. I started, in March, 1923, to rush that branch of litigation, and thought I would end it, but it has ended me.

Before the enactment of the Lever Art on August 10, 1917, which forbade the manufacture of whisky for beverage purposes, the entire number of licensed distilleries in the United States was 507; and during the fiscal year ended June 30, 1919, the last year when the production of beer for such purposes was permitted, the entire number of breweries in operation was 669. Under preprohibition conditions, there were practically no illicit plants except in certain secluded communities. During the fiscal year ending June 30, 1925 as we have seen, 172,537 illicit distilleries, stills, still worms, and fermenters were seized by the National Prohibition Unit, to say nothing of the vast amount of subsidiary property which was seized with them.

The same story of irrepressible law violation is disclosed by the record of arrests for drunkenness in the leading cities of the United States since the enactment of the Volstead Act. On the whole, the trend of these arrests has been steadily upward, with only such fluctuations as have been produced now and then by spasms of law enforcement, inspired by especially aggravated conditions. Arrests for drunkenness in Baltimore increased from 1785 in 1920 to 3258 in 1921, 4955 in 1922, 6235 in 1923, 6029 in 1924 and 5887 in 1925.

Every one of [32] cities show the same pronounced increase in arrests for drunkenness between 1921 and 1925. There is nothing local, there is nothing sectional, there is nothing regional about the phenomenon. That increase is manifest north, south, east, and west. In not a few of the 32 cities, north, south, east, and west, that I have tabulated, the number of arrests for drunkenness last year were even in excess of the number of arrests for drunkenness in 1916, before the enactment of the Lever Act, the first Federal prohibitory act.

The claim has been made that this record of arrests for drunkenness is misleading, because since the enactment of the Volstead Act police officers are quicker to arrest persons under the influence of liquor than they were before that time. This is certainly not so in Baltimore, the city with which I am most familiar, because the standing instructions of our police commissioner as to the degree of intoxication that justifies arrest are the same as those that obtained before the passage of the Volstead Act, and there is every reason, besides, to believe that Baltimore city policemen share the hostility to prohibition which is entertained by the great majority of the people of Baltimore. Even if different conditions exist in other cities, it should be borne in mind that, at the present time, drunkenness is not so visible to the policeman, however alert to arrest, as it was when drink addicts did not get drunk on bootleg liquor or home brew in the home, but on liquor at the corner saloon.

Even if arrests for drunkenness were not so numerous in our cities and towns generally in 1925 as they were in 1916, surely that fact is one which should not afford the prohibitionists any considerable degree of satisfaction. Puerile, indeed, not to say despicable, would be the power of the Federal Government, if in its war upon the human desire for drink it had exerted no contracting force whatever. It may be that the volume of liquor drunk in the United States at the present time is not so great as it was before the enactment of the Volstead Act; if, for no other reason, because marketed liquor of all sorts comes much higher now than it did before that time; but the contrary view has been urged with not a little plausibility, to say the least. Nor am I prepared to say that if the people of the United States were to experience a fresh accession of fatuity, the Federal Government might not be using its Army and Navy in police work, and by spending a hundred or so millions of dollars, wipe out the bootlegger, as the inquisition wiped out the Protestant in Spain to the infinite material and moral loss of that country; but there is no reason to believe that the Federal Government would ever be willing to stretch its power to such length

Some time ago, Mr. Emory R. Buckner, the United States district attorney for the southern district of New York, expressed the opinion that prohibition might be enforced in the State of New York the Federal Government, with the expenditure of $15,000,000 a year, and the aid of 1,500 enforcement agents; but from the catechism, to which he has just subjected himself, I find that he is now of the opinion that the Federal Government can not be induced to take the necessary steps to secure Federal enforcement of prohibition in the State of New York, and that the State of New York, itself, is apparently unwilling to undertake the task. Indeed a bill providing for State enforcement has just been defeated at Albany. Like a sensible man, therefore, he has reached the conclusion that under existing conditions, Congress should modify the Volstead Act so as to permit each State to define what shall be deemed nonintoxicating liquor.

One thing is certain, and that is that even were the bootleggers entirely exterminated that would simply stimulate to an unprecedented degree home distilling and wine making. The still and the fermenter would become as common in the home as the spinning wheel once was. Anyone who is not a hopeless dolt can, in a brief time, learn how to make palatable liquor; and it is no unknown thing that even inmates in our prisons to be discovered making intoxicating beverages with the simplest mechanical and vegetable means.

A few days ago General Andrews said that his program was: First, to dry up the alcohol diversion leaks; second, to control the supply of medicinal whisky; third, to check moonshine and reduce smuggling; and, fourth, to force those who insist on violating prohibition laws to depend on home stills for their supply.

I am afraid that this program will leave the general but little time for, refreshing rest or healthful recreation.

The withdrawals of denatured alcohol, which the bootlegger is so successful in renaturing, jumped-terms of ordinary progression do not suit the case from 22,388,824 wine gallons in 1921 to 81,808,273 in 1925. That this enormous increase in the use of industrial alcohol found its a largely into the channels of the bootleg industry is unquestionable. The amount that did so in 1925 is computed by Henry T. Rainey, the well-known dry Member of the House from Illinois, at 55,000,000 proof gallons, notwithstanding the efforts of the Federal Government to render it too poisonous and nauseous for beverage purposes.

Diversions of denatured alcohol have, of course, been swollen by the fraudulent diversion in one way or another of pure grain alcohol, too, and sometimes such diversions have been accomplished by sheer robbery and violence,: as when a band of from 30 to 50 malefactors, none of whom have ever been brought to justice, recently took possession of a warehouse at Westminster, Md., bound its custodian, and carried away in trucks about 100 barrels of whisky.

The amount of medicinal whisky diverted in New York City alone in 1925 for beverage purposes, through the instrumentality of false medical prescriptions, has been estimated by Mr. Buckner at as high as 275,000 gallons.

Moonshine, instead of being made as it was before the enactment of the Volstead Act, in a few crude, sequestered localities, is now made, as the daily discoveries of the Federal and State prohibition forces evince, in swamps, in mountain fastnesses, in dense thickets, on rivers, in attics, in basements, In garages, in warehouses, in office buildings, even in caves and other underground retreats. In other words, moonshine is almost as ubiquitous as the radiance of the moon itself.

It is stated in the last report of Mrs. Mabel Walker Willebrandt Assistant Attorney General, that during the Federal fiscal year 1924-25, and for a "reasonable" period of time prior thereto, over 300 foreign vessels have been engaged from time to time in smuggling liquor into this country. Throughout the same time illicit over and agencies have also been transporting liquor in large quantities into it, across the Canadian and Mexican boundary lines. By the Federal Department of Commerce the business of smuggling liquor into this country is thought to have amounted, in 1924, to about $40,000,000 in value; and so far as I know, there is no reason to believe that it amounted to any less sum in the year 1925. It is true that cargoes of great value are quite frequently taken from rum runners overhauled by the rum chasers of the Coast Guard. One valued at $100,000 was captured at New York a few days ago. Another, valued at $420,000, was captured in the same waters in January last, but incidents of this kind have, all along, been so common that there is little cause to think that the rum octopus will ever lack tentacles to hack. Indeed, every time it loses one at least two seems to spring up in its place.

I see it stated in the press that as soon as General Andrews has accomplished the objects above mentioned, he proposes to move on liquor making in the home. Indeed, he has just set his entering wedge for this purpose in the bill that he had introduced into the Senate last Friday by Senator Goff, of West Virginia. Of course, to be thoroughly consistent, he must not shrink even from the task of invading the sanctuary of the American home for the purpose of ascertaining whether a little home brew has become actually intoxicating or not; but certainly that is likely to prove the most tyrannical and inglorious of all the tasks that he will ever be called upon to perform. It is bad enough for the American taxpayer to have to pay the cost of maintaining a spy de luxe at the Mayflower Hotel, or to pay the salary of a sneak like the one in Maryland who recently wormed himself, by what were supposed to be honorable overtures of marriage into the confidence of a young woman for the purpose of inducing her to sell him a small amount of bootleg liquor.

As I see it, the end of American liberty would, indeed, be in sight if an organized system of espionage were to encompass the American home, which might not scruple even to solicit servants to betray the confidence of their masters, or to afford one member of a family an opportunity to wreak some festering grudge upon another.

Ever since I heard that even the home might not be spared by the enginery of the inquisition which prohibition has established in this country, the words of Lord Chatham, which were so familiar to our people when they were winning the liberties that have now been so lamentably abridged, have been haunting my memory:

The poorest man may in his is cottage bid defiance to all the force of the crown.

It may be frail; its roof may shake; the wind may blow through it; the storms may enter; the rain may enter; but the King of England can not enter.

It is sometimes said that the Volstead Act has not been successfully enforced because the Federal Government has not made a thoroughly sincere effort to enforce it. This statement is unwarranted. Never in the history of free institutions has any government more pertinaciously, sought to carry out a policy, obnoxious to a powerful popular sentiment, than has the Federal Government in its relations to the Volstead Act. If it has not had its way it has been only because of the vast amount of public hostility engendered by the artificial and impracticable nature of prohibition itself, and because of the extent to which the fidelity of many Federal prohibition and State police officials has succumbed to the corrupting guile of a secret and unlawful business conducted by daring And unscrupulous men, and patronized by reputable American citizens. Such an unnatural act is in itself an incessant incentive to faithless administration. General Andrews said last year that the bribery of Government officials is the chief obstacle in the way of the enforcement of the Volstead Act. Be that as it may, there can be no doubt that the higher officials of the Federal Government, and the many brave and honorable subordinates in the prohibition service, have done and that could be humanly done, under the circumstances, to make national prohibition a success. Congress has upheld it with a degree of persistency which has even drawn down upon its head the reproach, however unjust, of extreme subserviency to the Anti-Saloon League.

Beginning for the year 1921, with an appropriation to the Treasury Department for the enforcement of the national prohibition act of $6,350,000, congressional appropriations to the same department, for the same purposes, have increased from year to year, until, for the year 1926, they have amounted, to date, to $9,678,734.09, and, when to this amount are allocated the shares of the total amounts now appropriated for the general expenses of the Coast Guard and the Department of Justice, respectively, which are properly chargeable to the cost of enforcing the Volstead Act, there is good reason to believe that the current estimate that the enforcement of that act is costing the Federal Government at the present time some $30,000,000 per annum, is not excessive.

Both, President Harding and President Coolidge may be said to have done all that they could in the exercise of their executive authority to secure popular obedience to the mandates of the act; the former even going so far as to call all the governors of the States together at Washington for the purpose of impressing upon on them the importance of insisting upon its clue observance;

and the second, not only doing the same thing later, but also convoking at Washington a similar gathering of some of the great industrial leaders of the country.

As for the Supreme Court, the legality of the Volstead Act has been shielded by it from attack with the full measure of dispassionate impartiality that to its infinite honor it has always brought to bear upon the discharge of its high judicial duty, and surely only a most carping spirit could find fault with the manner in which our Federal district judges have met the burdensome responsibilities imposed upon them by an unworkable law Which must, at times, have sorely shaken their confidence in the wisdom of the legislative branch of the Government.

The disastrous and scandalous results which have followed the vain effort to enforce the Volstead Act may be briefly summarized. It has diverted into the pockets of foreign and domestic lawbreakers a large part of the immense tax revenue of $443,839,544.98 that the Federal Government was receiving from distilled spirits and fermented liquors in 1918, and that could be most profitably employed today toward the payment of our national debt and the reduction of taxation. Among the domestic lawbreakers are reasonably supposed to be not a few millionaires. Indeed, some of them have thriven to such an extent that their incomes have even become objects of cupidity to the Federal income tax department. That act has also led to the expenditure in Canada, Mexico, Cuba, the Bahamas, the Bermudas, and Europe of millions of dollars, which, but for it, might have circulated in the channels of trade and commerce in the United States.

It is believed by Gilson Gardner, the well-known newspaper writer, who has made a special study of Canadian liquor conditions, that of the total annual gross receipts of the Quebec Liquor Commission, 40 per cent, or the sum of $16,000,000, comes out of the purses of American visitors. It is thought that as many as 200,000 American tourists visit Montreal and Quebec each season, and that a large, if not the greater part of these migrants are drawn away from the United States by the liberal liquor laws of Canada. Compute also what they spend in Canada on other things than liquor and the magnitude of our pecuniary loss can be at least measurably calculated The Volstead Act has placed human happiness in more than one vital particular under the irritating and harassing domination of a sour, corrosive and narrow-minded Puritanism, which does not hesitate to avow its enmity even to such innocent recreations as smoking and dancing. It has for the first time brought the church deeply into politics, and helped to give point to the malignant observation of John Randolph of Roanoke, that no communities are so badly governed as those that are governed by women, except those that are governed by priests. It has established a settled commerce between the worthier and the unworthiest members of the community. It has created an underworld almost as thoroughly organized to the respectable world above it. It is responsible for the unprecedented phenomenon of thousands and thousands of reputable men and women, including ministers of the law itself, living in habitual disregard of Constitution and low. It has tended to bring all laws, including itself, into more or less disrespect. It works the grossest discrimination between the wealthy individual who has a supply of preprohibition liquor or does not lack the money with which to buy from the bootlegger at bootleg prices, and the humbler individual who has no such supply, and can not afford such prices, but it is forbidden even to make a small amount of wine or beer under his roof for his own use. In many instances, it has deprived the poor drunkard of the monitor, who could formerly admonish, rebuke, or even threaten him with a straight face, but can do so no longer. It has transferred distilling and brewing operations from the distillery and brewery to the home, and under the very eyes of young children.

When the Volstead Act went into effect one of the vine growers of California killed himself because the prospects for his business seemed so dark. His prophetic outlook was poor. Since that time, the vine areas of California have been very much enlarged; and a ton of California grapes commands a price many times as great as it did then. Last year, before the 24th day of October, 60,449 carloads of grapes were shipped eastward from that State, the bulk of which the California grape grower reported were intended to be converted into "fruit juice." I say nothing of the many other sources within and without the limits of the United States from which grapes were shipped to points in the United States for the same purpose; nor do I say anything of the vast amount of corn, sugar, and other materials that are used in home brewing.

A year or so ago, I went down into the Italian quarter of one of our great cities on a warm, sultry, summer night, when the doors and windows were open, and at one point, the atmosphere was so strongly impregnated with the odor of wine in the making that I turned to my companion and said that a prohibition agent would not need any search warrant but his nose in that locality.

The Volstead Act has converted the Federal Government, with its denaturing outfit of poisons and filth, into a more monstrous Caesar Borgia than any that medieval Italy ever knew. In other ways also, it has filled the bowels of the people with deadly concoctions. The Metropolitan Insurance Co., which has 17,000,000 industrial policies holders, writes me that between 1917 and 1920, the year that the Volstead Act went into effect, there was a decided downward trend in deaths among its policyholders from alcoholism, but that since 1920 there has been an upward trend; the figure for 1925 (2.9 deaths per 100,000 policyholders) being nearly five times the figure for 1920 (0.6). In a report rendered last year by the State Hospital Commission of the State of New York it was stated that alcoholic insanity had trebled in that State during the five years of national prohibition.

The Volstead Act has diminished the use of mild fermented liquors and stimulated the use of ardent spirits. The proportion of the latter consumed by American visitors to Canada is said to be altogether out of keeping with the amount consumed by Canadians. It has displaced the temperate, refreshing glass of beer or wine with the fiery pocket flask. The champions of prohibition "are obliged to admit that drinking among women is rapidly increasing," Bishop Thomas Nicholson, Chicago, president of the Anti-Saloon League, was reported in the press as declaring at the thirtieth annual convention of the league at Washington in January, 1924. Who ever saw women freely drinking cocktails before the advent of national prohibition? It has transformed the love of adventure and excitement which, within lawful bounds, is one of the most charming characteristics of youth in both sexes into a pit of destruction. After going over the face of a large part of the United States, Ernest W. Mandeville, a writer in the Outlook, says, "Women and young boys and girls of social classes that never took a drink before prohibition are now indulging in liquors which are a menace both to their morals and the health." To the same effect is the testimony of Police Commissioner Richard E. Enright, of New York, and the Washington City police department. "Inability of the prohibition law to enforce prohibition is causing an increase in the number of young boys and girls who become intoxicated," declared

Judge H. C. Spicer of the juvenile court at Akron, Ohio, a short time ago when two boys, aged 15 and 16 years, respectively, were arraigned before him. "During the past two years," he added " there have been more intoxicated children brought into court than ever before."

"The Volstead Act has settled like a blight upon the entire joyous side of human existence," I had occasion to say quite recently, "and its acrid and intolerant spirit, at times, by a perfectly natural process of transmigration, reappears in the shrouded activities of the bigoted Ku Klux Klan." It has bred a spirit of hypocrisy worthy of the saintly sinners who, we are told by Butler in his inimitable Hudibras, "Compounded for sins they were inclined to by damning those that had no mind to." It has fostered deceit, perfidy, espionage, and tyranny, in some of its meanest and most hateful aspects. It has lowered the prestige of the Federal Government. It has even led more than one sober American citizen who gave his blood or treasure freely to our national cause, during the World War to ask whether our forefathers did not shed their blood in the cause of American liberty at Bunker Hill and Camden in vain. It has done more than anything else has ever been done to destroy the nice balance between State sovereignty and the National sovereignty which the framers of the Federal Constitution wise wisely and beneficently devised. Its infatuated devotees have not even stopped short of petitioning the President to use the military arm of the Federal Government for the purpose of promoting its visionary objects, and more than one peaceful and reputable citizen, like the late Mr. Holt of Raleigh, N. C., have been shot down in cold blood by it's agents.

Worst of all is the extent to which the Federal service has been defiled by corruption, hatched by it, In his recent review in the New York Times of the means by which national prohibition was achieved, Mr. Wayne B. Wheeler, the general counsel of the Anti-Saloon League, tells us that he and his fellow prohibitionists early adopted the rule of making it safe for a candidate to be a dry, and that in prosecuting this rule, their expenses at one time amounted to about $2,500,000 a year; a sum well calculated, it must be admitted, to impart a sense of safety to the breast of a legislative candidate when he decided to espouse the prohibition cause. A valuable addition to this policy of "safety first" was the provisions of the Volstead Act which craftily bestowed upon the farmer the exceptional privilege of setting up ferments in fruit juices without regard to the wholly artificial standard of one-half of 1 percent which the act imposed upon the city beer drinker. Another valuable addition was the bait to legislative support held out in the clause of the Volstead Act which excepted from the Federal classified service, for the benefit of congressional place-hunters, all the field positions in the prohibition enforcement bureau.

The result of this exception has been pithily stated by that eminent Citizen, William Dudley Foulke, the former member of the United States Civil Service Commission, and once, at any rate, a prohibitionist. "They secured," he said "the passage of the law with the clause in it, and thereby made all these places the spoils of Congressmen, many of whom unscrupulously secured the appointment of scoundrels who accepted bribes, dishonored the service, and made the enforcement bureau what President Harding himself called it, 'a national scandal.'" These words were written in 1923. Since that time so many prohibition agents, including even some prohibition directors, and so many policemen and other officers, intrusted with the duty of enforcing prohibition, have soiled their hands with bribes, or been guilty of other gross forms of misconduct in connection with prohibition work that if all of them were known, nothing less than what Byron calls "the Recording Angel's black bureau" could undertake to list them all.

The corrupt prohibition agent or policeman is just as much a part of the bootleg industry as the bootlegger himself. Last year it took two Pullman cars to transfer to Atlanta the convicted policemen and prohibition agents corralled in a single round-up in Ohio. In May, 1925, a special grand jury in Morris County, N. J., was reported in the press as returning at one time 28 indictments against county officers and others for violations of the Volstead Act. About the same time, the Rev. Marna S. Poulson, superintendent of the New Jersey Anti -Saloon League, was reported in the New York Times as saying, in an address at a prohibition rally at Atlantic City, "I don't know of anyone who can make a dollar go further than policemen and dry agents. By frugality, after a year in the service, they acquire automobiles and diamonds."

Since the organization of the prohibition service to February 1, 1926, 875 persons have been separated from the Prohibition Unit mostly for official faithlessness or downright rascality. Nor does the total that I have given include delinquents not dismissed but only allowed to resign. Neither has the Coast Guard, that nursing mother of brave and devoted men, military as its discipline is, by any means escaped the contamination of prohibition. Since the duty was assigned to it of preventing the smuggling of liquor from the sea into the United States, 7 temporary warrant officers, 11 permanent enlisted men, and 25 temporary enlisted men have been convicted of yielding, in one form or another, to the seductions of money or liquor in connection with prohibition work. I am unable to say how many members of the force have been arrested but not convicted. On December 10, 1925, a United Press dispatch reported that the entire crews of two Coast Guard patrol boats which had been assigned to patrol duty off the coast of Florida had been court-martialed for conniving with bootleggers. On March 8, 1926, a dispatch to the New York Times from Providence, R. I., announced that Capt. Eli Sprague, who had been for 12 years the commander of the New Shoreham (Block Island) Coast Guard station, and had shared in the rescue of more than 500 persons, had been held for trial on two secret conspiracy indictments. On or about February 18, 1926, the Washington Daily News reported that Boatswain's Mate Joseph Libby, who had walked barefoot through ice and snow to obtain succor for his comrades whom he had left unconscious from extreme cold on patrol boat 126, had been dishonorably discharged from the Coast Guard for bootlegging.

In view of what I have said, it is not surprising that Dr. Horace Taft, head master of the Taft School at Watertown and brother of Chief Justice Taft, should have said a few days ago at a law-enforcement meeting at Yale, "The United States is threatened with the rotting of her moral foundations and of her political and social structure as a direct result of prohibition."

The Manufacturer's Record, of Baltimore, has given, with the aid of the general prohibition propaganda, wide currency to the statement that in 1917 Judge E. H. Gary, of the United States Steel Corporation, Frank A. Vanderlip, Thomas A. Edison, and a thousand other leading men of affairs signed a memorial expressing the opinion that the time had come for the Federal Government to take steps looking to prohibition; that in 1922 the Record addressed a letter to each of the memorialists, asking him whether he still favored prohibition; that only 7 per cent of the replies to these letters declared in favor of wine and beer, and that in 1925 similar letters were sent by the Record to the same persons, and that the replies to these letters were overwhelmingly in favor of prohibition. In other words, the Dutch had captured and were still in possession of Holland. These statements, have been analyzed by Mr. E. C. Horst, a prominent citizen of the State of California, and I have recently received from him a letter as follows:

The memorial is said to number 1,000. The memorial is short of 1,000 by 432. The memorial is signed by 568.

Of these 568 who signed the memorial there were only 216 who voted in the final referendum of the Manufacturers' Record, and of those 216 only 88 were manufacturers or business men. The remaining 122 were professional men not engaged in manufacturing or trading. The Manufacturers' Record of 1922 published replies from 438 people, while the Manufacturers' Record of 1925 published replies from only 215; that is to say, that 223 of the 438 people that favored prohibition in 1922 did not reply to the editor of the Manufacturers' Record when he asked them for dry indorsements in 1925.

To such proportions does the most pretentious bulletin ever circulated by prohibition propagandists in support of the claim that the vast majority of the employers of the United States are in favor of prohibition shrivel when exposed to the ray of truth. Nay, more, moved by the wish to probe the conditions surrounding the claim of the Manufacturers' Record to the very bottom, the Daily Commercial News, of San Francisco, obtained signed statements from all the 844 advertisers whose names appeared in the issue of the Record in which only 7 per cent of the first replies received by the Record were said to have favored wine and beer. The result of the probe is published in the issue of the News for Wednesday, February 17, 1926, in these words:

These 844 advertisers are scattered throughout the United States. One fourth of the total number are in the Southern States, of whom 48 per cent responded, and of these, 60 to 61 per cent replied over their signatures that they were in favor of legalizing light wine and 2-3/4 per cent beer; and 63 to 65 per cent of the votes state that most of their employees are in favor of legalizing beer and light wine. In the East, Central, and Middle Atlantic States the percentages in favor of legalizing light wine and beer are still higher.

It is confidently asserted that the extraordinary prosperity of the United States at the present time, as reflected in abundant employment, increased savings bank deposits, and the purchase of motor cars is referable to prohibition. At best, as I had occasion a short time ago to say, that kind of argument is founded upon such vague premises and fortified by such uncertain trains of reasoning as to be practically worthless. It is hardly worth my while to deny that the recent economic condition of the United States is not due to prohibition when there is no such thing as prohibition, or only such prohibition as unceasingly from year to year manifests itself in expanding criminal dockets and mounting arrests for drunkenness.

Prohibition does not exist in Canada outside of some of its maritime Provinces and Ontario, which, however, does not lack 4.4 per cent beer. Yet the economic welfare of Canada during the last few years, as evidenced in building and other, material activities, is so amazing that at times the Canadian dollar has commanded a premium over our dollar.

How is the general state of things that I have pictured to be corrected? I answer by frankly recognizing the fact that the human appetite for drink is just as natural as the human appetite for food or reproduction; that it can be regulated but not eradicated, except perhaps at a cost in terms of money and tyranny that modern civilization will not long endure, by amending the Volstead Act so as to allow the use of 2.75 per cent beer; and by amending the eighteenth amendment to the Federal Constitution in such a manner as to authorize the Federal Government to take over the entire management and control of the liquor traffic, so far as State local option shall permit it to be carried on at all.

This brings me to the consideration of what is known as the Quebec plan of Government liquor control, created by the alcoholic liquor act passed by the Quebec Legislature in February, 1921. This act provides for the appointment of five commissioners, known as the Quebec Liquor Commission, an official body which conducts the liquor trade in the name and for the benefit of the Quebec government. All the profits accruing from the trade fall into the consolidated revenues of the Province. The commission is given the monopoly of it, to the exclusion of all private interests in the Province, and spirits for beverage purposes can be imported and retailed only through its, organization. For this purpose the commission has established to date 90 stores, 40 of which are in the city of Montreal, and 10 in the city of Quebec, leaving 40 for the other cities of the Province. Spirits can be bought in these stores only between 9 o'clock in the morning and 6 o'clock in the evening on the first five week days and between 9 o'clock in the morning and 1 o'clock in the afternoon on Saturdays. Only one bottle may be purchased at a time by any one customer; and the liquor is delivered in sealed bottles, and must be taken away to be drunk at home. There is no place in the Province of Quebec where spirits can legallybe bought by the glass and drunk on the spot.

Regulations as to wine and beer are much more lenient. First, as to wines. They are sold without limitation as to quantity in every store of the commission where spirits can be had. Furthermore, a few stores have been established exclusively for the sale of wines. Thirdly, a number of hotels and restaurants are licensed to sell wine to their guests at meals. Beer may be brewed in the Province, or shipped in under license from the commission. Brewers are allowed to sell to grocery stores, hotels, restaurants, taverns, and clubs, licensed by the commission, for the retail of beer.

The purpose of, these arrangements to discourage the purchase of spirits and to encourage the purchase of wine and beer instead is manifest.

In addition to the 90 stores operated by the commission for the retail sale of wine and spirits, there are in the Province of Quebec 489 hotels and 59 restaurants licensed to serve wine and beer to their patrons at meals, 573 taverns licensed to retail beer to be drunk on the premises, and 1,238 grocery stores licensed to sell beer by the bottle to customers who are required to take it away.

The right of local option is jealously preserved Any municipality may by the action of the majority of its voters express its wish to remain or become dry. In that event, the commission can not grant a license within its bounds, but any person living in a dry district can buy direct from the commission one bottle of spirits at a time and any quantity of wine.

The greater part of the Province in area and about half of it in population is dry by virtue of local option, and during the four years that the Quebec alcoholic liquor act has been in force the respective importance of dry and wet territories and populations has not been materially modified.

The total sales of the commission during the four years of its operation have exceeded $72,000,000, of which amount some $25,800,000 has been paid to the Canadian Federal Government in taxes. During the same period the net revenue received by the Quebec liquor government from different sources, including sales, permits or licenses, and seizures has been around $19,800,000; out of which sum nearly $17,500,000 has been handed over to the, Quebec Government. Besides the commission has built up out of its revenue a working capital and surpluses amounting in the aggregate to $2,350,000. These particulars have been derived by me from a paper by Arthur St. Pierre in the Independent of October 10, 1925.

Even more satisfactory than the financial results have been the moral results of the system. One of its effects has been to diminish the consumption of spirits by promoting the consumption of wine, and thereby to help to usher in the social conditions which Jefferson had in mind when he said:

No nation is drunken where wine is cheap; and none sober where the dearness of wine substitutes ardent spirits as the common beverage. It is, in truth, the only antidote to the bane of whisky. * * * Its extended use will carry health and comfort to a much enlarged circle. Everyone in easy circumstances (as the bulk of our citizens are) will prefer it to the poison to which they are now driven by their Government.

In 1924-25 the sales of wine by the commission exceeded its sales of spirits by 23,814 bottles; while in 1923-24, they were less by 864,960 bottles.

Another effect has been to bring about a steady decline in drunkenness. The commission was organized on May 1, 1921. In 1920 the monthly average, for arrests for drunkenness in Montreal had exceeded 600; in 1921, after the organization of the commission, it was a little less than 550; in 1922 it dropped to 354; in 1923 to less than 300, and in 1924 to 243. According to a recent study made by Mr. William P. Eno, of Washington City, in 1923, such arrests per 100,000 of population in dry Boston were eight times what they were in wet Montreal.

Of course, the Quebec liquor plan can not be adopted by statute in the United States because of the limitations created by the eighteenth amendment, but it could be naturalized in this country by an amendment to that amendment, and such an amendment is the one proposed in the bill introduced by me into the Senate, which is now before you.

As subsequently altered by me, it reads as follows:

Subject to present prohibitory provisions in the constitution of any State, and to laws heretofore or hereafter enacted in pursuance thereof, and to all existing local option laws in any State, so long as said provisions or laws shall respectively remain in force, the Congress shall have the exclusive power, with such enforcement aid as may be lent it by any State and be accepted by it, to regulate but not to prohibit or unreasonably restrict the manufacture, sale' transportation, importation, or exportation of intoxicating liquors, including the power to authorize any Federal agency that it may designate for the purpose, with the aid of such private business agencies as it may be authorized by the Congress to employ, exclusively to undertake and conduct, manage, and control the manufacture, sale, and distribution of such liquors; but, with the approval of a majority of the voters in any county, parish, or incorporated city or town in any State upon which this article shall at the time be operative, at a special election held for the purpose, the legislature of such State shall have the Power to prohibit the manufacture, sale, or distribution of intoxicating liquors within the limits of such county, parish, or incorporated city or town.

The Congress shall be empowered to enforce this article by appropriate legislation.

The character of this amendment is almost too plain to require explanation. It confers upon Congress the power to enact a plan of liquor control which, like the Quebec plan, would be a combination of exclusive Government management and local option. This power, however, is expressly made subject to present prohibitory provisions in State constitutions, and to State local option laws wherever they now exist, and to any local option laws that the States may pass in the future. Such laws could conceivably, by local initiative throughout the United States, be given an expansion that , with existing systems of state-wide prohibition in the different States would make prohibition, backed by a genuine popular support, as completely coextensive, with the entire territory of the United States as it is now supposed to be, but so far as the liquor traffic would not be swayed by State action, it would be controlled by the national authority under such administrative restrictions and safeguards that the old right to ship liquor from wet territory to dry territory, which was one of the chief abuses of the past, could be cut down to any limits that suited the discretion of Congress.

The amendment recognizes the imperishable truth that communities are never so obedient to the laws as when they harmonize with their own special historic backgrounds and social customs, usages, and habits. In other words, it provides for the right of local self-government which is the cornerstone of all true liberty. It conserves whatever is good in existing prohibitory conditions. It would bar out the old saloon. It does not surrender national control over the liquor traffic in local communities, except to the extent that local communities signify at the polls their desire that it should be so surrendered, and it never surrenders national control for the purpose of enabling any local community to say that it will have any system of license except what Congress shall prescribe.

In other words, it has in mind as administration which would cling to all the workable results of the long agitation for national prohibition, and yet adjust itself with easy flexibility to all the local diversities of thought and feeling, prejudice, and predilection, which necessarily distinguish such a vast domain as that of the United States.

Ritchie and State Prohibition Enforcement

Presented here is a reprint of the speech on "The Enforcement of the Eighteenth Amendment and the Volstead Act from the point of view of the Individual States", which Governor Ritchie delivered before the Institute of Public Affairs at the University of Virginia on August 14, 1929. It represents a complete answer to the charge of nullification which has been flung at the Governor. So comprehensive and logical was this defense of the Governor's position that the contentions he raised then have not yet been disproved by anyone.

I am one of the many who think we erred in putting prohibition into the Constitution, and that we err doubly in our present methods of attempted enforcement. If it be conceded that this great social experiment may have been noble in motive, I am still convinced that twelve years of experimentation have proved it an ignoble failure. You may disagree with me as to this, but you are bound to agree that we face one of the most perplexing and irrepressible problems which democracy has ever been called upon to solve. And solve it we must; though I question whether we shall ever do so by the processes of party politics, because prohibition makes too many political cowards.

Somehow the same, sound, sincere men and women of the country, regardless of party loyalties or personal predilections, must be aroused and united to the urgent need of doing something. The present intolerable situation cannot continue. It suits neither the sincere wets nor the sincere drys. The time has come to cut out wild talk, mutual criminations and recriminations and personal abuse, and face the facts.

Nothing is gained by insisting that prohibition reflects the higher morality and the will of God; that all good men are *ipso facto* for it, and that he who is not is *ipso facto* a publican, a sinner and an enemy of mankind.

A condition and not a theory confronts us. The power and prestige of government is being impaired and the administration of law demoralized. The annual financial cost, direct and indirect, of this experiment is, I believe, rapidly passing the billion dollar mark; and out of it all we are developing new forms of crime, of corruption, of law defiance and maladministration.

National prohibition is not a success and the sooner we admit it the sooner we shall find a way to do something constructive. The appointment of a Presidential commission to study an increase in crime which where it exists every police chief knows is due to the present system of National prohibition is certainly an extraordinary phenomenon in Government and is itself a sufficient admission of failure.

It is my purpose first to discuss the claim that the States have either a legal or a moral duty to take over as a State proposition the enforcement of the eighteenth amendment.

There are no State enforcement acts in New York, Nevada, Montana, Wisconsin and Maryland. Of these States the first four had enforcement acts but repealed them. Maryland never passed one. The position of Maryland is simple enough, and I presume it is the position of these four other States also.

The eighteenth amendment gives the Federal Government and the several States concurrent *power* to enforce it by appropriate legislation. Some contend very earnestly that this imposes a concurrent *obligation* to enforce, —that the power implies the duty.

Maryland does not so construe it. Because we do not, we are accused by militant drys of treason, sedition, secession, nullification and every other high crime and misdemeanor in the catalogue of prohibition abuse.

All this is sheer nonsense. The people of Maryland are as patriotic, as law-abiding and as law-respecting as the people of any other State. No one has the right to say less for the people of New York, Nevada, Montana and Wisconsin. Maryland is not guilty of rebellion against the Nation or of contempt for the Constitution in not passing a State enforcement act and neither are these other States in repealing theirs. We are as solicitous as any State in the Union to find the solution for intemperance, but we want the right solution. Our position is a reasoned position, and I think the sound and intelligent one.

The duty of the people to *obey* the eighteenth amendment is not involved in this discussion. My State does not question the legal obligation of its citizens to obey the amendment and the Federal laws passed under it. Both are in as full force and effect in Maryland as they are in every other State.

Our position simply is that when the Constitution declares that the States shall have concurrent *power* with

43

the Nation to *enforce* the eighteenth amendment, this does not mean that the States are legally or morally *obliged* to exercise this power. They have the clear right to exercise it or not in their sound discretion.

No State is called upon to provide enforcement machinery for the Federal Income Tax law, or the Narcotic law, or the Mann Act or any other Federal enactment that I know of. All of those acts are in full force in every State, but no State sets up State machinery to enforce them. They are the laws of the Federal Government and the Federal Government sets up its own Federal machinery to enforce its own laws. Why then should any State be obligated to set up State machinery to enforce just one out of all the thousands of Federal laws,— the Federal prohibition law,—merely because the eighteenth amendment says that it has the power to do so?

At the recent Governors' Conference in New London I made the statement that whether the States exercise their power to enforce the eighteenth amendment "is optional with them. If they choose not to do so, they violate no legal or moral obligation."

Senator Borah did me the honor of replying to this in the New York Times of July 28, 1929, and he there stated, as forcefully as they can be stated, the arguments for the proposition that the States are under the duty of enforcing the amendment.

Senator Borah's position is that when the will of the people is expressed in the Constitution, "neither Congress nor the States can disregard this command;" that the second section of the eighteenth amendment confers concurrent power on the Nation and the States to enforce the amendment, and this legally and morally binds the

44

States as well as the Nation to enforce it; that "where the authority is given it creates correspondingly a legal and moral obligation to act."

I would be the last to contend that the States are not under both a legal and a moral obligation to play the full part in our government which the Constitution assigns to them and intends them to play. They are, of course. But no such duty as Senator Borah describes is assigned to the States by the eighteenth amendment. Any belief that it is rests upon a complete misconception of the actual situation.

It is true this misconception is prevalent among a great many people, who really seem to believe that the States are under some sort of a binding obligation to set up State enforcement machinery under the amendment, and it is an amazing and deplorable thing that discussions of this proposition, which lies at the very root of the rights and duties of the States with respect to enforcement, are usually confined to personal abuse and *ex cathedra* utterances, with little apparent attempt or desire to get at the truth about it.

Under our system of dual sovereignty the established general principle is that a State officer has no power to make an arrest for the violation of a Federal law, unless the Act of Congress authorizes such State officer to make arrests and while in that case the officer may exercise such authority, he cannot do so if the same is prohibited by the Constitution or laws of his State. Dallemagne vs. Moisan, 197 U. S. 169.

The Volstead Act does not purport or attempt to confer power on State officials to enforce either its provisions or the provisions of the eighteenth amendment, nor is there any other Act of Congress which does.

There is, therefore, no Federal legislation which can be said to impose any duty upon the States to enforce the amendment, and if any such duty exists it can only be because the amendment itself prescribes it.

The only possible *argument* for this is that Section 2, in declaring that the States shall have concurrent power to enforce the amendment, is a grant of power to the States and the source of their right to pass enforcement laws at all; that this power so granted the States coupled with the like power granted the Nation shows that the eighteenth amendment contemplated a joint or dual enforcement machinery, and that the States were to aid the Nation in this work; and that it is the duty of the States to do what the amendment contemplates they shall do, and pass appropriate enforcement machinery of their own.

I refrain from discussing how completely this would destroy our basic American principle of dual sovereignty, because it is perfectly clear that no such meaning as this was intended to be given or can be given to the amendment.

In the case of United States vs. Lanza, 260 U. S. 377, (1922), the Supreme Court held that the amendment was *not* "the source of the power of the States to adopt and enforce prohibition measures;" that the States always had that power, and that it had been guaranteed them by the Tenth Amendment; and that the purpose of declaring a concurrent power of enforcement in the States was "to negative any possible inference that in vesting the National Government with the power of country-wide prohibition, state power was excluded."

In other words, the concurrent clause was not intended to and did not give the States any power at all to pass State prohibition acts or acts to enforce the eighteenth amendment. The intention was simply to make it clear that the amendment did not take away from the States the power which they already had in this regard, and that they were still free to exercise this pre-existing power, although, of course, subject now to the prohibitory requirements of the amendment.

The Supreme Court further said that "the second section means that the power to take legislative measures to make the policy (prohibition) effective shall exist in Congress in respect to the territorial limits of the United States, and at the same time the like power of the several States within their territorial limits *shall not cease to exist.*"

In the later case of Herbert vs. Louisiana, 272 U. S. 312, (1926), a State law was before the court, and the *argument* was advanced "that the State in denouncing the manufacture of intoxicating liquor for beverage purposes as a criminal offense and in taking proceedings to punish the offenders, is exerting a power derived from the eighteenth amendment, and therefore that all that is done by the State in that regard must be taken as done under the authority of the United States." This is the only argument that can be made to support the proposition that the States are under any kind of a duty to pass State enforcement acts. The Supreme Court rejected this argument on the grounds stated in the Lanza case.

Consequently, the authority of a State to pass State prohibition laws, including laws to enforce the eight-

47

teenth amendment does not come from that amendment at all. It comes from the State's reserved powers, guaranteed by the Tenth Amendment; and the concurrent clause, instead of being a grant of power, was inserted merely to make clear that the States' reserved powers so far as prohibition is concerned, had not been destroyed by putting prohibition in the Federal Constitution.

In a word, the concurrent clause grants the power of enforcing the amendment to Congress, but it grants no power at all to the States. As to them it simply preserves their pre-existing sovereign power to enact State prohibition or enforcement measures, subject to the limits set by the amendment.

Since the State's power to enforce the eighteenth amendment does not come from the amendment at all,— since, as the Supreme Court said in the Lanza case, prior State prohibition laws "derive their force *as do all new ones consistent with it,* not from this amendment, but from power belonging originally to the States, preserved to them by the Tenth Amendment," it cannot possibly be said that the amendment impores any sort of obligation on the States to enforce it.

As Professor Howard Lee McBain, in his recent work "Prohibition, Legal and Illegal," correctly and succinctly says: "Manifestly if the States derive from the amendment no power to enact prohibition laws, they are of a certainty under no obligation, moral or legal, to enact such laws because of the amendment."

There is, of course, no higher or more binding or more final authority on this question than the Supreme Court of the United States. But let me supplement and reinforce their decision with the following remarks made during the debates on the eighteenth amendment by Rep-

48

resentative Webb, a leading Prohibitionist, who was at the time acting as spokesman for the House Judiciary Committee:

"Mr. Speaker and gentlemen of the House: I believe I will take up your time but briefly in explaining the committee amendments to this resolution as it passed the Senate. The first amendment adopted in the Judiciary Committee was the new section 2. As it passed the Senate it provided that the 'Congress' should have the power to enforce this article by appropriate legislation. Most of the members, including myself, of the Judiciary Committee, both wet and dry, felt that there ought to be a reservation to the State also of power to enforce their prohibition laws. And therefore we amended the resolution by providing that the Congress and the several States' shall have 'concurrent' power to enforce this article by appropriate legislation. So the amendment reads:

'The Congress and the several States shall have concurrent power to enforce this article by appropriate legislation.'

"I believe, regardless of our division on the dry and wet question, every Member will agree with us that this is a wise and proper amendment. Nobody desires that the Federal Congress shall *take away from the various States the right to enforce the prohibition laws of those States.* If we do not adopt this amendment from the committee there might be a fight in Congress every two years as to whether the States should be *given the right to help enforce this proposed article of the Constitution.* Because, as I see it, after the States have delegated to the Federal Congress power to do a certain thing, for instance to stop the manufacture and sale of alcoholic

49

liquors for beverage purposes, the question is whether the State has not turned over to the Federal Congress *the exclusive right to enforce it.*"

Therefore, in adopting the concurrent clause Congress had no thought of making it the *duty* of any State to pass a State enforcement act. The idea simply was not to let the eighteenth amendment *take away from the States the right* to pass any prohibition and enforcement acts at all.

President Hoover, in his inaugural address, ascribes part of the abuses which have grown up under the eighteenth amendment "to the failure of many state and local officials to accept the obligation under their oath of office zealously to enforce the law."

Senator Borah makes the same point, and asks: "May the Governor of a State remain quiet, is he under no legal or moral obligation to act, when violence challenges the Constitution which he has taken an oath to support?" And he further asks whether "the members of the State Legislature who take their oaths to support the Constitution of the United States under the second section of the eighteenth amendment satisfy their oaths if they refuse to legislate or to appropriate money to uphold and maintain the Constitution?"

Senator Borah's expressed position is that whenever the Federal Constitution undertakes to define any national policy, then every Senator, Congressman, Governor, legislator and other official, state or national, sworn to *support* the Constitution, becomes, by virtue of this oath, bound not only to support such national policy but *also to enforce it;* and if they do not he is convinced our government will go on the rocks. If this were so, the rock of ages would be strewn with no end of wrecks, for the course of history has not been charted along any such route.

But it is not so. No Governor, no member of the State Legislature, and no other State or local official has taken any oath which obligates him to *enforce* any Federal law, including the eighteenth amendment, by legislation, appropriation or otherwise. The oath to support the Constitution does not make any of them a Federal enforcement officer. It confers on them no duty to constitute themselves the machinery or to provide the means for enforcing Federal law.

The President holds no executive power in the States, and has no duty with respect to the enforcement of State laws. The Governors of the States hold no executive power in the Federal Government and have no duty with respect to the enforcement of Federal laws.

Under the American system of government the States owe no duty to the Nation to enforce the laws of the Nation and the Nation owes no duty to the States to enforce the laws of the States.

Federal officials are bound to enforce Federal laws and State officials are bound to enforce State laws, but neither Nation nor State is bound to enforce the laws of the other sovereignty.

The eighteenth amendment went far in invading the domain of the States when it regulated for all the States a subject which, under the Tenth Amendment, had always been theirs to regulate for themselves. But it did not go to the extent of imposing upon State governments or State officials the duty of *enforcing* Federal laws. If it had done that the dual system of sovereignty, without which our form of government cannot endure, would have been destroyed.

For these reasons the people of Maryland have the clear right to decide for themselves whether they will adopt a State enforcement act or not, and the people of every other State in this country have the same clear right.

As a State we do not defy the Federal law; we do not ignore it or try to nullify it. We put no obstacles whatever in the way of its full enforcement by the officials of the Federal Government which passed it. In every way we concede the right of the Federal authorities to enforce the Federal law in Maryland to any limit they see fit. We would not want to see the Marines so misused, but I expect we would not question the Government's legal right to call them out if Washington is willing to go along with Dr. Clarence True Wilson that far.

We recognize the principle of local option to the fullest extent. Nearly all the twenty-three counties of the State had gone "dry" before the eighteenth amendment was adopted, and through the tried and true processes of local self government we were mastering the liquor evil more effectively than can possibly be done under the present system. In the ten years since I became Governor, during which the amendment and the Volstead Act were, of course, in force, I have signed fifteen measures which the Legislature passed strengthening these local option laws for the counties. We concede the right of the communities in our own State to pass and strengthen and enforce such prohibition laws as their people see fit.

But we do exercise our sovereign right, which neither the eighteenth amendment nor any other advancing Federal power has yet taken away, not to incorporate the Volstead Act into Maryland State law.

I say the Volstead Act, because when people insist on a State enforcement act what they always mean is the enactment of the Volstead law as a State measure or of something more stringent or more arbitrary or more costly. In Maryland we decline to make the Volstead Act a law of the State. So long as the Federal government elects to enforce the eighteenth amendment by the Volstead law, just so long will we leave the enforcement of the amendment to the Federal government. We are under no duty to help relieve the Federal government of the burdens and the cost it has assumed under the Volstead law by making that law a Maryland measure and setting up our own State machinery to enforce it, and thus making the people of Maryland share its burdens and its costs; and we decline to do it.

We are not willing to see our present capable police system and its remarkably successful handling of crime and criminals jeopardized in order to try out this experiment.

I turn to the Illinois Crime Survey, compiled and published this year by the Illinois Association of Criminal Justice in cooperation with the Chicago Crime Commission, and read there the story of an organized underworld of crime, which enforces its decrees by bombs and death, and dedicates itself to commercialized vice, gambling, bootlegging, hijacking and racketeering, as well as to old established crimes like murder and robbery; and I recall that Illinois has a State prohibition act, the "Illinois Search and Seizure Law," and that the Chicago police are charged with its enforcement and that they also cooperate fully with the Federal authorities under the Volstead Act.

I see similar conditions, varying only in degree, in

other great cities of the country where State enforcement acts are in effect.

Then I turn to my home town, Baltimore City, and see there an amazing decrease in the number of major crimes during the past six years and an increase in arrests and an increase in convictions. Where crime waves exist and what may be their cause I leave others to expound; there is no crime wave in Baltimore, nor the semblance of any.

The Baltimore City Police and the Baltimore City Courts are not charged with the duty of enforcing a State Volstead Act, and the police do not arrest for violations of the Federal Volstead Act. The police and the courts are free to give their whole time to the detection and punishment of crime, and the result is there is far less crime than ever before.

The Maryland people want the Maryland police and the Maryland courts to keep on that way. We do not want our police subjected to the influences which experience everywhere shows go hand in hand with the enforcement of the Volstead Act. Now our criminal cases are tried within three weeks or less after the arrest. We do not want the dockets overwhelmed with cases under the Volstead law.

We are justified in saying that law and order is not promoted by a State Volstead act. There is infinitely more law and order in Baltimore City which has none than in many other great cities which have. It is our firm conviction that by declining to have our police and our courts undertake local Volstead enforcement, we have less corruption, less crime and a higher character of peace, harmony and orderly and efficient government than many of the enforcement States which also have large cities.

These are briefly our reasons for not wanting a State Volstead Act in Maryland. Surely they are not sinful or wanton or immoral or treasonable reasons. They are simple and easily understood, and appeal to us as the surest way to attain the highest measure of law and order in our State.

Yet we are told that this position is one of nullification. I have already shown that the Supreme Court itself has absolved us of any such charge. There is no duty, no obligation on any State to adopt a State Volstead or enforcement act if it does not want to.

But the truth is, Maryland's position, instead of being an effort at nullification, is in fact a protest against nullification. Maryland feels that Congress and its sister States have nullified certain rights and immunities guaranteed to it under the express and implied covenants of our Federal compact. They have nullified our right to govern ourselves in a domain where only self government can work. Our houses are no longer our castles; we are denied the right in certain cases to be judged by a jury of our peers; we can be halted and searched as we go about our lawful adventures, and can be hectored, browbeaten and even cold-bloodedly shot down,—all in the name of the law. We can be punished twice for the same offense, have our property seized for wrongs we did not ourselves commit, and we can have our homes padlocked on orders that are more executive than judicial. If all this is not the nullification of supposedly inalienable rights and liberties, what is it?

Yet Maryland as a State offers no resistance of any kind to the law which does these things. Maryland makes not the slightest attempt to abrogate it or to nullify it. We simply say it is Federal law, not Maryland law, and it is no part of our duty as a State to adopt it as our own and set up State machinery to carry it out. We leave its enforcement in our State to the Federal Government which made it. To call that nullification is wholly absurd.

There is no historic or legalistic sense in which the word "nullification" can possibly apply here. None of the five States which have no State enforcement acts seek to prevent the enforcement of the Federal prohibition laws within their confines; and nullification means affirmative resistance.

The doctrine of nullification, which made its first appearance in our history about 1799, was that each State had the right to decide for itself whether a given Act of Congress under certain circumstances was binding upon it. As to such Acts, it was claimed that each State had an equal right to determine the extent or method of its local observance or enforcement; and, under certain conditions, States claimed the right to destroy it, to treat it as "null and void and of no effect."

In the words of the living former Attorneys General of Massachusetts and other distinguished lawyers in advising the electorate of Massachusetts:

"Nullification as defined by the highest authority is the action of a State intended to *abrogate* within its limits the operation of a Federal law."

This political doctrine, like that of secession and old-time States' Rights, has gone forever into the discard. No State asserts it or practices it, and it is sheer buncombe to indulge in such accusations today.

If a State's failure to enforce a law or to try to enforce it, is to be called nullification, then all the States could be found guilty of it on many counts. All our Statute books are full of laws that are not enforced; laws that are ob-

56

solete; laws that we never try to enforce and that were never meant to be enforced; laws that are merely held over us *in terrorem;* laws that are palpably absurd or impossible. There is no State that really enforces its Sunday laws, its blue laws, its laws against profanity, or a hundred other legal prohibitions I could name. If all existing laws affecting business were enforced, big business would have to stop, or at least our Hoover prosperity would suffer a fatal chill.

I go one step further. If the inadequate enforcement of the eighteenth amendment or the failure to enforce it amounts to nullification, then not the States but Congress is the nullifier.

There are doubtless those who believe the eighteenth amendment can be enforced, but surely there is no one who thinks it is being enforced.

Of course Congress will never make an adequate effort to enforce the law. I mean adequate in the view of those who think it possible to enforce it. Mr. Doran, the Prohibition Commissioner, told the committee of Congress that this would cost the Government at least $300,000,000 a year. Congress will never appropriate any such sum and it will never create the gigantic enforcement machinery which would be required.

But if Congress does not do these things, the responsibility rests directly on its own shoulders. There is no escape from it. The eighteenth amendment places on the States no duty to enforce it. The States can help if they wish, but there is no duty. The dry spokesman of the House Judiciary Committee in reporting the amendment said so and the Supreme Court has settled it.

But it is, I submit, the duty of Congress to enforce the requirements of the Constitution. To meet that duty

57

Congress passed the Volstead law, and it is now the duty of Congress either to carry out that law by providing adequate appropriations and adequate machinery, or, if enforcement is not possible, to change the law so that enforcement will be possible.

Those who talk so glibly in this connection about treason, nullification and the sancitity of law, have a wrong conception of law, of its nature, origin and sanctions. They seem to think that some spiritual significance attaches to a legislative enactment, instead of recognizing it as a purely human product. Law gets its sanctions from the internal life and spirit of the community; from its customs, traditions, ideals, needs and aspirations. A law must be more than an experimental command, if it is to be obeyed. It must conform to the social needs and ideas of its time, and the element of popular consent and custom must enter, if any system of law or law enforcement is to have life and vitality. It must also comport with the moral sensibilities of the community. You see this illustrated in the wave of moral indignatioon that is sweeping over the nation because of these so-called prohibition-enforcement murders. These officers may be within their strict legal rights when they shoot, but such legal action none the less does violence to the fundamentals of law.

Here is the prime difficulty with the problem of prohibition enforcement. The country was not yet ready for the "noble experiment," and it has put the times out of joint. The law is not in tune with the popular will. They say it was passed by a majority of our people, but it certainly did not express the reasoned judgment of the majority. It was thrust upon us in a period of war unrest. It was passed while millions of our younger voters were over-sea defending the battle line of freedom. It was jammed through Legislatures in States where a referendum to the popular will would unquestionably have registered against it.

Now that it is being defied by so many millions, it has led to another enforcement fallacy, which befuddles many and finds favor even in quarters that know better, namely, that the best way to get rid of a bad law is to enforce it. I can think of no case in history comparable to prohibition where this theory has ever worked or even been tried in practice.

Most repeals come about because experience proves a given law unenforceable. We did not get rid of the Stamp Acts or the fugitive slave law by forcing repeal through enforcement. States like Kansas did not repeal their anti-cigarette laws, for example, because actual enforcement proved them to be foolish, but because experience proved them unenforceable. Many Sunday laws are objectionable even to their advocates, but they are never enforced so as to induce their repeal.

A lesson in the ethics of enforcement can be found in our experience with the Fifteenth Amendment. Here the white population of the southern States was suddenly confronted with a constitutional mandate which they justly believed would wreck the foundations of their civilization. They did not seek to prove that the way to get rid of it was to enforce it. They resisted it by any means at hand until they were able to find devices and legal fictions to outwit it. And this Fifteenth Amendment is still law. Forgotten, but not gone.

After all, you are putting a pretty hard job up to the States when you tell them they must enforce the Volstead

59

Act in order to get rid of it. Do you really believe it possible to enforce any law if to do so you must supplement the regular enforcement officers by calling out the Coast Guard on sea and the Marines on land, and enclose the Nation with barbed wire?

The real trouble is that for most people disobedience of the existing prohibition system does no violence to their conscience. They realize that the crimes created by these statutes are simply *mala prohibita*. No such attitude is ever taken against crimes that are *mala in se*. We do not have to prohibit murder, arson, burglary or offenses which social consciousness has long regarded as crimes; all we need do is inflict punishment. If the law did not punish, society, in self protection, would at once find a way to do so.

Because prohibition is not enforced, one might gather from current talk, even in high position, that our entire legal system is breaking down. This is absurd. Respect for law, like hostility to tyranny, is part of the very fibre of our national character. Our legal foundations are not tottering because millions decline to respect a law that is alien to human nature and to American institutions. All that sort of talk seems to me to grow out of a concerted effort to shift the public interest from the concrete issue of prohibition, on which so many disagree, to the abstract issue of law observance, on which really all agree. No one wants to be a law-breaker, so let us not befog the issue with abstractions. Our difficulty is not disrespect for law in general, but for this law in particular. Our problem is not law-enforcement, but enforcing obedience to this particular law, and when obedience can be hoped for only by force instead of by acquiescence, it is time to ask what is wrong.

It is now regarded as a sort of quasi-treason to talk about personal freedom in this connection. Yet it was precisely to protect the freedom of the individual in just such cases that we agreed to make our Federal Government one of limited powers; that we devised our Federal system of distributed sovereignties; formulated a written constitution; joined in the mutual covenants of a Bill of Rights. The impulse of it all was to protect our individual liberties so that each of us, from the highest to the lowest, could realize his desire to be let alone to live his own life in his own way, with due regard to the equal rights of all others to do likewise. This is still good Maryland doctrine, at least. And I think it is sound.

The ultimate practical difficulty, of course, is to know what best to do. We cannot unscramble this omelet; neither can we digest it. Something must be done. A house divided against itself cannot stand. I realize that discussion of this is not germane to the subject, but perhaps I may conclude by stating, as I have done before, my own conviction that the whole problem within the State should go back to the State, with power to enact workable laws in harmony with local ideals and the people's will. If popular government means anything it seems to me to mean this. Anyway I feel sure that sooner or later it will go back to the States both as a matter of right and of expediency. Neither our social nor our Federal system can stand the present strain. We have tried to nationalize prohibition, but if we are ever to get anything worth while, we must democratize the whole subject, and each State must be free from the coercion of other States. I see no other way out of the wilderness.

III. BAD FEATURES OF THE PRESENT SITUATION AND DIFFICULTIES IN THE WAY
OF ENFORCEMENT

1
CORRUPTION

As to corruption it is sufficient to refer to the reported decisions of the courts during the past
decade in all parts of the country, which reveal a succession of prosecutions for conspiracies,
sometimes involving the police, prosecuting and administrative organizations of whole
communities; to the flagrant corruption disclosed in connection with diversions of industrial
alcohol and unlawful production of beer; to the record of federal prohibition administration as to
which cases of corruption have been continuous and corruption has appeared in services which in
the past had been above suspicion; to the records of state police organizations; to the revelations
as to police corruption in every type of municipality, large and small, throughout the decade; to
the conditions as to prosecution revealed in surveys of criminal justice in many parts of the land;
to the evidence of connection between corrupt local politics and gangs and the organized
unlawful liquor traffic, and of systematic collection of tribute from that traffic for corrupt
political purposes. There have been other eras of corruption. Indeed, such eras are likely to
follow wars. Also there was much corruption in connection with the regulation of the liquor
traffic before prohibition. But the present regime of corruption in connection with the liquor
traffic is operating in a new and larger field and is more extensive.

2
THE BAD START AND ITS RESULTS

Too often during the early years of prohibition were arrests made and prosecutions instituted
without sufficient evidence to justify them. In very many instances, unwarranted searches and
seizures were made, which resulted in the refusal by Commissioners to issue warrants of arrest,
or in the dismissal of the prosecution by the courts. In many instances, the character and
appearance of the prohibition agents were such that the United States attorney had no confidence
in the case and juries paid little attention to the witnesses. Thus some of the most important
causes were lost to the Government. On the other hand, the prohibition agents were more
concerned to secure a large number of arrests or seizures than to bring to the District Attorneys
carefully prepared cases of actual importance. It is safe to say that the first seven years'
experience in enforcing the law resulted in distrust of the prohibition forces by many of the
United States attorneys and judges.

It must be said that enforcement of the National Prohibition Act made a bad start which has affected enforcement ever since. Many things contributed to this bad start.

(a) The Eighteenth Amendment was submitted and ratified during a great war. The National Prohibition Act was passed immediately thereafter. During a period of war the people readily yield questions of personal right to the strengthening of government and the increase of its powers. These periods are always characterized by a certain amount of emotionalism. This was especially true of the World War. These enlargements of governmental power, at the expense of individual rights are always followed by reactions against, the abuses of that power which inevitably occur. Periods following great wars are generally characterized by social discontent and unrest which frequently culminate in peaceful or violent revolutions. We have been passing through this secondary phase.

The Eighteenth Amendment and the National Prohibition Act came into existence, therefore, at the time best suited for their adoption and at the worst time for their enforcement. The general reaction against and resentment of the powers of government was inevitable. It could not fail to find expression in opposition to those laws which affected directly and sought in large measure to change the habits and conduct of the people. This attitude has been manifest in the non-observance and resistance to the enforcement of the prohibition laws.

The ratification of the Amendment was given by legislatures which were not in general elected with any reference to this subject. In many instances, as a result of old systems of apportionment. these legislative bodies were not regarded as truly representative of all elements of the community. When ratifications took place a considerable portion of the population were away in active military or other service. It may be doubted if under the conditions then prevailing the results would have been any different if these things had not been true yet these circumstances gave grounds for resentment which has been reflected in the public attitude toward the law and has thus raised additional obstacles to observance and enforcement.

(b) In the second place, the magnitude of the task was not appreciated. It seems to have been anticipated that the fact of the constitutional amendment and federal statute having put the federal government behind national prohibition would of itself operate largely to make the law effective. For a time, there appeared some warrant for this belief. For a time, uncertainty as to how far federal enforcement would prove able to go, lack of organization and experience on the part of law breakers, and perhaps some accumulated private stocks and uncertainty as to the demand and the profits involved, made violations cautious, relatively small in volume, and comparatively easy to handle. But soon after 1921 a marked chance took place. It became increasingly evident that violation was much easier and enforcement much more difficult than had been supposed. The means of enforcement provided proved increasingly inadequate. No thorough-going survey of the difficulties and consideration of how to meet them was undertaken, however, until violations had made such headway as to create a strong and growing public feeling of the futility of the law.

(c) A third cause was lack of experience of federal enforcement of a law of this sort. The subjects

63

of federal penal legislation had been relatively few and either dealt with along well settled common law lines, or narrowly specialized. There was no federal police power and the use of federal powers for police purposes became important only in the present century. The existing federal machinery of law enforcement had not been set up for any such tasks and was ill adapted to those imposed upon it by the National Prohibition Act. But it was sought to adapt that machinery, or to let it find out how to adapt itself, without much prevision of the difficulties. Inadequate organization and equipment have resulted.

(d) A fourth cause which had serious incidental effects was the attempt to enforce the National Prohibition Act as something on another plane from the law generally; an assumption that it was of paramount importance and that constitutional guarantees and legal limitations on agencies of law enforcement and on administration must yield to the exigencies or convenience of enforcing it.

Some advocates of the law have constantly urged and are still urging disregard or abrogation of the guarantees of liberty and of sanctity of the home which had been deemed fundamental in our policy. In some states concurrent state enforcement made an especially bad start with respect to searches and seizures, undercover men, spies and informers; and by the public at large the distinction between federal and state enforcement officers was not easily made. Moreover, the federal field force as it was at first, was largely unfit by training, experience, or character to deal with so delicate a subject. High-handed methods, shootings and killings, even where justified, alienated thoughtful citizens, believers in law and order. Unfortunate public expressions by advocates of the law, approving killings and promiscuous shootings and lawless raids and seizures and deprecating the constitutional guarantees involved, aggravated this effect. Pressure for lawless enforcement, encouragement of bad methods and agencies of obtaining evidence, and crude methods of investigation and seizure on the part of incompetent or badly chosen agents started a current of adverse public opinion in many parts of the land.

(e) Another cause was the influence of politics. No doubt this influence of politics is inevitable in any connection where very large sums of money are to be made by manipulation of administration, and where control of patronage and through it of interference or noninterference with highly profitable activities may be made to yield huge funds for political organizations and as means to political power. In the enforcement of prohibition politics intervened decisively from the beginning, both in the selection of the personnel of the enforcing organization and in the details of operation. This political interference was particularly bad some years ago in connection with the permit system. When inquiry was made into large scale violations, when permits were sought by those not entitled to them, when attempt was made to revoke permits which had been abused, recourse was frequently had to local politicians to bring to bear political pressure whereby local enforcement activities were suspended or hampered or stopped. Nor was this the only source of interference. For some time over-zealous organizations, supporting the law, brought pressure to bear with respect to personnel and methods and even legislation which had unfortunate results. Only in the last few years has enforcement been reasonably emancipated from political interference.

(f) Constant changes in the statute and in the enforcing organization have also had an unfortunate effect. In eleven years the statute was amended or added to in important particulars four times. In that time the central organization as set up originally has twice been changed radically. In that same period the system of permits in connection with industrial alcohol has been changed three times. In consequence it may be claimed with good reason that administration of the law has not been as effective as it might have been.

(g) Another cause, which must not be overlooked, is lack of administrative technique in connection with the tribunals set up under the law. The National Prohibition Act gives to the supervisors of industrial alcohol powers of granting, renewing, and revoking permits -which may involve large investments and no inconsiderable businesses. Thus a system of administrative tribunals has been set up to pass on what may amount to very important property rights. The operation of administrative tribunals of all kinds, necessary as they obviously are, is giving serious concern, largely because of their lack of technique and lack of experience and the inherent difficulty of providing effective control. Perhaps nowhere are the results of this lack of technique more apparent than in connection with the administrative tribunals under the National Prohibition Act.

In some places administrative hearings with respect to permits are carried on as quasi-judicial proceedings, with the dignity of a court and with judicial methods. In others there is no settled procedure or systematic conduct of the proceedings, and in consequence there is want of uniformity, want of predictability, and often not a little dissatisfaction. In consequence there has been much variation in the attitude of the federal courts towards these tribunals. Where the courts have not supported or are not supporting the decisions of the administrators, it will be found as a rule, that the administrative tribunals in that particular locality are not, or until very recently were not, such in their personnel or in their procedure as to command judicial confidence. The evil that some of these tribunals did in the past lives after them in an unfortunate judicial attitude toward administration of the permit system in more than one important center.

(h) Another cause was lack of coordination of the several federal agencies actually or potentially concerned in enforcing prohibition, and consequent relative failure of cooperation until attention was given to this matter within the past few years.

Federal administration has always been more unified than that of the states. Yet friction and want of cooperation in law enforcement, as between different bureaus or services whose functions bear on the same fields or overlap, has been a common phenomenon which the exigencies of enforcing prohibition have merely made more prominent. Want of traditions of cooperation and departmental or bureau esprit de corps made it unlikely that services organized in different departments would cooperate heartily; and the services among which cooperation was to be promoted were distributed in the Department of the Treasury, the Department of Justice, the Department of Agriculture, and the Department of Labor. But even when the different agencies were in the same department, our traditions of independent individual administration led to habits or tendencies of non-cooperation among administrative bureaus. In some localities not long since there was often friction, and more often want of sympathetic common action between the customs authorities and the prohibition agents. There is evidence before us of "occasional co-operation" between the prohibition and the narcotic and immigration services as recently as a year ago. It is not much more than a year since a coordinator of the customs border patrol, coast guard and prohibition agencies was set up at one of the most important centers of importation of liquor in the United States. But for a decade those services were under one department.

When the services are organized in different departments, want of cooperation is even more to be expected. Before transfer of prohibition enforcement to the Department of Justice, there was not infrequent lack of cooperation between United States marshals and prohibition administrators. Within a year, in some places, there has been lack of cooperation between United States attorneys and prohibition administrators. Not long ago there was often much want of accord between them and even sometimes public disagreement. Recently there was want of cooperation between the prohibition administrator, or his agents, and agents of the Department of Agriculture in a section where enforcement is particularly difficult.

Thus enforcement has fallen short of what it should have been partly because of this tradition and these habits of non-cooperation between department and department, bureau and bureau, and service and service. But non-cooperative federal enforcement had gone on for a decade before much was done to co-ordinate the different federal activities and bring them into some unified system.

(i) Finally, enforcement was relied on in and of itself without any reinforcing activities to promote observance. After the passing of the National Prohibition Act, the educational activities toward a public opinion opposed to the use of intoxicating liquor gradually lost their impetus and largely became dormant. For a decade little or nothing has been done in this connection although such activities were peculiarly needed in an era of relaxing of standards of conduct and general free self-assertion. As a result too heavy a burden was put upon enforcement from the beginning and during the critical period in its history.

3

THE STATE OF PUBLIC OPINION

From the beginning ours has been a government of public opinion. We expect legislation to conform to public opinion, not public opinion to yield to legislation. Whether public opinion at a given time and on a given subject is right or wrong is not a question which according to American ideas may be settled by the words, "be it enacted." Hence it is futile to argue what public opinion throughout the land among all classes of the community ought to be in view of the Eighteenth Amendment and the achieved benefits of national prohibition. So long as state cooperation is required to make the amendment and the statute enforcing it effectual, adverse public opinion in some states and lukewarm public opinion with strong hostile elements in other states are obstinate facts which can not be coerced by any measures of enforcement tolerable under our polity. It is therefore a serious impairment of the legal order to have et national law upon the books theoretically governing the whole land and announcing a policy for the whole land which public opinion in many important centers will not enforce and in many others will not suffer to be enforced effectively. The injury to our legal and political institutions from such a situation must be weighed against the gains achieved by national prohibition. Means should be found of conserving the gains while adapting, or making it possible to adapt, legislation under the amendment to conditions and views of particular states.

Improved personnel and better training of federal enforcement agents under the present organization may well effect some change in public opinion, especially in localities where indignation has been aroused by crude or high handed methods formerly in vogue. But much of this indignation is due, to the conduct of state enforcement, which affects opinion as to enforcement generally. A change in the public attitude in such localities should follow an overhauling of state agencies.

We are not now concerned with the various theories as to prohibition, or with public opinion thereon, except as and to the extent that they are existing facts and causes affecting law observance and enforcement.

It is axiomatic that under any system of reasonably free government a law will be observed and may be enforced only where and to the extent that it reflects or is an expression of the general opinion of the normally law-abiding elements of the community. To the extent that this is the case, the law will be observed by the great body of the people and may reasonably be enforced as to the remainder.

The state of public opinion, certainly in many important portions of the country, presents a serious obstacle to the observance and enforcement of the national prohibition laws.

In view of the fact, however, that the prohibition movement received such large popular support and the Eighteenth Amendment was ratified by such overwhelming legislative majorities, inquiry naturally arises as to the causes of the present state of public opinion. There appear to be many causes, some arising out of the structure of the law the conditions to which it was to be applied, and the methods of its enforcement. Others, inherent in the principle of the act, may now be stated.

The movement against the liquor traffic and the use of intoxicating liquors for beverage purposes was originally a movement for temperance. The organizations which grew out of this movement and were potent in its development, were generally in their inception temperance organizations having as their immediate objectives the promotion of temperance in the use of alcoholic beverages and, as a means to this end, the abolition of the commercialized liquor traffic and the licensed saloon, which were the, obvious sources of existing abuses. In many of those states where prohibition laws were adopted and saloons abolished, provision was made for the legal acquisition of limited amounts of alcoholic liquors for beverage purposes. It was only when the Eighteenth Amendment was adopted that total abstinence was sought to be established by fiat of law throughout the territory of the United States or even in many of those states which had adopted limited prohibition laws.

There are obvious differences, both as to individual psychology and legal principle, between temperance and prohibition. Temperance assumes a moderate use of alcoholic beverages but seeks to prevent excess. Even though the ultimate objective may be total abstinence, it seeks to attain that objective by the most effective regulation possible and by the education of the individual to the avoidance of excess and gradual appreciation of the benefits of abstinence. To those holding this view, the field of legitimate governmental control over personal conduct is limited accordingly. Prohibition makes no distinction between moderate and excessive use. It is predicated upon the theory that any use of alcoholic liquors for beverage purposes, however, moderate and under any conditions, is antisocial and so injurious to the community as to justify legal restraint. To those who entertain this view the effort to enforce universal total abstinence by absolute legal mandate is logical. There is, therefore, a fundamental cleavage in principle between those who believe in temperance and those who believe in prohibition which it is difficult to reconcile under the traditional American attitude toward the law already discussed.

When the original temperance movement developed into one for prohibition, the immediate objective was the abolition of the commercialized liquor traffic and the legalized saloon. As between the alternatives of supporting prohibition or the saloon, those who favored the principle of temperance naturally supported prohibition; and, by a combination of the two groups, brought about the adoption of the Eighteenth Amendment and the National Prohibition Act.

When these measures became operative the situation was changed. The legalized liquor traffic and open saloon were abolished, and few desire their return. The question was no longer one between prohibition and the saloon but whether prohibition or the effort to enforce universal total abstinence by legal mandate was sound in principle or was the best and most effective method of dealing with the problem. On this question there was an immediate and inevitable cleavage between those who believed in prohibition and those who believed in temperance. Those who favored prohibition on principle naturally supported the law and demanded the most vigorous measures for its enforcement. Those who favored temperance on principle, while regarding the abolition of the legalized traffic and the saloon as a great and irrevocable step forward, yet looked upon the effort to require and enforce the total abstinence upon all the people, temperate and intemperate alike, by legal mandate, as unsound in principle and an unwarranted extension of governmental control over personal habits and conduct. They recognized and insisted upon the exercise of the right of the government to regulate and control the production, handling, and use of intoxicating liquors to the full extent necessary to prevent excessive use or other conduct which would be injurious to others or the community, but did not approve of the attempt to extend that power to the prevention of temperate use under conditions, not, in their view, injurious or antisocial. The abolition of the commercial traffic and the open saloon were so obviously steps in the right direction that for a time many of those holding this view acquiesced in the law or gave it passive support, but as its operations became more manifest and methods and efforts of enforcement developed, this acquiescence or indifference changed into non-observance or open hostility. Thus an ever widening difference was developed between those groups who by their united efforts for the abolition of the saloon had made possible the adoption of the Amendment and the National Prohibition Act.

Of course, there had been at all times a very substantial portion of the normally law-abiding people who had actively opposed the Eighteenth Amendment on principle. Many of these accepted and observed the law when once it was passed. When it became apparent that the results expected were not being realized, when the effects of the operations of the law and of the methods of enforcement which they deemed invasions of private rights became manifest, their opposition became aroused. This opposition was now, for reasons stated above, largely increased from the ranks of those who had formerly supported the law to get rid of the saloons, but felt that it went too far-who really favored the principle of temperance but did not favor prohibition. The cumulative result of these conditions was that from its inception to the present time the law has been to a constantly increasing degree deprived of that support in public opinion which was and inessential for its general observance or effective enforcement.

4
ECONOMIC DIFFICULTIES

Another type of difficulties are economic. Something has been said already of those involved in ease of production. The constant cheapening and simplification of production of alcohol and of alcoholic drinks, the improvement in quality of what may be made by illicit means the diffusion of knowledge as to how to produce liquor and the perfection of organization of unlawful manufacture and distribution have developed faster than the means of enforcement. But of even more significance is the margin of profit in smuggling liquor, in diversion of industrial alcohol, in illicit distilling and brewing, in bootlegging, and in the manufacture and sale of products of which the bulk goes into illicit or doubtfully lawful making of liquor. This profit makes possible systematic and organized violation of the National Prohibition Act on a large scale and offers rewards on a par with the most important legitimate industries. It makes lavish expenditure in corruption possible. It puts heavy temptation in the way of everyone engaged in enforcement or administration of the law. It affords a financial basis for organized crime.

5
GEOGRAPHICAL DIFFICULTIES

A different type of difficulties may be called geographical. For one thing the proximity of sources of supply from the outside along almost 12,000 miles of Atlantic, Pacific and Gulf shore line, abounding in inlets, much of it adjacent to unoccupied tracts offering every facility to the smuggler, speaks for itself. But in addition the chief sources of supply from the outside are immediately accessible along nearly 3,000 miles of boundary on the Great Lakes and connecting rivers. Likewise we must take account of 3,700 miles of land boundaries. Our internal geography affords quite as much difficulty. Mountainous regions, such swamp areas as the Dismal Swamp and the Everglades islands in the great rivers such as the Mississippi, forested regions and barrens, are everywhere in relatively close proximity to cities affording steady and profitable markets for illicit liquor. Here also are the best of opportunities for unlawful manufacture.

6
POLITICAL DIFFICULTIES

What may be called political difficulties grow out of the limits of effective federal action in our polity, the need of state cooperation and the many factors operating against it, the tradition of politics and political interference in all administration, and the tendency to constant amendment of the law to be enforced.

It must be borne in mind that the federal government is one of limited powers. Except as granted to the United States or implied in those granted, all powers are jealously reserved to the state. Certain traditional lines of federal activity had become well developed and understood. Policing, except incidental to certain relatively narrow and specialized functions of the general government was not one of them. Importation, transportation across state lines, and the enforcement of excise tax laws were natural subjects of federal action. But prohibition of manufacture, distribution and sale within the states had always been solely within the scope of state action until the Eighteenth Amendment. This radical change in what had been our settled policy at once raised the question how far the federal government, as it was organized and had grown up under the Constitution, was adapted to exercise such a concurrent jurisdiction.

Nor was it merely that a radical change was made when the federal government was given jurisdiction over matters internal in the states. It was necessary also to adjust our federal polity to a conception of two sovereignties, each engaged independently in enforcing the same provision, so that, as it was supposed, wherever and whenever the one fell down the other might step in. Endeavor to bring about a nationally enforced universal total abstinence, instead of limiting the power devolved on the federal government to those features of the enforcement of the amendment which were naturally or traditionally of federal cognizance, invited difficulty at the outset. But difficulties inhered also in the conception of the amendment that nation and state were to act concurrently, each covering the whole of the same ground actually or potentially; each using its own governmental machinery at the same time with the other in enforcing provisions with respect to which each had a full jurisdiction.

There are four possibilities in such a situation (1) a strong, centralized, well-organized federal police; (2) full voluntary cooperation between state and nation; (3) a voluntary petition between state and nation in which each may be relied on to carry out zealously the part assigned to it, and (4) abdication of part, leaving to the states, if they care to exercise it full control over the field which the nation surrenders.

Attempts to bring about and maintain the requisite cooperation between national and state enforcement of prohibition encounter adverse public opinion in many important localities and are hampered by a bad tradition as to cooperation of state and federal governments and by irritation in communities which feel that the ideas of conduct and modes of life of other communities are being forced upon them.

We have a long tradition of independence of administrative officials and systematic decentralizing of administration. In consequence disinclination to cooperate has pervaded our whole polity, local, state, and federal; and for historical reasons since the Civil War there has been more or less latent, or even open, suspicion or jealousy of federal administrative agencies on the part of many of the states. Concurrent state and federal prohibition has shown us nothing new. It has repeated and recapitulated in a decade the experience of 140 years of administration of nation-wide laws in a government. In the beginnings of the federal government, it was believed that state officials and state tribunals could be made regularly available as the means of enforcing federal laws. It was soon necessary to set up a separate system of federal magistrates and federal enforcing agencies. We had no traditions of concerted action between independent governmental activities and it was not until the World War that we succeeded in developing a spirit of cooperation at least for the time being. In spite of that experience, the Eighteenth Amendment reverted to the policy of state enforcement of federal law, and again there has been not a little falling down of enforcement between concurrent agencies with diffused responsibility. The result was disappointing. Too frequently there has been a feeling, even in states which had prohibition laws before the National Prohibition Act, that enforcement of prohibition was now a federal concern with which the state need no longer trouble itself. Thus there has often been apathy or inaction on the part of state agencies even where local sentiment was strong for the law. It is true the good sense and energy of some prohibition directors and vigorous action on the art of some state executives have at times brought about a high degree of cooperation in more than one jurisdiction. Sometimes this cooperation is local and fitful, sometimes and in some places it is complete, and sometimes it is well organized and coordinated. But there are no guaranties of its continuance.

It seems now to be the policy of federal enforcement to make on its own motion a partition of the field, leaving all but interstate combinations and commercial manufacture to the state. This relinquishing of much of the field of concurrent jurisdiction, to be taken on by the states or not as they see fit, is a departure from the program of the Eighteenth Amendment.

All administration in the United States must struggle with a settled tradition of political interference. At the outset of enforcement of prohibition, the choice of enforcement agents was influenced for the worse both by politicians and by pressure of organizations. Positions in the enforcement organization were treated from the standpoint of patronage. Since the magnitude of the task could not have been appreciated, it was assumed that methods of filling federal administrative positions -which had on the whole sufficed as to other laws would suffice here. Thus the enforcement organization at first was not at all what the task called for. Moreover, political interference went beyond the filling of positions in the administrative organization. There was constant complaint of interference by politicians with the granting and revoking of permits, with efforts at enforcement and with the details of administration. Political interference has decreased, but as our institutions are organized and conducted, it will always be a menace to effectual enforcement.

7
PSYCHOLOGICAL DIFFICULTIES

A number of causes of resentment or irritation at the law or at features of its enforcement raise difficulties for national prohibition. A considerable part of the public were irritated at a constitutional "don't" in a matter where they saw no moral question. The statutory definition of 'intoxicating" at a point clearly much below what is intoxicating in truth and fact, even if maintainable as a matter of legal power, was widely felt to be arbitrary and unnecessary. While there was general agreement that saloons were wisely eliminated, there was no general agreement on the universal regime of enforced total abstinence. In consequence many of the best citizens in every community, on whom we rely habitually for the upholding of law and order, are at most lukewarm as to the National Prohibition Act. Many who are normally law-abiding are led to an attitude hostile to the statute by a feeling that repression and interference with private conduct area carried too far. This is aggravated in many of the larger cities by a feeling that other parts of the land are seeking to impose ideas of conduct upon them and to mold city life to what are considered to be their provincial conceptions.

Other sources of resentment and irritation grow out of incidents of enforcement. In the nature of things it is easier to shut up the open drinking places and stop the sale of beer, which was drunk chiefly by working men, than to prevent the wealthy from having and using liquor in their homes and in their clubs. Naturally when the industrial benefits of prohibition are pointed out, laboring men resent the insistence of employers who drink that their employees be kept from temptation. It is easier to detect and apprehend small offenders than to reach the well organized larger operators. It is much easier to padlock a speakeasy than to close up a large hotel where important and influential and financial interests are involved. Thus the law may be made to appear as aimed at and enforced against the insignificant while the wealthy enjoy immunity. This feeling is reinforced when it is seen that the wealthy are generally able to procure pure liquors, where those with less means may run the risk of poisoning through the working over of denatured alcohol or, at best, must put up with cheap, crude, and even deleterious products. Moreover, searches of homes, especially under state laws, have necessarily seemed to bear more upon people of moderate means than upon those of wealth or influence. Resentment at crude methods of enforcement, unavoidable with the class of persons employed in the past and still often employed in state enforcement, disgust with informers, snoopers, and under-cover men unavoidably made use of if a universal total abstinence is to be brought about by law, and irritation at the inequalities of penalties, even in adjoining districts in the same locality and as between state and federal tribunals -- something to be expected with respect to a law as to which opinions differ so widely -- add to the burden under which enforcement must be conducted.

Resentment is aroused also by the government's collecting income tax from bootleggers and illicit manufacturers and distributors upon the proceeds of their unlawful business. This has been a convenient and effective way of striking at large operators who have not returned their true incomes. But it impresses many citizens as a legal recognition and even licensing of the business, and many who pay income taxes upon the proceeds of their legitimate activities feel strongly that illegitimate activities should be treated by the government as upon a different basis.

Any program of improvement should seek to obviate, or at least reduce to a minimum, these causes of resentment and irritation.

It will be perceived that some of them are due to differences of opinion as to total abstinence and could only be eliminated by bringing about a substantial unanimity on that subject throughout the land, or by conceding something to communities where public opinion is adverse thereto. Others are due largely to inherent features of all enforcement of law which have attracted special attention in connection with a matter of controversy. These may be met in part by improvements in the machinery of enforcement, by improvements in the general administration of criminal

72

justice, and by unifying or reconciling public opinion, Still others are due to unfortunate but to no small extent remediable incidents of enforcement. Federal enforcement has been steadily improving in this respect. If state enforcement agencies in many jurisdictions could be similarly improved, the effect ought to be seen presently in a more favorable public opinion.

8
THE STRAIN ON COURTS, PROSECUTING MACHINERY, AND PENAL INSTITUTIONS

Our federal organization of courts and of prosecution were ill adapted to the task imposed on them by the National Prohibition Act. Serious difficulties at this point soon became apparent and enforcement of national prohibition still wrestles with them. The program of concurrent federal and state enforcement imposes a heavy burden of what was in substance the work of police courts upon courts set up and hitherto employed chiefly for litigation of more than ordinary magnitude. In the first five years of national prohibition, the volume of liquor prosecutions in the federal courts had multiplied by seven and federal prosecutions under the Prohibition Act terminated in 1930 had become nearly eight times as many as the total number of all pending federal prosecutions in 1914. In a number of urban districts the enforcement agencies maintain that the only practicable way of meeting this situation with the existing machinery of federal courts and prosecutions is for the United States Attorneys to make bargains with defendants or their counsel whereby defendants plead quilt to minor offenses and escape with light penalties. Hence a disproportionate number of federal liquor prosecutions terminate in pleas of guilty: In the year ending June 30, 1930, over eight-ninths of the convictions were of this character. Since enactment of the Increased Penalties Act, 1929, prosecutors have proceeded by information for minor offenses in most cases, thus facilitating the bargain method of clearing the dockets. During the year ending June 30, 1930, whereas for the federal courts as a whole 41.4 per cent of the convictions resulted in sentences to some form of imprisonment, in three urban districts in which there was obvious congestion the percentages were 6.3, 3.9 and 5.0, respectively. The meagerness of the result in proportion to the effort shows the seriousness of the difficulty under which the enforcement of national prohibition has been laboring. But this is not all. The bargain method of keeping up with the dockets which prevails of necessity in some of the most important jurisdictions of the country, plays into the hands of the organized illicit traffic by enabling it to reckon protection of its employees in the overhead. In some of our largest cities sentences have been almost uniformly to small fines or trivial imprisonment. Thus criminal prosecution, in view of the exigencies of disposing of so many cases in courts not organized for that purpose is a feeble deterrent. The most available methods of enforcement have come to be injunction proceedings and seizure and destruction of equipment and materials.

Lawyers everywhere deplore, as one of the most serious effects of prohibition, the change in the general attitude toward the federal courts. Formerly these tribunals were of exceptional dignity, and the efficiency and dispatch of their criminal business commanded wholesome fear and respect. The professional criminal, who sometimes had scanty respect for the state tribunals, was careful so to conduct himself as not to come within the jurisdiction of the federal courts. The effect of the huge volume of liquor prosecutions, which has come to these courts under prohibition, has inured their dignity, impaired their efficiency, and endangered the wholesome respect for them which once obtained. Instead of being impressive tribunals of superior

73

jurisdiction, they have had to do the work of police courts and that work has been chiefly in the public eye. These deplorable conditions have been aggravated by the constant presence in about these courts of professional criminal lawyers and bail-bond agents, whose unethical and mercenary practices have detracted from these valued institutions.

Prosecutors, federal and state, have been affected no less than courts. They have been appointed and elected too often under pressure of organizations concerned only with prohibition, as if nothing else were to be considered in the conduct of criminal justice. Their work has been appraised solely in terms of their zeal in liquor cases. Under the pressure to make a record in such cases, it has not always been easy to keep up the right standards of forensic conduct and methods, and speeches such as had not been known in common law courts since the 17th century have become not uncommon in our criminal courts in the last decade. High-handed methods, unreasonable searches and seizures, lawless interference with personal and property rights, have had a bad effect on the work of prosecution at a time when the general condition of American administration of justice was imperatively demanding improvement.

Injurious effects upon the administrative machinery of the courts have been equally apparent. Instances of difficulty in procuring execution warrants by United States marshals, scandals in the carrying out of orders for the destruction of seized liquors, failure to serve orders in padlock injunction cases, and carrying on of illicit production and distribution under protection of a marshal or his assistants, in many places have brought the executive arm of the federal courts into disrespect, where until recently its efficiency was universally believed in. The procuring of permits, the giving of legal advice to beer rings and organizations of bootleggers and the acting as go-betweens between law-breakers and political organizations with a view to protection on one side and campaign contributions on the other, have made conspicuous a type of politician lawyer who had been absent from the federal courts in the past.

Nor have these bad effects been confined to the criminal side of the federal courts. There has been a general bad effect upon the whole administration of justice. There has been a tendency to appraise judges solely by their zeal in liquor prosecutions. In consequence the civil business of the court's has often been delayed or interfered with. Zealous organizations, dictating appointments, interfering with policies and seeking to direct the course of administering the law cooperating with other unfortunate conditions when the law took effect, brought about crude methods of enforcement. The gross inequalities of sentence made possible by the Increased Penalties Act, 1929, has added to the difficulties of the administration of criminal justice.

A policy, announced at one time, of dealing in the federal courts only with large-scale violations, with organized smuggling, diversion, and wholesale manufacture and transportation-leaving police cases to the state courts-was not generally successful for several reasons. Some states have no laws, and, in view of the clear implication of Section 2 of the Eighteenth Amendment, the federal government could not be expected to acquiesce in a general system of open violations in such states. Some states or localities, after the National Prohibition Act, began to leave all enforcement, or at least the brunt thereof, to the federal courts. In these states, too, the policy of Section 2 of the Amendment called for federal action. Moreover petty prosecutions often have an important place in a program of reaching larger violators. Before repeated offenders may be brought within the provisions of the statute as to second and subsequent offenses, it is necessary to prosecute them for a first time even if only for a relatively slight violation. Such prosecutions of small offenders may also be the means of inducing employees to confess and thus aid in detecting those who are behind them. Nor may we overlook the desire of federal agents and officials to make a record for liquor prosecutions and the difficulty of catching and convicting large-scale as compared with small-scale violators.

The operation of the National Prohibition Act has also thrown a greatly increased burden upon the federal penal institutions which seems bound to increase with any effective increase in enforcement. The reports of the Department of Justice show that the total federal long term prison population, i. e., prisoners serving sentences of more than a year, has risen from not more than 5,268 on June 30, 1921 to 14,115 on June 30, 1930. The number of long term prisoners confined in the five leading federal institutions on June 30, 1930 for violation of the National Prohibition Act and other national liquor laws was 4,296 out of a total of 12,332. The percentage of long term violators of the National Prohibition Act and other national liquor laws to total federal prisoners confined in the five leading federal institutions on June 30, 1930 was therefore something over one-third. This constituted by far the largest class of long term federal prisoners so confined, the next largest classes being made up of those sentenced for violation of the Dyer Act (the National Motor Vehicle Theft Act) and the Narcotic Acts, the percentage of whom on June 30, 1930 were, respectively, 13.2% and 22% of the total.

The figures above set out include only persons serving sentences of more than one year, and do not include the very large number of individuals confined in county jails and other institutions for violation of the National Prohibition Act under shorter sentences.

The recital of these figures is sufficient to indicate the gravity and difficulty of the problem from the, penal housing standpoint, which the effective enforcement of the National Prohibition Act presents.

9
THE INVITATION TO HYPOCRISY AND EVASION INVOLVED IN THE PROVISION AS TO FRUIT JUICES

Reference has been made to the anomalous provision of Section 29, Title 2, of the National Prohibition Act as to the manufacture of nonintoxicating cider and fruit juices exclusively for use in the home. If these are not "liquor" within the act, it 'is hard to see why the provision was needed. If they are, and the provision so suggests by saying that the penalties for the manufacture of "liquor" shall not apply to them, there is a discrimination between beer of lower alcoholic content, which certainly is not a "fruit juice," and wine of distinctly higher content. Moreover, the failure to fix the meaning of "non-intoxicating" in this connection, leaving it a question of fact to be passed on by the jury in each case, in effect removes wine-making from the field of practicable enforcement. Why home wine-making should be lawful while home-brewing of beer and home distilling of spirits are not, why home wine-making for home use is less reprehensible than making the same wine outside the home for home use, and why it should be penal to make wine commercially for use in homes and not penal to make in huge quantities the material for wine-making and set up an elaborate selling campaign for disposing of them is not apparent. if, as has been decided, the provision means to sanction home making of wine of greater alcoholic content than permitted by Section 1, it is so arbitrary, so inviting of evasion, and so contrary to the policy announced in Section 3 that it can only be a source of mischief.

10
NULLIFICATION

It is generally admitted and indeed has been demonstrated by experience that state cooperation is necessary to effective enforcement. In states which decline to cooperate and in those which give but a perfunctory or lukewarm cooperation, not only does local federal enforcement fail, but those localities become serious points for infecting others. As things are at present, there is virtual local option. It seems to be admitted by the Government and demonstrated by experience that it is substantially impracticable for the federal government alone to enforce the declared policy of the National Prohibition Act effectively as to home production. Obviously, nullification by failure of state cooperation and acquiesced-in nullification in homes have serious implications. Enforcement of a national law with a clearly announced national policy, such as is set forth in Section 3 of the National Prohibition Act, cannot be pronounced satisfactory when gaps of such extent and far-reaching effect are left open.

11
HOW FAR ARE THESE BAD FEATURES NECESSARILY INVOLVED IN NATIONAL PROHIBITION?

As to the prevailing corruption, it has its foundation in the profit involved in violations of the National Prohibition Act. Hence it could be put an end to, or at least greatly reduced, by eliminating or reducing that profit. Also it could be materially reduced by better selection of personnel, both in the federal enforcing organization and in state police, administrative and prosecuting organizations. But it may be queried whether the profit in violation of the National Prohibition Act is likely to be eliminated or largely reduced so long as so many people and the people in so many localities are willing to pay considerable sums to obtain liquor, and so long as the money available for corruption is so wholly out of proportion to what is practicable in the way of salaries for those concerned with enforcement.

As to the state of public opinion, the way toward improvement is chiefly through education. Unhappily, since the National Prohibition Act the whole emphasis has been upon coercion rather than upon education. In addition many, at least, of the causes of resentment at national prohibition could be removed and thus a more favorable public attitude could be induced. On the other hand, it may be urged that it is too late to educate public opinion in those communities where a settled current adverse to national prohibition has set in. Also, care must be taken lest some of the changes in the law, necessary to remove what have become sources of irritation, may involve relaxation of enforcement so as to react unfavorably upon other features of the situation. The main difficulty will be to reconcile the population in our large urban centers to the policy announced in section three of the National Prohibition Act. How far this is possible is a matter of judgment on which opinions differ.

So also as to the profit involved in violations. How far as a practical matter this may be eliminated by more ample provision of machinery for enforcement and stimulating more complete cooperation in the enforcement of the law as it stands depends upon a judgment as to what may be achieved in places where there is hostile or lukewarm public opinion. At bottom, this question is linked to the preceding one.

The strain on federal courts and federal prosecuting machinery, grows out of the inadequacy of the organization of federal courts and of the federal prosecuting system to the task imposed upon it. To a degree, this inadequacy could be remedied. But it may be a question how far it is expedient to set up what would be in effect a system of federal police magistrates in order to enforce the National Prohibition Act in jurisdictions where the police will not deal with lesser violations to which the present federal judicial organization not adapted. If such violations are not prosecuted somewhere, either in state or in federal tribunals, there is to that extent nullification. While this bad feature of the present situation is not inherent in prohibition, it is closely connected with the question of cooperation between state and federal governments and of concurrent jurisdiction as contemplated by the Eighteenth Amendment, and what is done by way of remedy must depend upon the conclusions reached with respect to possibilities of cooperation.

Finally, with respect to the provision in Section 29 of Title 2 of the National Prohibition Act relation to home production of the bad or potentially bad, features of the present situation could be and ought to be eliminated by the simple process of making the provision in this respect uniform with those of the rest of the act. Removal of the anomalous provision in Section 29 would do away with what threatens to be a serious impairment of the legislatively announced policy of national prohibition.

X - CONCLUSIONS AND RECOMMENDATIONS

1. The Commission is opposed to repeal of the Eighteenth Amendment.

2. The Commission is opposed to the restoration in any manner of the legalized saloon.

3. The Commission is opposed to the federal or state governments, as such, going into the liquor business.

4. The Commission is opposed to the proposal to modify the National Prohibition Act so as to permit manufacture and sale of light wines or beer.

5. The Commission is of opinion that the cooperation of the states is an essential element in the enforcement of the Eighteenth Amendment and the National Prohibition Act throughout the territory of the United States; that the support of public opinion in the several states is necessary in order to insure such cooperation.

6. The Commission is of opinion that prior to the enactment of the Bureau of Prohibition Act, 1927, the agencies for enforcement were badly organized and inadequate; that subsequent to that enactment there has been continued improvement in organization and effort for enforcement.

7. The Commission is of opinion that there is yet no adequate observance or enforcement.

8. The Commission is of opinion that the present organization for enforcement is still inadequate.

9. The Commission is of opinion that the federal appropriations for enforcement of the Eighteenth Amendment should be substantially increased and that the vigorous and better organized efforts which have gone on since the Bureau of Prohibition Act, 1927, should be furthered by certain improvements in the statutes and in the organization, personnel, and equipment of enforcement, so as to give to enforcement the greatest practicable efficiency.

10. Some of the Commission are not convinced that Prohibition under the Eighteenth Amendment is unenforceable and believe that a further trial should be made with the help of the recommended improvements, and that if after such trial effective enforcement is not secured there should be a revision of the Amendment. Others of the Commission are convinced that it has been demonstrated that Prohibition under the Eighteenth Amendment is unenforceable and that the Amendment should be immediately revised, but recognizing that the process of amendment will require some time, they unite in the recommendations of Conclusion No. 9 for the improvement of the enforcement agencies.

11. All the Commission agree that if the Amendment is revised it should be made to read substantially as follows:

Section 1. The Congress shall have power to regulate or to prohibit the manufacture, traffic in or transportation of intoxicating liquors within, the importation thereof into and the exportation thereof from the United States and all territory subject to the jurisdiction thereof for beverage purposes.

12. The recommendations referred to in conclusion Number 9 are:

1. Removal of the, causes of irritation and resentment on the part of the medical profession by:

(a) Doing away with the statutory fixing of the amount which may be prescribed and the number of prescriptions;

(b) Abolition of the requirement of specifying the ailment for which liquor is prescribed upon a blank to go into the public files;

(c) Leaving as much as possible to regulations rather than fixing details by statute.

2. Removal of the anomalous provisions in Section 29, National Prohibition Act, as to cider and fruit juices by making some uniform regulation for a fixed alcoholic content.

3. Increase of the number of agents, storekeeper-gaugers, prohibition investigators, and special agents; increase in the personnel of the Customs Bureau and in the equipment of all enforcement organizations.

4. Enactment of a statute authorizing regulations permitting access to the premises and records of wholesale and retail dealers so as to make it possible to trace products of specially denatured alcohol to the ultimate consumer.

5. Enactment of legislation to prohibit independent denaturing plants.

6. The Commission is opposed to legislation allowing more latitude for federal searches and seizures.

7. The Commission renews the recommendation contained in its previous reports for codification of the National Prohibition Act and the acts supplemental to and in amendment thereof.

8. The Commission renews its recommendation of legislation for making procedure in the so-called padlock injunction cases more effective.

9. The Commission recommends legislation providing a mode of prosecuting petty offenses in the federal courts and modifying the Increased Penalties Act of 1929, as set forth in the Chairman's letter to the Attorney General dated May 23, 1930, H. R. Rep. 1699.

There are differences of view among the members of the Commission as to certain of the conclusions stated and as to some matters included in or omitted from this report. The report is signed subject to individual reservation of the right to express these individual views in separate or supplemental reports to be annexed hereto.

Geo W. Wickersham
Chairman

HENRY W. ANDERSON

NEWTON D. BAKER

ADA L. COMSTOCK

WILLIAM I. GRUBB

WILLIAM S. KENYON

FRANK J. LOESCH

PAUL J. MCCORMICK

KENNETH MACINTOSH

ROSCOE POUND

SEPARATE REPORT OF HENRY W. ANDERSON

Introduction

This Commission was created for the purpose of making a "thorough inquiry into the problem of the enforcement of prohibition under the Eighteenth Amendment and laws enacted in pursuance thereof, together with the enforcement of other laws." The essential purpose was not so much to find that abuses existed in law observance and enforcement, for this was already known, as to ascertain the nature and extent of these abuses and the causes therefor, and to suggest definite and constructive remedies. This purpose was clearly stated by the President in a brief address to the Commission at the time of its organization in which he said: "It is my hope the Commission shall secure accurate determinations of fact and cause, following them with constructive, courageous conclusions, which will bring public understanding and command public support of its solutions."

After eighteen months of investigation and study the Commission is now submitting its report on the problem of prohibition enforcement. I am unable to agree with some of the discussion in the report, or to concur in some of the conclusions--especially Conclusions numbered 6 and 9 as they are expressed, and Recommendations 3 and 8. My chief objections to the report, however, are due to its failure to draw definite conclusions as to certain essential aspects of the problem, or to present constructive remedies. The right is reserved therein to the members of the Commission to express their individual views as to any matters contained in or omitted from the report in separate or supplemental statements to be annexed thereto. I am signing the report subject to this reservation.

With the essential facts as stated in the report I concur. Confronted by these facts, I am forced to the view that the causes for existing conditions and the solution of the present problem must be sought in fundamental social and economic principles which are ignored or violated in the existing system of national prohibition. These causes should be critically analyzed to the end that they may be understood and effective remedies devised to meet them. The essential conclusions, both as to present enforcement and the enforceability of the existing law, should be clearly stated.

A constructive solution of this problem should now be proposed. It is my purpose to do this--to present as a substitute for the present system a definite plan of liquor control, in conformity with our scheme of government, based upon sound social, political and economic principles, the essential elements of which have been tested in our own experience, and which, if adopted, will in my view provide a solution of the problem. The facts stated and discussed in the report of the Commission can lead only to one conclusion. The Eighteenth Amendment and the National Prohibition Act have not been and are not being observed. They have not been and are not being enforced. We have prohibition in law but not in fact. The abolition in law of the commercialized liquor traffic and the licensed saloon operated entirely for private profit was the greatest step forward ever taken in America looking to the control of that traffic. The saloon is gone forever. It belongs as completely to the past as the institution of human slavery.

On the other hand the effort to go further and to make the entire population of the United States total abstainers in disregard of the demand deeply rooted in the habits and customs of the people, ran counter to fundamental social and economic principles the operations of which are beyond the control of government.

As a result we are confronted by new evils of far-reaching and disturbing consequence. We are in grave danger of losing all that has been gained through the abolition of the legalized liquor traffic and the saloon. The fruitless efforts at enforcement are creating public disregard not only for this law but for all laws. Public corruption through the purchase of official protection for this illegal traffic is widespread and notorious. The courts are cluttered with prohibition cases to an extent which seriously affects the entire administration of justice. The prisons, Sate and National, are overflowing, but the number of lawbreakers still increases. The people are being poisoned with bad and unregulated liquor to the permanent detriment of the public health and the ultimate increase of dependency and crime. The illicit producer, the bootlegger and the speakeasy are reaping a rich harvest of profits, and are becoming daily more securely entrenched. The enormous revenues (estimated at from two to three billion dollars per annum) placed in the hands of the lawless and criminal elements of society through this illegal traffic are not only enabling them to carry on this business in defiance of the government, but to organize and develop other lines of criminal activity to an extent which threatens social and economic security. The country is growing restive under these conditions. The situation demands some definite and constructive relief.

The liquor question is obscuring thought, dominating public discussion, and excluding from consideration other matters of vital concern, to an extent far beyond its actual importance in our social and economic life. It must be solved or the social and political interests of our country may be seriously compromised.

We should profit by the lessons of our own history. America way the only nation of the civilized world which had to invoke the horrors of civil war to rid itself of the blight of human slavery. We allowed emotion and prejudice to obscure thought, and tampered with the situation by evasion and compromise, with tragic results. We are doing the same today. The whole world, including America, after years of suffering, is in a condition of social unrest and economic depression. Confidence in the integrity and capacity of government is shaken. It is no time for tampering with this problem. A definite solution is demanded.

We learn from experience. Progress is attained through the constant process of trial and error. Organized society has not exhausted its resources for dealing with the liquor question. Between the one extreme of a legalized traffic conducted solely for private profit, and the other extreme of absolute prohibition, lies a great middle ground of unexplored territory. Social organization is never absolute; the truth is generally to be found in this middle ground.

The abolition of the legalized traffic conducted solely for private profit has cleared the field. Holding at any cost the position thus gained we can take it as a point of departure for a new offensive against the existing evils. Then, by methods adapted to present conditions, based upon sound principles and experience, we can accomplish their defeat. If other means of evading reasonable social restraints are then devised we may by proper modification of the line of action conquer them, and continue in this process until through effective control and higher social development the ultimate objective shall be obtained.

I. THE CAUSES FOR EXISTING CONDITIONS

No law can be enforced unless it has the general support of the normally law abiding elements of the community.

The conception of natural or inherent rights of the individual as limitations upon the power of government and of majorities has been generally accepted in America since the Declaration of Independence. Whether this is sound it is useless to enquire. The existence of this conception is a stubborn fact of first magnitude. The distinction in principle between temperance and absolute prohibition by law is manifest. Public opinion is substantially unanimous in support of the abolition of the legalized saloon. But a large number of those who favor temperance and are unalterably opposed to the commercialized liquor traffic, including many who do not use alcoholic beverages in any way, regard the effort to enforce total abstinence by law upon the temperate and intemperate alike as unsound in principle and as an undue extension of governmental power over the personal conduct of the citizen. They feel that the present law attempted too much--went too far in its invasion of personal rights. This state of opinion among a large and increasing proportion of the normally law abiding people of the country is an important factor in the situation. It has its sources in fundamental principles and political conceptions which are beyond the reach of government. This attitude of public opinion constitutes an insuperable obstacle to the observance and enforcement of the law.

Another fundamental cause for existing conditions is to be found in the character and structure of the Eighteenth Amendment. That Amendment is a rigid mandate controlling both Congress and the states. It is the first instance in our history in which the effort has been made by Constitutional provision to extend the police control of the federal government to every individual and every home in the United States. The practical and political difficulties which have resulted therefrom are manifest. It imposed upon the federal government the obligation to enforce a police regulation over 3,500,000 square miles of territory, requiring total abstinence on the part of 122,000,000 people who had been accustomed to consume over 2,000,000,000 gallons of alcoholic beverages per annum. This was certainly an ambitious undertaking for any government.

The cooperation of the several States was contemplated but the Amendment inevitably operated to defeat this expectation. It aroused the traditional jealousy of the States and the people thereof as the right of local self-government in matters affecting personal habits and conduct. As a result no less than eight states, containing one-fourth of the entire population of the United States, either have no enforcement law or have repealed or voted to repeal such laws. The people of other states are obviously contemplating similar action. Many states are indifferent as to enforcement. Comparatively few are actively of effectively cooperating in the enforcement of the prohibition laws. In view of the statement of every Federal Director, or Commissioner of Prohibition, from the beginning, confirmed by the unanimous finding of this Commission, that the National Prohibition Act cannot be enforced without the cooperation of the states, this situation seems to require only a simple syllogism to demonstrate that this law cannot be enforced at all.

Even more important and controlling causes for the existing situation are to be found in the social, political and economic conditions to which the law is sought to be applied.

The Eighteenth Amendment and the National Prohibition Act undertake to establish one uniform rule of conduct as to alcoholic beverages for over one hundred and twenty million people throughout the territory of the United States. This large and widely scattered population contains elements of nearly every race in the world. Many of them are but recently derived from their parent stocks. They still cling, in a greater or less degree, to the social conceptions of the races from which they sprang, and to the habits and customs of their inheritance.

The social, political, and economic views of these elements and groups are correspondingly varied and often conflicting. This variety or conflict of view finds direct expression in their personal habits, and is reflected in the thought and political organizations of the communities in which they live. Some of the political divisions of the country have had centuries of existence with settled habits and fixed social customs. Others are but the recent outgrowths of frontier life and have all those characteristics of independence, and of resentments of social control, incident to pioneer conditions.

Few things are so stubborn and unyielding as habits and conceptions of personal or political conduct which have their roots in racial instincts or social traditions. As a consequence of this truth--so often ignored--the development of that social and institutional cohesion which is essential to the spirit and fact of nationality is always a matter of slow and painful evolution. It can not be hurried by mandate of law. It comes only through the influence of association and understanding, through the development of common ideals and interests, the reluctant yielding of individual freedom to the demands of social organization.

Experience indicates that if the effort is made to force this development by legal mandate the result is social discomfort and resentment, frequently finding expression in passive refusal to observe the law, or in resistance. If normal development is sought to be unduly limited or restrained it finds expression in social unrest or disorder and, if carried to its ultimate conclusion, in revolution.

The operation of these principles has been manifest in every stage of the social and political life of the United States. The original colonists came to America with minds strongly influenced by the principles of individual liberty which dominated the thought of Europe during the seventeenth and eighteenth centuries. This individual consciousness was accentuated by conditions of life in the New World. It found its first united expression in the American Revolution. Even then these separate and independent communities were held together with difficulty for the protection of their common interests and in the face of a common enemy. When the war was over they, jealous of any central control, immediately began to draw apart.

The resulting disorganization and the dominant influence of a few great leaders made possible the adoption of the Federal Constitution. The declared purpose of that instrument was to bring about a "more perfect union." The people were not ready for nationality. It was not attempted. The federal government was given control only over matters of general interest. The states remained as agencies through which the varied and sometimes divergent interests and social conceptions of the several localities might find expression; as schools for the training of the people in the difficult adventure of self government and for the gradual development of social, political, and economic life into a more cohesive nationality.

As the older communities became settled and individual freedom of action became limited by necessary social restraints, the more adventurous elements moved on to the frontier. New states were organized to begin again the difficult process of social adjustment. The frontier only disappeared late in the last century.

In the meantime, successive tides of immigration have brought into this confused and divergent social order new elements of various races, customs and ideals which have created strong cross currents in the stream of American life and have tended to affect its flow.

Under modern conditions, the progress of the United States toward that stage of social uniformity and cohesion which would admit of national regulation of matters affecting personal habit and conduct has been more rapid than that of older nations, but it appears yet to be far from actual attainment. The social and economic outlook, habits and customs of the urban and industrial communities of the East are necessarily different from those of the agricultural communities of the South or West, of the more recently settled areas of the frontier. Those of different races and nationalities are still more widely divergent. If a topographic map should be made of the social conditions and stages of institutional development of the entire United States, it would present an aspect as rough, and with variations as acute as the physical surface of the country. If we should then undertake to fit one rigid plane to every part of this highly irregular and unyielding surface, it would give some idea of the difficulties of adjusting a national law of this character to every community and to each individual of the United States.

These conditions are clearly reflected in the attitude of individuals and communities toward the observance and enforcement of the prohibition laws. Those who had been accustomed to use alcoholic beverages--who saw no harm in their moderate use and no reason why they should be denied this privilege--sought other sources of supply in disregard of the law. Public irritation and resentment developed. There was a revisal of sectionalism due to the feeling in urban and industrial communities that the law was an effort on the part of the agricultural sections to force their social ideals upon other sections to force their social ideals upon other sections to which those ideals were not adapted. On the other hand, there was, on the part of those communities which favored the law, resentment against those which resisted its enforcement. These things are not only prejudicial to the observance and enforcement of the prohibition law; they go much further, and affect adversely the normal operations of our entire national life.

The economic conditions to which the Amendment and law are to be applied are of equally fundamental character and of even more conclusive significance. It has already been stated that prior to the adoption of the Amendment, the people of the United States consumed more than

84

two billion gallons of alcoholic liquors per annum. Neither the Amendment nor the law could eradicate this demand. It had its sources in the customs and habits of the people themselves. The business and agencies through which the demand had been legally supplied were destroyed. The supply within the country, except that in private possession or in bonded warehouses, disappeared. The legal channels of supply from beyond our borders were obliterated. The demand remained.

Where a demand exists and that demand can be supplied at an adequate profit, the supply will reach the point of demand. Interference with or obstruction of the sources or channels of supply may affect the cost, and thus for a time reduce the effective demand as to those who are unable or unwilling to pay the increased price, but to the extent that the sources of the demand will provide the profit necessary for the supply the demand will be met. It was due to this elementary law that in the earlier years of prohibition, before the agencies of illegal domestic production could be developed, the purchase and use of alcoholic liquors were more largely confined to persons of means who could afford to pay the higher cost.

The operation of this economic law explains the failure of state regulation and state prohibition. State regulation undertook to control the supply at the point of outlet and sale. It did not touch the demand. Generally no effort was made to control the amount or source of supply or the profit. Such regulation therefore operated to increase the pressure of the supply at the point of attempted control and thus to increase sales to overcome this obstruction. It thus tended to augment the very evils which it sought to prevent. State prohibition undertook to control the supply at its source or point of entry but could not eradicate the demand, hence the supply reached the point of demand either through channels beyond the control of the state or through illegal production within the state.

When national prohibition was adopted, the operation of this principle was merely extended. During the earlier period of national prohibition, the existing sources of supply were the liquor in bonded warehouses, the diversion of industrial alcohol and the smuggling from other countries. Since it was less difficult to open illegal channels for a supply which already existed than to create illegal agencies for new production, the supply during these earlier years came largely from these sources. The withdrawals from bonded warehouses upon illegal or improperly granted permits were at first considerable. This was afterwards checked or the supply was exhausted. The diversion of industrial alcohol was extensive in the earlier years of prohibition, and appears to have reached its maximum at about 1925 and 1926. As other sources of domestic supply have been developed this has decreased. Smuggling reached its highest point at about 1926. With the development of less costly means of domestic supply smuggling has gradually decreased until it is now in large measure confined to the more expensive foreign wines and liquors, purveyed to people of means. In the meantime methods and agencies of illicit distilling, brewing and wine making have been developed and improved to a point where the existing demand is to a large extent supplied from these sources. The amount and quality are steadily rising and the prices falling. There is clear evidence that the drinking among some of the less prosperous classes of the population is increasing to a corresponding degree. Unless means are devised which will be far more effective than any yet employed or suggested to check this process it will inevitably continue, regardless of the present law, until the demand reaches the point of saturation approximating that which existed prior to the adoption of the Eighteenth Amendment.

It was the hope of many that with National Prohibition there would be a gradual decrease in the demand for alcoholic beverages until in a reasonable time it would substantially disappear. In the present study of the subject nothing has been discovered in past experience, or in operation of social and economic principles which would furnish any foundation for this hope. The lessons of human experience, the operations of economic law and the evidence as to present tendencies all indicate the contrary. In addition to the essential principles stated, the existence of an unregulated supply of alcoholic liquors at falling prices, the psychological appeal in gratifying a forbidden taste, the adventure of breaking a sumptuary law and the romance which surrounds the leaders of this illicit traffic, all have their profound effect, especially upon youth, and clearly indicate that the hope that there would be a decrease in demand was and is an illusion.

It would be difficult to find a more complete example of the force of the inexorable laws of supply and demand and of the principles discussed in their operation against the government than in the history and effect of prohibition in the United States.

This need not continue. The essential principles of successful strategy applied by organized society against its enemies, military or civil, are always the same--to hold them in check as far as practicable, while striking at their basic resources. With the illegal liquor traffic the prime resource lies in the profits of the business. Remove this and the business will end. The irresistible forces of social and economic law may be directed against this traffic with quite as decisive results as they have hitherto, under state regulation and state and national prohibition, been directed against the government and in favor of the lawbreaker. This may be demonstrated by a few simple and familiar illustrations from both military and economic history.

In the Civil War in America the northern armies, with all the power and resources of the federal government, could not get to Richmond in four years. In the meantime the navy was closing the ports and cutting off the supplies of food and munitions. When this was finally accomplished the southern armies were helpless. The more men they had the weaker they were. They surrendered in the field. Also in the World War the armies were blocked. It then became a question of supply. When the submarine campaign failed and the allied blockade succeeded with the addition of American resources, the armies of the central powers crumbled. The same was true of the Grand Army of Napoleon at Moscow. The Russians did not fight him directly. They cut off his supplies. The result was prompt and decisive.

The same principles have operated in our regulation of industrial corporations. So long as the states of the federal government undertook to regulate railroads by direct or frontal attack it was of no avail. The resources of these corporations were too large, their influence too great. They controlled industry through rebates and sometimes exercised their influence through corruption. Their activities affected the entire social and business life of America. With their immense financial and political power the problem was far more difficult than the present problem of the control of the liquor traffic. When the federal government, through the Interstate Commerce Commission, took control of the revenues through the fixing of rates, limited the return based on value, controlled the expenditures for construction and operation as well as the issue of securities, fixed the method of keeping accounts, regulated the operations, stopped rebating and eliminated passes and special privileges--thus controlling the sources of their power--the problem was solved. These measures of control must be constantly perfected and changed to meet new conditions, but the Commission has flexible powers readily adapted to this end. We have thus established in principle and in operation the best and most effective system of public regulation of privately owned and operated agencies in the world, and have solved a problem which once seemed insoluble in the face of the opposition of the most powerful financial interests in America. They now accept and approve the system.

The same is true as to the Federal Reserve Banks. The most difficult of all things to regulate and control is money. For nearly a century our banking system was a source of constantly recurring trouble. Finally the Federal Reserve Banks were established, with profits limited to a fixed percentage on the capital, owned and operated privately under government regulation. These institutions are not primarily interested in profit, for beyond the limited return this goes to the government. Both national and state banks are members of the system. The Federal Reserve Board with large and flexible powers can meet changing conditions in different sections of the country. In its essentials the problem which vexed America for years and caused many social and economic evils is solved.

The same principles that operated successfully in military strategy and in the regulation and control of legal, yet recalcitrant, corporate interest may be applied to the struggle of organized society against lawlessness in any form, including the liquor traffic. So long as human nature remains unchanged and lawlessness is profitable it will persist. Make lawlessness unprofitable by holding it in check as far as practicable and by using the forces of social and economic law against it, instead of trying to enforce direct control in violation of those principles, and the results will be successful.

The principles of economic law are fundamental. They cannot be resisted or ignored. Against their ultimate operation the mandates of laws and constitutions and the powers of government appear to be no more effective than the broom of King Canute against the tides of the sea.

There are other secondary or contributing causes for existing conditions such as matters of organization and incidents of enforcement, some of which are discussed in the report. I do not concur in the view there expressed that "general unfitness" of the organization, especially in the earlier years of national prohibition, was in "large measure" responsible for the "public disfavor in which prohibition fell". The difficulties encountered in the creation of the organization and training of personnel for a task of this character are manifest, but these cannot properly be appraised apart from a consideration of the conditions of social and economic confusion in the period following the World War. There was, and probably is, a considerable amount of bribery and corruption in the organization. This cannot be condoned. It is only fair, however, to the men engaged in this task to consider its nature and circumstances before issuing verdicts of general condemnation based upon individual cases of delinquency. Men have moral as well as physical limitations. If the people provide a law of this character and then send into action for its enforcement, throughout the territory of the United States, a small field force of from 1,000 to 1,500 underpaid men against a lawless army running into tens of thousands, possessed of financial resources amounting to billions, ready to buy protection at any cost, the people must expect unsatisfactory results and heavy moral casualties. These conditions, to the extent that they have existed, have naturally tended to discredit the law. The same is true as to public killings, unwarranted searches and seizures, deaths from poisoned alcohol and other similar incidents of enforcement. There is a feeling on the part of many people, including earnest supporters of this law, that there must be some effective means of solving this problem which would not require the shooting of people upon the highways, the invasion of the sanctity of the home or the poisoning by the government of substances which are known to be used in beverages--especially where the purchase and use of such beverages is not even an offense against the law. These incidents of enforcement organization and method are deplorable. They have been contributing causes for the present state of irritation and resentment. I cannot find, however, that they have been or are fundamental or controlling factors in the larger situation. The understanding and ultimate solution of this problem must be found not in these incidental causes, but in those major causes which have their sources in the social and economic principles by which society itself is controlled, which human laws, constitutions and governments are powerless to resist.

It might be within the physical powers of the federal government for a time to substantially enforce the Eighteenth Amendment and the National Prohibition Act. But under existing conditions this would require the creation of a field organization running high into the thousands, with courts, prosecuting agencies, prisons, and other institutions in proportion, and would demand expenditures and measures beyond the practical and political limitations of federal power. This would inevitably lead to social and political consequences more disastrous than the evils sought to be remedied. Even then the force of social and economic laws would ultimately prevail. These laws cannot be destroyed by governments, but often in the course of human history governments have been destroyed by them.

Upon a consideration of the facts presented in the report of the Commission, and of the causes herein discussed, I am compelled to find that the Eighteenth Amendment and the National Prohibition Act will not be observed, and cannot be enforced.

II. CONSIDERATION OF SUGGESTED REMEDIES

Many plans for meeting the existing situation have been suggested. They tend either to ignore essential limitations in our system of government, or are opposed to the lessons of experience, or violate fundamental social or economic principles. Only a few of the more important will be mentioned.

The proposal for the repeal of the Eighteenth Amendment, remitting the problem to the control of the several states, is strongly urged. I am unqualifiedly opposed to such repeal.

The repeal of the Amendment would immediately result in the restoration of the liquor traffic and the saloon as they existed at the time of the adoption of the Amendment in those states not having state prohibition laws. The return of the licensed saloon should not be permitted anywhere in the United States under any conditions.

For fundamental reasons already discussed, state regulation and state prohibition substantially failed before the adoption of the Eighteenth Amendment. With further improvements in means of transportation and other social and economic changes which have since taken place, those measures would be even less effective today. I can see no sound reason for going back to systems which have already failed, and which afford no reasonable probability of future success.

As to the repeal of the National Prohibition Act, leaving the Amendment unchanged, the objections seem equally conclusive. This would be open nullification by Congress of a Constitutional provision. The repeal of the law would leave the Amendment without any provision for its enforcement. It would remain as a limitation upon the powers of both Congress and the States. No system of regulation or control -- except State prohibition -- could be adopted or continued since this would be prohibited by the Amendment. The license to the violators of the law and general social confusion which would result are difficult to measure.

The proposal that the law be amended so as to permit the sale of light wine and beer is objectionable both on principle and from a practical standpoint. If the limit of alcoholic content were placed so low that the beverage sold would not be intoxicating in fact it would not satisfy the demand. If it were placed high enough to be intoxicating in fact, it would to that extent be nullification of the Amendment. Under this plan, we would have saloons for the sale of light wine and beer, and bootlegging as to liquors of higher alcoholic content. We would then have the evils of both systems and the benefits of neither. The opportunities for evasion of the law as to prohibited liquors would be enormously increased. Norway tried a system of prohibition as to liquors of an alcoholic content of more than 12 percent. It failed. There were international complications involved, but chiefly because of the domestic evils resulting from the system, it has been abandoned and a system similar in principle to that of Sweden has been substituted.

The various suggestions as to National or State dispensaries cannot be accepted, for obvious reasons. Whatever may have been the results in other countries, a system of this kind is certainly not adapted to the political conditions or to the dual system of government in the United States. Our past experience with this system has been unfortunate.

I regret that I cannot concur in the view that further trial be made of the existing system before reaching a final conclusion as to its enforceability. Aside from the difficulties as to the future determination of the results of this trial, in my view a study of the facts and existing conditions, as presented in the report, and of the fundamental and controlling causes therefore, leads inevitably to the conclusion that the Amendment and law cannot be enforced.

I concur in the recommendation of the report that the Eighteenth Amendment be modified as therein stated. But the National Prohibition Act would still be in force. No substantial change in the Act, or substitute therefore, is suggested. We cannot stop there. We have found that the law is not being observed or enforced. We have found causes for these conditions which clearly show that it cannot be enforced by any means within the reasonable limitations of federal power. An effort must be made at least to find some effective solution for the problem. I shall therefore go further and present as a substitute for the existing law, should the Amendment be modified, a complete plan of liquor control.

III. PROPOSED PLAN OF LIQUOR CONTROL

Any plan for the control of the liquor traffic must meet three fundamental requirements, (1) it must be based upon sound social, political and economic principles; (2) it must be adequate to scope and structure to meet every element of the problem; and (3) it must be practical in operation.

1. The Principles and Requirements of the Plan

The essential principles and requirements to which any plan of liquor control must conform may be briefly stated.

(a) It must preserve the benefits which have been gained through the abolition of the legalized liquor traffic and the saloon conducted solely for private profit.

(b) It must provide for the effective control and regulation of individual conduct with respect to the use of alcoholic liquors to the extent that such conduct is anti-social or injurious to others; but it must respect and protect freedom of individual action when that is not anti-social or injurious to the community. This will remove public irritation and resentment against the law, and will insure that support from the normally law-abiding elements of the community which is essential to its observance and effective enforcement.

(c) It must be sufficiently flexible to admit of ready adaptation to changing conditions and methods of evasion. It must restore the traditional balance between the functions of the Federal and State governments, defining the duties of each with sufficient clearness to prevent overlapping, and leaving sufficient elasticity to permit of mutual adjustment. It must give to the federal government adequate power to insure uniformity of control as to those aspects of the problem which are of general concern or proper federal cognizance. It must leave to the states the maximum of discretion consistent therewith, both as to the policy to be adopted in dealing with the problem, and as to methods of local control, to the end that it may be adapted to the public sentiment of the people and to local conditions within the states. This would permit of the ready adjustment of the plan to the varied social, racial and institutional conditions existing throughout the United States and within the several states.

(d) It must conform to the requirements of sound economic principles, and recognize the irresistible power of the law of supply and demand. It must take the profit out of every phase of the illegal traffic, and employ the force of economic law to defeat that traffic, instead of attempting to oppose the principles, permitting them to operate in favor of the law-breaker. We have seen that the failure to conform to this requirement has operated to defeat every system for the regulation or control of the liquor traffic in America.

(e) Finally, the profits of the liquor traffic should be used for the destruction of that traffic and the prevention of crime. To the extent that the demand for alcoholic beverages cannot be prevented it must be tolerated, but the supply should be restricted to the full extent that this can be done without opening the way for the profitable operations of the illegal traffic. To this end the demand, insofar as it cannot be prevented, should be supplied by privately owned and operated agencies created for this purpose under strict government regulation. They should be required to supply wholesome products at prices and under conditions to be fixed by Federal and State commissions. By thus furnishing a better product at lower prices it would at once become impossible for the illicit traffic to continue. The profits in excess of a return, fixed by law, on the capital invested should go into the treasury of the federal or state government, as the case might be. After paying all expenses of the governments in connection therewith the remainder of such profits should be segregated into special funds, federal or state, to be appropriated by Congress and the respective state legislatures in their discretion for education, public health, the improvement of housing conditions and other social purposes of similar nature. In this way, instead of having the proceeds of this traffic go to finance lawless and criminal activities as at present, they would be used to eliminate the breeding grounds of crime and ultimately to remove those conditions which are most potential in inducing the excessive use of intoxicating beverages.

2. The Scope and Structure of the Plan

I

It is proposed that as soon as practicable, by appropriate action of Congress and of the States, the Eighteenth Amendment be modified or revised, as recommended by the Commission, to read as follows:

"The Congress shall have power to regulate or to prohibit the manufacture, traffic in or transportation of intoxicating liquors within, the importation thereof into, and the exportation thereof from the United States and all territory subject to the jurisdiction thereof, for beverage purposes."

This modification would bring the Amendment into conformity with the traditional principles of our system of government. By conferring power upon Congress, it would give to the Amendment the necessary flexibility. The power to prohibit should be given to the end that if the proposed modification is adopted the National Prohibition Act would continue in force thereunder until Congress enacted some other plan, thus avoiding any break in the system of control and preventing the restoration of the saloon anywhere in the United States. Under the proposed Amendment as modified, Congress would have full power (1) to continue the present system of absolute national prohibition, or (2) to remit the matter in whole or in part to the States, or (3) to adopt any system of effective control. Since greater flexibility is one of the outstanding needs of the present system, this modification should be made even if the policy of absolute national prohibition is to be continued.

II

That Congress should then create a bipartisan National Commission on Liquor Control, which should have full power under such laws as Congress might enact to regulate and control the manufacture, importation, exportation, transportation in interstate commerce, and also the sale, as and to the extent hereinafter stated, of intoxicating liquors of more than one-half or one percentum alcoholic content, for beverage purposes; and to exercise similar regulation and control over alcoholic liquors for other purposes, and of industrial alcohol, to the full extent necessary to render the system of control of such liquors for beverage purposes effective. The powers of the Commission as to the regulation and control of the traffic indicated and of the agencies created for the purposes thereof should be fully as complete as those of the Interstate Commerce Commission over railroads and should in every respect be adequate for the purposes of the plan.

III

That Congress should create a National Corporation for the purposes of the plan, all of the stock of which should be privately owned, or in its discretion a number of such corporations, such as one for each judicial circuit, with the powers and duties generally stated below. Since one corporation, with branches throughout the country, would simplify operation and regulation, the plan will be stated on that basis. This corporation should have the usual powers of a commercial corporation to the extent necessary for the purposes of the plan except as herein limited. It should be vested with the exclusive right and power (to be exercised under the control and regulations of the National Commission) of manufacture, importation, exportation and transportation in interstate commerce, and of sale as and to the extent hereafter stated, of all alcoholic liquors for beverage, as well as for medicinal and sacramental purposes in, within or from the territory of the United States or subject to the jurisdiction thereof. The charter of the corporation should contain appropriate provisions for amendment or repeal by Congress; for the issue and redemption of its securities; limiting the return upon its capital; and providing for its operation and management, all of which should be subject to the control of the Commission.

The financial plan of the corporation, to be fixed in its charter and in operation subject to the control of the Commission, should provide for an issue of stock of only one class to be sold at par, to be entitled to cumulative dividends limited to such rate upon the actual capital invested as might be determined by Congress, or with its authority by the Commission. A rate of not less than 5% nor more than 7% is suggested. The corporation should be permitted to retain from its earnings not exceeding 2% per annum on its invested capital as a reserve against contingencies and as an amortization fund for the retirement of its capital should Congress desire to change the plan of control, or for any other reason. This fund should be held, used and invested under orders of the Commission. All earnings in excess of the permitted return and amortization fund should be paid into the treasury of the United States to be held as a special fund to be disposed of by Congress as hereinafter provided.

In the event of the liquidation of the corporation for any cause, it should be done under the direction of the Commission. After payment of its obligations and the par value of its stock with any accumulated dividends thereon the remainder of its assets, including any balance of the reserve or amortization fund, should be paid into the treasury of the United States to be held as a part of the special fund.

IV

It should be required by law that alcoholic liquors for beverage, medicinal or sacramental purposes of over one-half of one percent alcoholic content by volume (not including industrial alcohol) might be manufactured, imported, exported, transported in interstate commerce, or sold as and to the extent thereafter stated, solely by the National Corporation, or its branches approved by and operating under such bonds as to their employees as might be prescribed by the Commission. The Commission should have power to prescribe the alcoholic content of the various kinds and grades of liquors.

All alcoholic liquors so acquired or produced should be promptly placed in bonded warehouses of the Corporation, which should be located at convenient points throughout the country approved by the Commission. Before shipment, every container thereof should bear a label of the Corporation showing the kind, amount and alcoholic content of the liquor contained therein, certified by the Corporation. The Corporation should only be allowed to make sales and shipment of such liquors in any state to a corporate agency created by such state, similar in general character to the National corporation, for the purpose of the purchase and distribution and local sale of such liquors within the state if and to the extent permitted by the laws thereof. If the State at its option elected not to adopt the system, it could establish or continue prohibition, in which event it would have to enforce its own laws within the State, but the federal law would not permit sales or shipments into that State by the National Corporation except through the State in bond. Every aspect of the operations outlined would be subject to the control and regulation of the Commission and appropriate penalties would be prescribed for violations of the law or of such regulations.

V

The price at which the various liquors should be sold by the National Corporation should be fixed or approved by the Commission after hearing in proper cases, and should be posted at appropriate places. The prices should be based primarily upon and scaled upward on the basis of alcoholic content – the lower prices on low alcoholic content liquors such as light wine and beer, and the highest prices practicable on high alcoholic content liquors, such as whiskies and brandies. The prices should be such as on the one hand to limit the use and, on the other hand, not high enough to permit the illegal traffic in or sale of such liquors. The price should be adequate to provide for the operating requirements of the National Corporation on the basis of accounting and expense to be approved by the Commission; for a small ad valorem tax which might be imposed by the government to provide for its expenses in connection with the system; for the permitted return upon the invested capital of the Corporation; and for the reserve or amortization fund. The entire remaining revenue would go into the special fund in the treasury of the United States to be disposed of by Congress. The price should be as nearly uniform as possible throughout the country.

VI

The National Corporation should sell and transport only to state agencies created for the purposes of local distribution and sale within the state. This would be entirely optional with the State. If any State desired to establish or continue prohibition, it could do so. In the event it would have to enforce its own law within the State, but would be protected by the federal government from any supply from outside. If a State commission and a State corporation similar in character and structure to the National agencies discussed, with similar powers and functions within the State. The State agencies would have to conform in general outline to a plan prescribed by the National

Commission in order to insure uniformity throughout the country as to matters of general consequence, but as to local questions they would be subject entirely to State control and could easily be adapted to the varied social and economic conditions within the State. Matters of price, return and other financial and operating details within the State would be controlled by the State commission along the same lines as already discussed, and the surplus revenues from operations within the State would go into the State treasury as a special fund to be disposed of by the legislature of the State. The State agency would purchase from the nearest branch of the National Corporation, and shipments would be made in bottles or containers under the seal of that corporation to such branch of the State agency as might be directed. The State agency would, with the approval of the State commission, establish branches and local sales agencies at convenient points. The State could permit local option as to the establishment of a sales agency in any given community. These agencies should be in buildings where no other commercial activity is carried on, should be open only at certain hours of the day, on such business days as might be prescribed by state law or regulation. The sales employees should be required to give surety bonds to insure good character and protect against abuses. Sales should be permitted only in original packages or units under seal of the National Corporation and not opened within a limited distance of the agency. Other necessary regulations would be prescribed by the State commission as to local operations.

Sales should be limited to persons holding license books, which should be issued by the State agency nearest the fixed abode or voting place of the holder under regulations of the Commission. The bolder should be required to sign an agreement in this book to account for the purchases made thereunder at any time on request and to the satisfaction of the State corporation or State commission. This book should be good for purchase at any state agency in the United States, subject to regulations of the National and State commissions. All purchases should be entered in this book and the entry signed by the employee making the sale. The amount of wine and beer below an alcoholic content to be fixed from time to time by the appropriate Commission might or might not be limited, but the amount of high alcoholic liquors should be limited to a reasonable quantity in any month, having regard to the proper use by the purchaser with a view to limiting the use and preventing purchases for illegitimate purposes. The requirement for accounting for purchases would further protect this situation. Special permits could be issued under regulations upon showing of special requirements, and provision could be made for limited special books for foreign visitors and transients. Upon conviction for violation of the law, for drunkenness or other cause provided by law, the book could be cancelled for such time as might be prescribed. All state and national regulations should seek to restrict sales and use as far as may be done, without leaving a possible demand which could be supplied at a profit by bootleggers. The essential purpose must be to drive the illicit producer and trader out of business and keep them out by directing against them the force of the law of supply and demand, and fixing prices with which they cannot possibly complete. Within these limits, the regulations should operate to reduce the demand. No advertisement of alcoholic liquors or solicitations of purchasers should be permitted.

VII
The excess revenues from the operations of the national corporation would go into the federal treasury, and those from the operations of the state corporation and its branches would go into the

state treasury. These revenues, which now go entirely to the lawless and criminal classes, would undoubtedly be very large. They would be subject to disposition by Congress and the state legislatures respectively. They should be set aside as special funds in the respective treasuries, and used for educational purposes, especially as to the evils resulting from the use of alcoholic beverages and for the eradication and prevention of those conditions which cause excessive drinking, or which tend to create a demand for intoxicating beverages.

To this end, it is proposed that the revenues derived by the federal government from the plan, including the excess earnings of the National Corporation, should be set aside in the Treasury as a special fund from which the expenses of the Government, including those of the National Commission incurred in connection with the system, should first be paid. The Commission should be required to collect accurate facts and statistics as to the operation and social economic results of the system in the United States and of systems of liquor control in all foreign countries and the effects of such systems, and of the use of intoxicating liquors upon individual, social and economic life; to publish the same in bulletins for distribution without cost to colleges, schools, libraries, and other educational agencies, and to individuals. These publications should be in popular terms but should be scientific and factual, similar to those now issued by the scientific agencies of the government. The cost thereof, including distribution, should be paid out of this fund.

Such proportion of the remainder of the fund as Congress might determine should be distributed among the several states upon an equitable basis and should be used by them as stated below. The remainder of the fund should be appropriated by Congress to be used by the proper federal agencies for scientific investigations of social and economic conditions related to crime and dependency at their source, to the extent that these matters are within the proper cognizance of the federal government.

The larger proportion of the National fund could be apportioned to the states since matters of social regulation and improvement are properly within their jurisdiction. After paying the expenses of the State Commission and other regulation expenses, the State could use the surplus revenues derived from the excess earnings of the State Corporation (if created), together with its proportion of the National fund, for education, public health (including medical services for the poorer rural districts) the improvement of housing conditions and elimination of slums urban and rural, the prevention and abatement of delinquency, the care of the poor, the improvement of economic security, and other similar social activities which tend to eliminate the sources of crime and delinquency, and to remove those conditions of social and economic hardship and stress by which the demand for alcoholic stimulants is largely induced.

3. The Practical Operation of the Plan

Every principle and feature of this plan, except as to the specific use of excess profits, is now in operation either in the present system of government regulation of railroads, or in the Federal Reserve Bank system, or in both. The principle and practice of private ownership and operation under government regulation are too well established to require discussion. Even as to the use of the excess profits (which is only a suggestion and not an essential part of the structure of the plan) the same principle is in operation with respect to both railroads and banks. The profits of railroads in excess of 5-3/4 per centum return fixed on value are subject to recapture and use under government control for the development of the transportation services. The profits of the Federal Reserve Banks in excess of the limited return on capital and a permitted reserve go into the federal treasury.

Any statement of a plan of this character covering so large a field may seem complicated. In operation it would be simple. All liquor imported or produced would be the property of the National Corporation, and would be put into bonded warehouses at convenient points under strict government regulation and control. Accurate accounts thereof would be kept as prescribed by the Commission. It could be sold and transported only to state agencies under seal of the National Corporation and proper regulations. There would be no leakage in this process because (1) the essential employees of the Corporation would be bonded, (2) the product would have to be accounted for to the Commission, and (3) there would be no demand for or profit in illegal liquor so long as a reasonable supply could be obtained legally. Smuggling and illicit production would end since no one would buy bootleg liquor of doubtful quality at high prices when good liquor could be obtained at fair prices. The profit in the illegal traffic would be eliminated.

When the liquor reaches the State agency, it could be sold only under national and state regulations. Sales could be made only to holders of permit books. These books would be issued under regulations of the State Commission, with safeguards against transfer or improper use, and would be subject to cancellation for any violation of the laws or regulations. The amount which any holder could purchase, certainly of high alcoholic content liquors, would be limited as far as it might be possible to do so without opening a demand for an illegal supply. The holder would be required to sign an agreement to account for all purchases on request. The amount purchased would be entered in the book and the entry signed by a bonded employee of the corporation. The liquor so purchased would be in the original package or container of the National Corporation, bearing its seal and showing the alcoholic content. The prices to the purchaser would be fixed from time to time by the State Commission to meet existing local conditions, subject to adjustment by the National Commission for the purpose of general uniformity as in the case of intrastate rates of railroads.

If a State elected to continue prohibition, it could do so. It would enforce its own laws within the State. Full protection would be provided against shipments from without the State. There would be only two possible sources of supply of legal liquor. The federal law would prohibit shipments of liquor by the National Corporation into such State. This source would be completely controlled. Purchases of liquors under the plan in an adjoining state would also be effectively controlled. No liquor could be obtained except on permit books issued as above stated. The amount of the purchase would thus be limited to personal requirements, and the purchaser would have to account for the same on request of the State agency. It would be impossible to secure liquor for illegal shipment or sale.

Illegal production in an adjoining State would be prevented by economic law as well as by federal and state statues. The illegal producer could not manufacture and sell bootleg liquor in competition with good liquor supplied by the State agency at lower prices than he could meet.

Deprived of a local market, he certainly could not manufacture for the purpose of shipment into another State having prohibition, in violation of the laws of both States and of the federal law. The door would thus be effectively closed against every source of supply from without the State.

An analysis of this plan of control both as to structure and operation shows that it meets every aspect of the present problem; that it is in conformity with the principles and requirements outlined above. It is predicted upon our own successful experience in dealing with problems involving similar principles of private ownership and operation with adequate government regulation. It fully preserves the benefits gained through the abolition of the legalized traffic and the saloon. It is flexible and may readily be adapted to varying local conditions as well as to new situations or new efforts at evasion which may arise. It is in conformity with our political system, contemplates effective action of both state and federal governments in their appropriate jurisdictions, and the adjustment of these activities to each other with a maximum of discretion to the States consistent with effective liquor control.

It also conforms to essential economic principles and brings the force of these principles into play against the smuggler, illicit producer and bootlegger, instead of permitting them to operate as at present against the government and in favor of the criminal class. To the extent that there is an unavoidable and existing demand for alcoholic beverages, it meets that demand by legal but controlled supply of wholesale products, instead of having it supplied with dangerous or deleterious stuff through illegal channels. It takes from the lawless and criminal classes the enormous profits of the present illegal traffic, by which public service is being corrupted, and crime developed and organized, and applies these resources to educating the people as to the evils resulting from the use of alcoholic liquors, the elimination of the chief sources of crime, and the relief of the social and economic stress which tends to produce the desire and demand for alcoholic stimulants. It tends through effective control and the operation of natural laws to progressively reduce the demand and ultimately to eliminate this evil from our social and economic life. It should result in an effective solution of the present problem.

Conclusion

The problems of American life may best be solved through the study of our own experience in the successful application of sound principles, under our system of dual governments, to our peculiar social and economic conditions.

A study of the conditions in or experience of other countries is helpful only to the extent that it illustrates the operation of principles which underlie and are common to all social and economic organization.

It was with this thought in mind that the plan for the regulation and control of the liquor traffic herein presented was developed. When it became evident as a result of the present investigation and study that the existing system of national prohibition was not being observed or enforced, that owing to social and economic conditions in the United States, and to the operation of fundamental social and economic laws, it could not be enforced, a study was first made of our own experience in applying the principles involved in this problem to other phases of our national organization, and the results of that experience. It was found that in the familiar system of joint state and federal regulation of railroads, extending over a period of forty years, every principle involved in the present problem of liquor control had been successfully applied to conditions different as to the facts, but similar as to the essentials. The same was found to be true in less degree with the Federal Reserve Bank system. These two agencies present a body of experience in the successful application of fundamental social and economic laws to varied and complicated human conditions not to be found elsewhere. The present plan was then formulated, based upon those principles and that experience.

A study was then made of foreign systems of liquor control. Some of the countries were visited, interviews held with government officials and citizens of every class, and checked by personal investigations of the operations of the several systems. The system which has been in force in Sweden for more than ten years, which is similar as to many principles but different as to many details from the plan herein proposed, is by far the most successful of any existing system of liquor control. These studies abroad entirely confirmed the view that the plan proposed is sound in principle and practical in operation; that it is adapted to our system of government, and to social and economic conditions in America; that if adopted, it should remove this vexing problem from our political life, and result in its constructive solution.

We must not lose what has been gained by the abolition of the saloon. We can neither ignore the appalling conditions which this Commission has found to exist, and to be steadily growing worse, nor submit to their continuance. The time has arrived when the interest of our country we should lay aside theories and emotions, free our minds from the blinding influence of prejudice and meet the problem as it exists. Forgetting those things which are behind we must bring into action against existing evils the great reserve of American common sense, guided by practical and successful experience. By this means, we shall advance the cause of temperance and achieve an effective solution of the liquor problem.

As appears from their separate statements filed with the report, this plan is recommended for consideration by Commissioners KENYON, LOESCH, MACKINTOSH, McCORMICK and POUND. The endorsements of Commissions KENYON and McCORMICK are subject to the condition stated in their memoranda to the effect that they favor a further trial of the present law before definitely recommending the adoption of a substitute.

HENRY W. ANDERSON

Washington, D.C., January 7, 1931

SEPARATE REPORT OF MONTE M. LEMANN

Under the language of the Appropriation Act which provided funds for the work of the Commission, it is the duty of the Commission to inquire into the enforcement of the Eighteenth Amendment and the laws enacted in pursuance thereof. I construe this language as a mandate to assume the Eighteenth Amendment as the established national policy. The wisdom, advantages and desirability of prohibition in the abstract, it be enforceable, are not, as an original question, within the province of the Commission, whose primary function it is to ascertain the facts bearing upon the problem of enforcement and to make such recommendations as the ascertainable facts may seem to justify.

Except with respect to the machinery of enforcement, the amount of scientifically provable facts bearing upon the enforcement of the eighteenth Amendment made available to the Commission is small, and the material before the Commission consists chiefly of statements and reports by persons whose positions give them special opportunities for observation and entitle their estimates upon the issues of fact to more weight than those of the ordinary individual. As to the machinery of enforcement, omitting the machinery of the courts and penal institutions, an extended study has been made for the Commission by Messrs. Henry S. Dennison and Albert E. Sawyer and their staff. That study presents in considerable detail the history, development and present situation of the federal forces dealing with prohibition enforcement, excluding the federal courts and penal institutions. The facts collected in this study, some of which are set out in the report of the Commission, are sufficient, I think, to support the conclusions that (a) even upon the most restricted theory of the proper field of federal activity, the organization for the enforcement of the National Prohibition Act is and always has been inadequate, (b) the uncertainty and changes attending the early history of the Prohibition Bureau and the poor quality of the field force prior to the extension of Civil Service prevented the organization from operating with reasonable efficiency prior to the reorganization of 1927 and for some time thereafter, (c) the federal machinery for the enforcement of the National Prohibition Act has not yet had an opportunity to demonstrate the most that it can accomplish, and (d) a substantial improvement in enforcement may reasonably be expected with increased personnel and equipment.

The machinery of enforcement may, in my judgment, without disproportionate expense, be made adequate to cope with the industrial alcohol and smuggling aspects of the enforcement problem.

The entire number of plants holding permits to produce ethyl alcohol, exclusive of breweries conserving the alcohol driven off, was on June 30, 1930, forty-nine(1) plants, of which two produced no alcohol during the fiscal year ending June 30, 1930, were owned by twenty-one corporations on June 30, 1930. These figures were furnished to the Commission by the Technical Division of the Bureau of Industrial Alcohol. It is, I think, reasonable to assume that those directing these enterprises will not connive at violation of the law, but even if they were disposed so to do, their number and the location of their plants is sufficiently limited to permit of adequate supervision. During the fiscal year ending June 30, 1930, there were in the entire country only sixty-seven denaturing plants in operation and of these there were basic permits held on June 30, 1930, by only seven which might be termed independent. Of these two were subsidiaries of large corporations and used all of the denatured alcohol which they produced, so that there were in fact on June 30, 1930, only five actually independent denaturing plants(2). Enactment of legislation prohibiting independent denaturing plants would entirely remove any possibility of difficulty as to them. The study made by Messrs. Dennison and Sawyer calls attention to the difficulty presented by the so-called coverhouse, or establishment purchasing from permittees products made by them from specially denatured alcohol, for resale to illegitimate denaturing plants. The difficulty with respect to these coverhouses arises from the fact that under existing legislation there is doubt as to the Government's authority to examine the records of persons purchasing products manufactured from specially denatured alcohol or to require reports from such persons, for the purpose of determining the ultimate disposition made of the products so purchased. This difficulty may also be met by appropriate legislation.

The new process for the manufacture of synthetic alcohol from petroleum is likely to cause some added difficulty in dealing with the problem of industrial alcohol, but not beyond the reasonable power of the federal government to meet. It must be borne in mind that even with the abandonment of prohibition, the federal government would continue to be faced with the problem of supervising industrial alcohol plants and preventing diversion of industrial alcohol in order to protect the government's taxes, although it is true that the incentive to divert would then be confined to evasion of the tax.

As to legitimate cereal beverage plants or breweries, there were in force on June 30, 1930, in the entire country only two hundred and seven permits authorizing the operation of such plants(3). These plants were inadequately supervised, but it would require only a relatively small force of men (estimated at four men for each brewery) to supply this supervision, and no serious difficulty in enforcement appears to be presented at this point.

Upon the facts presented, I have also reached the conclusion that the difficulties of enforcement with respect to smuggling are exaggerated. Of course, it always will be impossible entirely to prevent all smuggling of liquor. It is also impossible to completely prevent the smuggling of other commodities. Conceding that a greater difficulty is presented in the case of liquor, it seems reasonable to conclude that a moderate increase in personnel and in the number of first-class destroyers assigned to the Coast Guard service, an addition to the patrol service of faster boats, radio equipment and silencing devices, accompanied by an increase of two or three hundred men in the Customs service, would eliminate most of the smuggled liquor. In this connection it may be observed that the official statistics of the Canadian government with which the Commission has been furnished show that the quantity of all alcoholic beverages declared for export from that country to all points was 4,816,291(4) imperial gallons in the year ended March 31, 1930. The figures include alcoholic beverages declared for export not only to the United States (prior to the recent ban by the Canadian government of such exports), but also all liquors exported to St. Pierre and Miquelon, Central America and other countries. While it is true that the ratio of increase in the quantity of liquor declared for export from Canada to St. Pierre and Miquelon and Central American points has been considerable, the total amount of liquor so exported remains relatively small. In the fiscal year ended March 31, 1930, the total quantity of alcoholic beverages exported from all Canadian ports to St. Pierre and Miquelon was 1,038,980 gallons(5). Assuming that the entire quantity of liquor exported from Canada found its way into the United States--an assumption which seems beyond the possible fact--the total quantity would not be as great as commonly supposed. In addition to liquor declared for export through regular channels, some may be surreptitiously brought into the United States directly from Canada, but the quantity so introduced can be acquired only by individual purchasers in Canada and it does not appear that in the aggregate it could bulk very large. A consideration of these figures suggests that much of the liquor which is purchased upon the assumption that it is imported actually represents moonshine spirits distilled and sold under fictitious labels. In considering the problem arising in the prevention of smuggling and the frequently referred to extent of our land and water external boundaries, it must again be borne in mind that a serious burden is likely to be thrown upon the federal government if prohibition is abandoned in carrying out the federal task of preventing smuggling of liquor from wet states into dry states, since interstate roads, both primary and secondary, far exceed the international highways. The great increase in mileage of paved roads, made possible by federal aid and large state bond issues, and the extent of the use of automobiles would make this difficulty one of no inconsiderable proportions, in meeting which active local cooperation would be necessary.

As the foregoing indicates, while industrial alcohol and smuggling present some serious difficulties, they seem to me to be quite within the power of the federal government alone to deal with without any unreasonable expenditure or unduly large organization. The great problem in the enforcement of the National Prohibition Act lies in the ease with which spirits are manufactured in stills both upon a large and small scale and the facility and extent to which wine and malt liquors may be and are made in and outside of homes. The increase in the production of corn sugar in this country from 157,276,442 pounds in 1919 to 896,121,276 pounds in 1929(6), without adequate explanation in ascertainable legitimate use, is one indication of the extent to which the illicit manufacture of liquor in stills has increased. Cane and beet sugar, corn meal, other grains and molasses also afford other easily available material for the illicit manufacture of alcohol in stills. It is conceded that it is impossible to do more than guess at the total quantity of alcohol which is currently available from these sources; but the estimate of the Bureau of Prohibition of the Department of Justice for the fiscal year ending June 10, 1930(7), which is the lowest that I have seen for that year, places the total amount possibly manufactured from corn, cane and beet sugar, corn meal or other grains, and molasses at 29,950,000 gallons of absolute alcohol, equal to 59,900,000 gallons of 100 proof alcohol. The Bureau of Prohibition in the Department of Justice has also estimated the possible illicit production of wine and malt liquor during the fiscal year ending June 30, 1930, to be 118,320,300(8) and 683,032,000 gallons respectively. There is no method by which the correctness of these estimates can be checked with reasonable precision, but the expert information that the Commission has been able to obtain does not warrant any conclusion that the estimates, in general, are above the fact. The figures above quoted are exclusive of liquor estimated as possibly placed in circulation through smuggling and diversion of industrial alcohol. The total estimates reflect a probable per capita circulation of intoxicating liquor which, while still considerably less than before prohibition, is much too great to sustain any claim of reasonable enforcement or observance of the Eighteenth Amendment(9). In the year ending June 30, 1930, according to the annual report of the Commissioner of Prohibition, there were seized 16,180 distilleries, 8,138 stills, 4,152,920 wine gallons of malt liquor and 34,183,427 wine gallons of mash(10). Yet the statements made to the Commission indicate that intoxicating liquor is readily obtainable in every city of consequence in the country.

To break up the manufacture and distribution of intoxicating liquor made on this scale in thousands of stills and apparatus for the manufacture of wine and home brew scattered throughout the nation, both in cities and at many lonely spots in the country, the field force in the prohibition service on June 30, 1930, aggregated 1,786 for the entire country, made up as follows:

Agents 1,484 Investigators 109 Special agents 193 Total 1,786

Messrs. Dennison and Sawyer have recommended an increase of 60 percent in the number of prohibition agents and of 100 percent in the number of investigators and special agents. The adoption of these recommendations would mean the employment of 890 additional agents and 302 additional investigators and special agents, or an aggregate addition to the field force of 1,192, bringing the total prohibition field force for the entire country to approximately 3,000. The apparent conclusion that so moderate an increase would permit effective dealing with the enforcement problem I understand to be based upon the theory that by concentration upon the large, conspicuous cases and the organizing minds which direct the distribution of illicit liquor, the sources of supply may be effectively broken up(11).

Mr. Dennison is a business executive and organizer of proven capacity and success. His judgment must therefore command respectful attention. Except, however, upon the theory that with improved efficiency in the federal enforcement agencies that could also be obtained more cooperation from state enforcement agencies, it does not seem reasonably likely that even upon the proposed plan of concentration upon sources of supply (which appears to me a proper administrative policy) a federal field force of approximately three thousand men could effectively prevent the operation of stills, the manufacture of home brew, beer and wine and the distribution of intoxicating liquors throughout the country. To accomplish a result of this magnitude in a country of the size of the United States would, in my judgment, require the services of many thousands of enforcement officers. Such a federal police force could not be maintained consistently with our governmental system.

Assuming that it were in fact feasible and desirable for the federal government to maintain a police force of the size requisite to cope with the illicit manufacture and sale of intoxicating liquor throughout the country, there would be required a corresponding increase in federal courts and federal penal institutions if the federal government were to carry the burden of enforcement without local aid. According to the reports of the Commissioner of Prohibition and Attorney General for the fiscal year ending June 30, 1930, there were terminated in that year in the federal courts 52,706 criminal cases under the National Prohibition Act, involving 72,673 persons as defendants, of which there were convictions in 44,484 cases (54,085 defendants). 74.4% of the defendants in cases terminated were convicted. Of the persons convicted 48,577 of 89.8% pleased guilty (a ratio which did not exceed the ratio in other federal criminal cases but which may be more significant in prohibition cases because of their far greater number) (12). In the same year there were 8,224 civil injunction suits disposed of in favor of the United States and 3,668 temporary injunctions obtained in prohibition cases in addition to approximately 3,000 libel suits (13). The Commission has now under way a field study of the business of the federal courts in thirteen important districts. This investigation should make available for the first time detailed facts with respect to such matters as the time now actually spent in federal courts upon enforcement of the prohibition law, the manner in which that enforcement is dealt with, the extent to which it interferes with other business of the courts, and the possibility of any substantial and compensating relief to those courts from other changes in their jurisdiction or from the repeal of such statutes as the Dyer Act relating to the theft of motor vehicles. I should have preferred to express no opinion upon the federal court situation until this investigation had been completed, but upon the material now available in the reports of the Attorney General and the Bureau of Prohibition, it is difficult to avoid the conclusion that at least in many of the larger cities of the country the federal court organization could not meet increased demands from prohibition cases except by increases in the number of judges, court rooms and incidental equipment(14). Reflection has convinced me that the bill authorizing the United States Commissioners to pass in the first instance upon petty cases is open to serious objection and would not in practical operation relieve the congestion existing in federal courts in metropolitan areas.

If the increase in the field enforcement force recommended by Messrs. Dennison and Sawyer should be made, the increased efficiency of the field force should, in the ordinary course, be reflected in an increased number of cases for prosecution in the courts and especially in the number of serious cases requiring much time for trial.

In addition to the court problem, there is also to be considered the situation with respect to penal institutions. Assuming that the field forces were increased and that the courts were able to adequately dispose of prohibition cases, an increase in the number of convictions and in the gravity of sentences must be expected. The reports of the Commissioner of Prohibition show that the percentage of convictions receiving jail sentences increased from 28.5% in 1928 (15) to 33.7% in 1929 (16) and 41.4% in 1930 (17), and the average sentence in days per jail sentence imposed increased from 120.7 in 1928 (18) to 140 in 1929 (19) and 227.7 in 1930 (20). This has already resulted in a considerable increase in the number of violators of the National Prohibition Act actually confined in federal institutions. The number of long term liquor law violators confined in the five principal federal institutions increased from 1,887 on June 30, 1929 (21) to 4,296 on June 30, 1930, at which date the liquor law violators comprised 34.8% of the total population of these institutions. This was substantially more than the percentage of violators of the narcotic acts (which was 22%) or of the motor vehicle act (which was 13.2%) (22). Of the 10,496 federal long term prisoners received from the courts during the year ending June 30, 1930, 4,722 or 45% were sentenced for violation of the Prohibition Act, while the number of such prisoners received under sentence for violation of the Narcotic Act was 1,752 (16.7%) and those received under sentence for violation of the Dyer Act was 1,458 (13.9%). The reports of the Attorney General for the fiscal years 1928 and 1929 are not made on a precisely comparable basis but they indicate that the prohibition law violators received in federal institutions under long term sentences in those years were 2,530 and 3,589 respectively (23). These figures indicate a steady increase in the number of prohibition law violators flowing to federal institutions, an increase which it would seem must be accelerated as enforcement became more effective. The figures quoted include only federal long term prisoners. Until recently no information was available as to federal short term prisoners held in county and municipal institutions, but figures recently received (24) from the Bureau of Prisons of the Department of Justice show that in the year ending June 30, 1930, there were received from the courts under short term sentences for liquor law violations a total of 21,427 prisoners and that on June 30, 1930, there were present in county and municipal institutions 5,680 prisoners under sentence in federal liquor cases (which figures includes long term prisoners awaiting transfer to federal penitentiaries as well as short term prisoners sentenced to jail). As more men are arrested for violation of the National Prohibition Law and more are adequately tried, convicted and sentenced, the burden upon the federal penal institutions seems bound to continue to increase at a rapid rate.

With respect to all the agencies required for enforcement, police, courts and prisons, the conclusion seems inevitable that the federal government alone cannot bear the burden of the enforcement of the Eighteenth Amendment. Adequate enforcement of the Amendment would require the assistance of local police officers as well as the machinery of state courts and penal institutions supplemented by a large measure of voluntary observance. The problem of enforcing the Eighteenth Amendment, therefore, reduces itself to an inquiry as to the possibility of securing the necessary cooperation from the states and cities and of arousing public opinion in favor of the enforcement and observance of the law. That such cooperation and public opinion do not now exist, at least in most urban districts, upon any effective scale, seems reasonably clear from the general statements and reports made available to the Commission and the amount of intoxicating liquor in circulation. According to the 1930 census, of the total population of the United States, 122,755,046, 30%, or 36,325,736, live in cities of more than 100,000 inhabitants each and 49,242,777, or 40%, live in cities of more than 25,000 inhabitants each. If the law is not enforceable in cities of the country where the use of alcoholic beverages is most likely to be abused, it cannot be considered as enforceable in the proper sense as a national instrument. What may be accomplished in the direction of securing the necessary cooperation and in the arousal of public opinion is a matter of judgment upon which men will react differently with different qualities of temperament and as to which the judgment of no ordinary individual, and least of all mine, is of particular significance. I was originally disposed to indulge some optimism in the matter upon the theory that improved Federal enforcement might bring a change in the attitude of those who were now purchasing and drinking liquor and that improvement in public opinion might be attained by more consideration of the great difficulties involved in alternative plans of liquor control and of the danger of corruption, political intrigue, and economic and social abuse which they involve, as well as by emphasis upon law observance and appeals to citizens to abstain from subsidizing violation of law aggravated at times by corruption and violence. But I find it impossible to justify such optimism in the face of the arguments stressed in the report of the Commission emphasizing the popular objections to the regime of a prohibitory law and the reasons which many persons have for believing these objections well founded. Without considering the validity of the objections and reasons thus stressed, as to which opinions will widely differ, it seems to me clear that they do not justify failure to observe the law. Their existence among great numbers of people including many respectable citizens must, however, be recognized as a fact, and it is not open to doubt that leaders of opinion everywhere are regularly and openly drinking intoxicating liquor, which can be furnished only in violation of the Eighteenth Amendment. After considering the arguments made in the report of the commission, I cannot find any reasonable ground for the expectation that public sentiment, especially in urban districts, can be changed to the extent necessary to bring about the local cooperation required for the general enforcement and observance of the law. I have reached this conclusion with reluctance because I am deeply sensitive to the difficulties in finding any substitute method of controlling the liquor traffic which will avoid the dangers of intemperance, corruption, and political abuse found in the regulatory provisions prevailing prior to the adoption of the Eighteenth Amendment.

When alternatives to national prohibition are considered, the same state of public opinion, emphasized in the majority report, which leads me to the conclusion that the local cooperation necessary for the enforcement of the National Prohibition Act cannot reasonably be expected, seems to me to require the conclusion that repeal is the only consistent alternative. With great deference to the opinion of those who are so much better qualified than I to consider the matter, I do not think that to substitute for the Eighteenth Amendment a provision leaving the matter to Congress is any solution. Unless the Commission, after its opportunity for study, is prepared to recommend to Congress a concrete plan for dealing with the situation, the suggestion that the matter be referred to Congress seems to me not a dispose of the problem or to make any substantial advance in its disposition. Moreover, this proposal would mean that the liquor question would play a large part every two years in the election of Congress, that a fixed national policy of dealing with it would never be assured (25), and that all the political influence of the liquor interests would be introduced actively into our national affairs. It is suggested that this would be preferable to having these interests active with each state legislature, but relegation of the matter to Congress would carry no assurance even of this accomplishment, since Congress doubtless would not undertake to force any state to be wet which desired to be dry, and that issue would still have to be fought out in each state. If it be a fact that no law can be adequately enforced which is contrary to local public opinion, no recommendation can consistently be made that the matter be left to Congress so as to enable the majority of that body to impose its view upon every community. If Congress should undertake to prohibit the saloon, the difficulties of effective federal enforcement in cities would not be substantially less than they are now in the absence of local public opinion and effort by local law enforcement agencies. If local opinion is against the saloon, as it should be, it will assert itself through state law. Nor is there any need for any amendment to the Constitution to permit of federal control in the matters which would fall properly within the field of federal control upon proper recognition of local public opinion. The power to regulate interstate commerce is adequate to permit Congress to control interstate movements from the wet states into dry states under a law of the general nature of the Webb-Kenyon act.

In considering the experience of Sweden and of the Canadian provinces in connection with systems of government control, it must be observed that while the per capita consumption of spirits under these systems showed a considerable drop in the earlier years of their operation, it has shown a quite steady per capita increase in both the Dominion of Canada (26) and Sweden in the last several years (27). I have not given elaborate consideration, however, to the operation of these systems, because I think the evils which would flow from any federal dispensary system, either through direct government control or through a corporation the net profits of which above a limited extent would inure to the government, would present governmental difficulties as serious as are encountered in our present system. If an experiment with governmental control is to be undertaken, it appears to me better that it should be undertaken by individual states than by the federal government. It seems reasonably certain that any attempt to embark upon a paternalized permit system would not succeed in this country, would open the door to considerable corruption, and would transfer the bootlegger from the rich man to the poor man as his field for operation.

Summarizing, my conclusion is that the Eighteenth Amendment cannot be effectively enforced without the active general support of public opinion and the law enforcement agencies of the states and cities of the nation; that such support does not now exist; and that I cannot find sufficient reason to believe that it can be obtained. I see no alternative but repeal of the Amendment.

I do not favor the theory of nullification, and so long as the Eighteenth Amendment is not repealed by constitutional methods, it seems to me to be the duty of Congress to make reasonable efforts to enforce it, however grave the doubts as to ultimate success. The additions to the field forces and equipment which are set out in detail in the Dennison-Sawyer study appear to be a moderate proposal in this direction and would involve no seriously disproportionate expense for the effort at prohibition enforcement as compared with moneys otherwise expended for governmental operation. I therefore concur in the recommendations that the number of prohibition agents, inspectors, storekeeper gaugers, warehousemen, investigators and special agents should be increased as recommended in that report with corresponding increases in the Customs Bureau and in the personnel and equipment of the Coast Guard. I do not think that any improvement in enforcement of the Eighteenth Amendment would result from an amendment of the National Prohibition Act so as to permit the manufacture of so-called light wines and beer. If the liquor so manufactured were not intoxicating, it would not satisfy the taste of the great majority of those who are now drinking intoxicating liquors, and if it were intoxicating, it could not be permitted without violation of the Constitution. Such legislation would moreover add to the difficulties of enforcement because if the permissible alcoholic content were increased, it would become harder to determine when the law had been violated. I agree that consistency requires that the National Prohibition Act should be amended so as to place cider and fruit juices upon the same basis as other intoxicating liquors; that independent denaturing plants should be prohibited; that there should be legislation adequate to eliminate the coverhouse problem in industrial alcohol; and that details with respect to the use of liquor for medicinal purposes should be provided for by regulation rather than by statute. These recommendations for immediate improvement in the machinery of enforcement represent, I think, a reasonable extension of federal efforts at enforcement which it is the duty of Congress to make so long as the Eighteenth Amendment remains in the Constitution.

MONTE M. LEMANN
Washington, D.C., January 7, 1931

Footnotes:

(1) In 1923, the number was seventy-six. See Annual Report Commissioner of Internal Revenue, page 33.

(2) This information was also furnished to the Commission by the Technical Division of the Bureau of Industrial Alcohol.

(3) Annual Report, Commissioner of Prohibition--1930, page 90.

(4) "The Control & Sale of Liquor" (a mimeographed report issued by the Dominion Bureau of Statistics in 1930), page 17.

(5) Report of Consul General Linnell to State Department, Nov. 21, 1930.

(6) The 1919 figures are taken from the U.S. Bureau of the Census, Biennial Census of Manufactures (1921), p. 89. The 1929 figures are taken from the Census Bureau, Department of Commerce, Census of Manufactures (1929). Release of July 7, 1930.

(7) "Possible Production of Illegal Liquor in the United States for the Fiscal Year Ending June 30, 1930," Bureau of Prohibition, Department of Justice, September, 1930.

(8) Subsequently reduced by 3,154,866 gallons deducted as the legal production of wine, leaving a corrected estimate of 115,165,434 gallons.

(9) The total quantity of intoxicating liquors estimated by the Bureau of Prohibition to be possibly in circulation from all sources in the year ending June 30, 1930, was approximately 69,820,218 proof gallons of spirits, 118,476,200 gallons of wine and 684,176,800 gallons of malt liquor. In the year ending June 30, 1917, the quantities of intoxicating liquors consumed were 167,740,325 proof gallons of spirits, 42,723,376 gallons of wine and liquors consumed were 167,740,325 proof gallons of spirits, 42,723,376 gallons of wine and 1,885,071,304 gallons of malt liquor. The figures last quoted are taken from the United States Statistical Abstract for 1922, page 697.

(10) Annual Report, Commissioner of Prohibition, 1930--page 111. The figures quoted do not include still worms or fermenters seized, the number of which was large.

(11) The authors of the study add, however, that small violators cannot be entirely neglected and that cooperation of local law enforcement officers is needed in dealing with them.

(12) A field study into the relationship between pleas of guilty and sentences would be necessary before any considered statement on this point could be made. An examination of the table in the Annual Report of the Commissioner of Prohibition, 1930, page 118, shows that the percentage of pleas of guilty is as high in some districts where substantial jail sentence are given in a large proportion of cases as in districts where jail sentences are rare and very short. It may be that in the first class of districts sentences are more severe where the defendant pleads not guilty and is convicted after trial so that an inducement to plead guilty is in fact offered.

(13) The figures are taken from the Annual Report, Commissioner of Prohibition, 1930, page 118; Annual Report, Attorney General of the United States, 1930, page 100.

(14) The report of the Conference of Senior Circuit Judges (Annual Report of the Attorney General of the United States, 1930, page 4) describes the congestion in the federal district courts as continuing to be a major problem and recommends the appointment of five additional district judges. The Conference Report refers to suggestions made for the creation of additional districts and requests the Attorney General to make a survey as to the feasibility of consolidations or changes in existing districts. The total number of criminal cases pending in the federal courts on June 30, was in 1929 31,153 and in 1930, 35,849. That the increase was due entirely to prohibition cases is indicated by the fact that the total number of such cases pending on June 30 increased from 18,385 in 1929 to 22,671 in 1930. The percentage of prosecutions pending under the Prohibition Act to total criminal prosecutions increased from 59.0 percent at June 30, 1929, to 63.2 percent at June 30, 1930. The number of prosecutions instituted under the National Prohibition Act increased only slightly from 56,786 in the fiscal year 1929 to 56,992 in the fiscal year 1930. But while the new prosecutions instituted thus increased only to the extent of 206, the cases pending at the end of the fiscal year increased by 4,286 from June 30, 1929, to June 30, 1930. Of this increase 3,040, according to a statement of the Department of Justice, were in the Southern District of New York, leaving a net increase of 1,246 for the rest of the country. A statement compiled by the Department of Justice shows that of the ninety-one federal districts in the United States, there were eleven districts each of which, either at the beginning or at the end of the fiscal year 1930, had more than 500 prohibition cases pending, and nine districts each of which had more than 300 such cases pending at one of such dates. Four of the eleven districts were included in those for which additional judges were recommended by the 1930 Conference of Senior Circuit Judges.

(15) Annual Report, Commissioner of Prohibition, 1928, page 95.

(16) Annual Report, Commissioner of Prohibition, 1929, page 109.

(17) Annual Report, Commissioner of Prohibition, 1930, page 118.

(18) Annual Report, Commissioner of Prohibition, 1928, page 99.

(19) Annual Report, Commissioner of Prohibition, 1929, page 113.

(20) Annual Report, Commissioner of Prohibition, 1930, page 118.

(21) Annual Report, Federal Penal and Correctional Institutions, 1929, page 61.

(22) Bureau of Prisons, Department of Justice, unpublished data released December, 1930.

(23) The above figures are taken from the Annual Reports of the Attorney General; the year 1930, page 315; the year 1929, following page 298; the year 1928, following page 292.

(24) Unpublished data released December, 1930.

(25) The suggestion that Congress might then elect to return to Prohibition does not seem to

carry far. If Prohibition cannot succeed when given status as a fixed national policy by constitutional provision, it does not seem reasonable to hope that it could succeed when its continuance was open to attack every two years, or that the necessary organization for enforcement could be maintained and developed in the face of a constant doubt as to the permanency of the policy.

(26) "The Control and Sale of Liquor in Canada." Canada Department of Trade and Commerce, Dominion Bureau of Statistics, Ottawa, 1930, page 19.

(27) Annual Reports of Swedish Royal Liquor Control Board (Rusdryeksforsaljning).

STATEMENT BY GEORGE W. WICKERSHAM

I have signed the report of the Commission, although as is probably inevitable when eleven people of different antecedents and temperaments endeavor to agree upon a contentious subject, it is more or less of a compromise of varying opinions. In so far as it states facts, I believe it to be generally accurate. Every effort has been made to make it so. I should have preferred to have it state more facts and fewer broad generalizations from unstated facts. But the difficulties in securing accurate statistics, owing to the unsystematic and unscientific manner in which they are commonly kept in this country, often makes it impossible to get reliable statements of fact, although there may be sufficient available information to afford a fairly reliable basis of generalization.

I am in entire accord with the conclusions "that enforcement of the National Prohibition Act made a bad start which has affected enforcement ever since"; that "it was not until after the Senatorial investigation of 1926 had opened people's eyes to the extent of law breaking and corruption that serious efforts were made" to coordinate "the federal services directly and indirectly engaged in enforcing prohibition," and that not until after the act of 1927 had extended the Civil Service law over the enforcement agents, were there the beginnings of such an organization as might have been expected to command the respect of other services, the courts and the public, and thus secure reasonable observance of the law and enforcement of its provisions as well as other laws are enforced. Until then, too, enforcement largely had expended itself upon a multitude of prosecutions of petty offenders; it measured success in enforcement by the number of cases – most of which were trivial and in few of which were substantial penalties imposed. I cannot believe that an experiment of such far reaching and momentous consequence as this of National Prohibition should be abandoned after seven years of such imperfect enforcement and only three years of reorganization and effort to repair the mistakes of the earlier period. The older generation very largely has forgotten and the younger never knew the evils of the saloon and the corroding influence upon politics, both local and national, of the organized liquor interests. But the tradition of that rottenness still lingers, even in the minds of the bitterest opponents of the Prohibition law, substantially all of whom assert that the licensed saloon must never again be restored. It is because I see no escape from its return in any of the practicable alternatives to Prohibition, that I unite with my colleagues in agreement that the Eighteenth Amendment must not be repealed and differing with some of them, I have been forced to conclude that a further trial should be made of the enforceability of the Eighteenth Amendment under the present organization, with the help of the recommended improvements. I am entirely in accord with the views expressed in the Report that Prohibition cannot be accomplished without the cooperation of the States and the active support of public opinion. This cooperation has been and still is sadly lacking in many States. Even where there is an adequate State law and a good State law enforcement organization, public sentiment often prevents enforcement. The crucial inquiry respecting the National situation is whether it be too late to expect or to hope for any more favorable turn in public opinion as a result of better organization and methods of enforcement and a campaign of exposition of the evils of the old state of affairs and the dangers of a return to the saloon and corrupt saloon politics. I think that if a proposed amendment to the Constitution simply repealing the Eighteenth Amendment, were to be passed by the requisite majorites in both houses of Congress and submitted to the States, to be considered by Conventions called for the purpose in each State, the delegates to be chosen in an off year and the Conventions to be held in a year when there is no presidential election, we should have intelligent discussions of the question and a result which would reflect the sober informed and deliberate opinion of the people. Such a procedures might remove the issue from party politics. If the result were to support the Eighteenth Amendment, public opinion would promote observance and sustain a reasonable, intelligent enforcement of the law such as would furnish a test of Prohibition that would conclusively demonstrate whether or not it is practicable. If the preponderating opinion should oppose Prohibition, the way would be opened to a revision of the Amendment such, for example, as the one recommended in our report.

Even then there would remain the difficult question of how to allow the manufacture and sale of intoxicating liquors without the return of the saloon. The best method thus far suggested is a modification of the Swedish system. Yet I have great doubts if such a system would work in our country. I think the pressure to obtain books authorizing purchase of liquor would be so irresistible, that all benefits of the system would be lost; of else, the intrigues of organized liquor interests would exert such influence in Congress, that the distinctive characteristics of the system would be destroyed and an abundance of liquor soon flow for all who wished it. The whole subject is one of great difficulty. There is room for difference of opinion on most of the elements involved. Therefore, despite the well financed active propaganda of opposition to Prohibition and the development of an increasingly hostile public opinion, I am not convinced that the present system may not be the best attainable, and that any substitute for it would not lead to the unrestricted flow of intoxicating liquor, with the attendant evils that in the past always were a blight upon our social organization.

GEORGE W. WICKERSHAM
Washington, D.C., January 7, 1931

STATEMENT BY ADA L. COMSTOCK

The material which has been brought before the Commission has convinced me that adequate enforcement of the Eighteenth Amendment and the National Prohibition Act is impossible without the support of a much larger proportion of our population than it now commands. Moreover, the conditions which exist today in respect to enforcement and which, in my opinion, can be modified only slightly by improvements in administration, tend to undermine not only respect for law but more fundamental conceptions of personal integrity and decency. For these reasons, I am one of the members of the Commission who favor an immediate attempt at change. As I still hope that federal regulation of the liquor traffic may prove more effective than that of the states, I favor revision of the amendment rather than its repeal.

ADA L. COMSTOCK.
Washington, D.C., January 7, 1931

STATEMENT BY NEWTON D. BAKER

In my opinion, the Eighteenth Amendment should be repealed and the whole question of policy and enforcement with regard to intoxicating liquors remitted to the Senate.

If, for practical reasons, immediate repeal bethought unattainable, a submission of the Amendment suggested in the report of the Commission would test the present sentiment of the country and, if the Amendment were adopted, would accomplish the double result of removing an arbitrary and inflexible police regulation from the Constitution, where it seems to me it should never have been put, and of giving Congress the power to adapt federal legislation on the subject, from time to time, to the realities of the situation as they may develop.

I have signed the report of the Commission because it is a fair finding of the facts disclosed to us by such evidence as was available, and because it is clear that so long as the Constitution and law remain as they now are, the recommendations of the report should be carried out to aid the Executive, charged with the duty of enforcement.

The efforts now being made to enforce the law are sincere and intelligent and aided and supplemented, as recommended in the report, a higher degree of effectiveness will be certain to follow, but in my opinion, the problem is insoluble so long as it is permitted to require a nation-wide federal enforcement of a police regulation, at variance with the settled habits and beliefs of so large a part of our people.

NEWTON D. BAKER
Washington, D.C., January 7, 1931

STATEMENT BY WILLIAM I. GRUBB

I am one of the members of the Commission, who believe that prohibition under the Eighteenth Amendment is entitled to a further trial before a revision or repeal of the Amendment is recommended. I join in the findings of fact and all the ultimate conclusions of the general report of the Commission (except that recommending that the Amendment be revised immediately, without awaiting a further trial), but not in all of the general observations.

My reasons for thinking that prohibition under the Amendment is entitled to a further trial are twofold. The first is that it is an experiment, which has not been completed, and has not yet had a fair trial, and the second is that no satisfactory substitute for it has been presented or shown to exist.

I

I agree with the conclusion of the report that enforcement and observance of the law have never been and are not now adequate or satisfactory, and do not warrant its continuance, unless a change is probable within a reasonable time. I agree also in the finding of the report that there has been an improvement in the efficiency and character of enforcement methods, since the enforcement unit was placed under Civil Service, and since the transfer of the unit to the Department of Justice. Improvement in the machinery alone will not accomplish satisfactory enforcement. It will require also a favorable change in the attitude of the public towards the law. Voluntary observance of a law of this nature is essential. So long as the majority of the people do not observe it, the law is powerless to enforce it. I believe that the use of only clean and efficient methods of enforcement, together with adequate appropriations to accomplish efficiency, may change the present hostile attitude of the public to one of voluntary observance and approval, that will within a reasonable time for such an end, bring about a proper enforcement of prohibition. So long as improvement continues, the experiment cannot be considered completed, and should not be abandoned. If, and when, improvement ceases or when it is demonstrated that the improvement, though continuing, will not result in a changed public opinion, favorable to the law, so that enforcement can be made reasonably effective, the experiment should be abandoned. The time required for the completion of the experiment cannot be determined in advance, but will work itself out during the progress of the trial. The result of a further trial is a matter of prophecy, not of fact, as to which there can now be no certain ascertainment. In view of the present improvement, and the possibility of its resulting in successful observance and enforcement of the law in the future, I think the experiment should be accorded a further trial.

II

This conclusion is reinforced because of the fact that no satisfactory substitute for prohibition under the Amendment has yet been presented or shown to exist. Repeal of the Amendment would remit the control of the liquor business to the States, except so far as it was susceptible of Federal control through the powers of interstate commerce and taxation. Prohibition is conceded to have produced two great benefits, the abolition of the open saloon and the elimination of the liquor influence from politics. Remission to the States would assure the return of the open saloon at least in some of the States, and the return of the liquor interest to the politics of all of them. Revision of the Amendment by vesting in Congress the exclusive control of the liquor business

112

would make certain the return of the liquor influence in national politics, and possibly the return of the open saloon in all the States. The authority of Congress under its taxing and commerce powers would be inadequate to protect a State desiring prohibition, in securing it, when it had neighbors who permitted the manufacture and distribution of intoxicating liquors. Vesting in Congress the power to regulate or prohibit without recommending a specific plan of regulation or control, furnishes no solution of the liquor question, and would leave it to constant agitation in Congress and the Country, until the happening of the remote contingency of a solution satisfactory to all parties. As to the systems of other countries, they may be classified into prohibition, ownership and operation by governments or governmental agencies, private operation under regulation and taxation, or without restrictions. The finding of the Commission is adverse to operation by government agencies. In this finding, I concur. Private operation without restrictions is impossible. This leaves for consideration, regulated private operation and prohibition. Private operation, under a high license, proper closing regulations, forbidding the sale to minors and incompetents, and drinking on the premises where sold, seems the only practicable system, excluding prohibition. This was the system that preceded prohibition. The difficulty experienced with it then was that the regulations were impossible of enforcement, and the liquor business came to such a disregard of them, as led to prohibition. An abandonment of prohibition and a return to regulated private operation would be a step backward in the evolution of the liquor question, and one that should not be taken until all hope of a reasonable enforcement and observance of prohibition under the Amendment and the enforcement laws had disappeared.

Believing that the time has not yet come, I think there should be a further trial, and that there is a possibility under improved enforcing methods and personnel, and increased and adequate appropriations for equipment and additional personnel, together with a resulting sympathetic feeling of the public towards the law, of reasonable observance and enforcement being accomplished within a reasonable period. If proper enforcement and observance are not then had, or if a better and more satisfactory system is shown to exist, it will be time enough to abandon prohibition, and to adopt the better substitute.

W. I. GRUBB
Washington, D.C., January 7, 1931

STATEMENT BY WILLIAM S. KENYON

In signing the general report of the Commission, the right is reserved to each member to express his or her individual views as to matters therein discussed. It is not an easy matter for eleven individuals to agree on any report concerning the problem of prohibition enforcement and of necessity there must be some give and take in order to reach any conclusions.

I desire, as to some of the propositions, to submit a few observations.

I use the term, "prohibition laws," to cover all the laws passed by Congress to carry out the Eighteenth Amendment, and the terms "witnesses" and "evidence" to cover names and statements of parties before us.

In the report is this: "A division of opinion exists in view of the foregoing considerations as to whether enforceability of the law has been fairly tested." It seems to me the evidence before us is sufficient to demonstrate that at least up to the creation of a Bureau of Prohibition in the Department of Justice the enforceability of the prohibition laws had never been subjected to any fair and convincing test. Whether in view of the bad start in the enforcement program and the maladministration of the same up to said time there has been created a public sentiment against the law that makes it impossible for enforceability to have any fair chance, may be a debatable proposition. From my viewpoint, it is unfortunate that the hearings of the Commission on prohibition have been in secret, which compels us to file a report based in part on secret evidence. If the evidence produced before us could have been made public, I think it would have given to the country a true picture of why reasonable enforcement of the prohibition laws could not have been expected.

The Commission, of course, had no authority to grant immunity to witnesses, nor did it have the power of subpoena to compel attendance, which facts bore somewhat on the policy adopted of secrecy.

Notwithstanding this policy, it is permissible, I think, to refer to some evidence of witnesses before us who did not enjoin secrecy, without giving the names except in instances where the witness may have publicly stated the same thing.

There are many reasons why the prohibition laws have never had a fair chance of reasonable enforcement. I refer to some of them.

Up to the time of the recent transfer to the Department of Justice of prohibition enforcement, responsibility therefore was in the Treasury Department. It did not logically belong there. The higher officials of the Treasury Department were skilled in finance but not in law enforcement, and with some exceptions, had little heart in the enforcement of these laws. This naturally dampened any enthusiasm for enforcement on the part of enforcement forces all down the line.

Another reason is that a large part of the personnel up to the time at least that employees of the Prohibition Bureau were placed under the Civil Service were the kind who would not ordinarily have been selected to enforce any law. The report points out the tremendous overturn and in a general way the political influences surrounding the appointment of prohibition enforcement agents. Prior to the covering into the Civil Service of employees of the Prohibition Bureau, appointments of prohibition agents to a large extent were dictated through political influence and by political bosses. These appointments were regarded as political patronage. We have had before us experts from the Civil Service Commission from whom we have learned that even after the prohibition agents were placed under Civil Service, this political interference persisted, that some of the worst men had the strongest political backing. An examination of the Civil Service records would tell the story. Some of the prohibition agents, whose appointments were attempted to be forced by political influence were men with criminal records. Some apparently sought the positions because of the opportunity for graft and boasted of what they could make therein.

Others were entirely incompetent. It has been stated before us by those who should know that at least fifty per cent of the men employed as prohibition agents prior to the time they were placed under Civil Service were unfit for the position and incompetent as law enforcing officers. The turnovers in the prohibition personnel prior to Civil Service show a shocking condition. The situation is probably somewhat better now, and better men are being secured. There have been many honest, capable and patriotic officials in the prohibition service--men of the highest character, such as Prohibition Administrators John D. Pennington, S. O. Wynne, Thomas E. Stone, Alfred Oftedahl and others. I do not mean to criticize the entire personnel, nor by mentioning these to disparage all of the others. Some of the personnel have been excellent, some indifferent, some indifferent, some corrupt.

Major Chester P. Mills, who honestly tried to enforce the law as Prohibition Administrator of the Second Federal District of New York, has told in articles published in Collier's Weekly in 1927 the story of attempted political influence in the appointment of prohibition agents in his district, and has repeated practically the same story before us. In these articles he said that "three-fourths of the 2,500 dry agents are ward heelers and sycophants named by the politicians." Politicians, some of them high in national affairs, attempted to force upon him men with criminal records – some the very lowest grade of vote-getters--which apparently was the test of the politician for good prohibition agents. Prohibition was expected evidently by some politicians to furnish a fine field for the operation of the spoils system in politics. Their expectations have been largely realized. One of the leading political bosses of New York City informed Mills that he must let him control the patronage in his office or he would have to get out. Another told him that efficiency must give way to patronage. One agent with a criminal record whom he discharged was reinstated after Mills ceased to be Administrator, and was continued in office until about a year ago, when he was indicted for alleged conspiracy to violate the provisions of the National Prohibition Act. One of the parties whom it was insisted he should appoint had shortly before shot a man in a row in a speakeasy, another had been found with burglar tools upon him. Major Mills tried to do an honest job and soon discovered, according to his statements, that he was not wanted on the job, and to use his language, was kicked "up-stairs to an innocuous zone supervisorship."

In one district the evidence shows that a prohibition agent was transferred prior to an election because his enforcement activities were injuring the party and interfering with the collection of funds for the campaign. Some officers were directed by political bosses to let up in their activities and "lay off" on their work until after some particular primary or election.

Another reason, somewhat closely associated with the character of the personnel, as to why the law has not been better enforced, is corruption. After every war there is a tragic era of graft and corruption, but all of the corruption under prohibition cannot be attributed to the aftermath of the war.

The profits in the unlawful making and vending of intoxicating liquors have been so enormous that the funds to invest in protection have been large, and the temptation to many men in the service on small salaries has been difficult to withstand. Evidence before us by those accurately acquainted with the workings of prohibition in the great cities, shows that in many of them the supposed enforcement of prohibition has been reeking with corruption, and has been a complete fiasco. The grand jury investigation at Philadelphia in 1928 disclosed that some of the police force were depositing more in the banks than their salaries amounted to. Bootleggers' accounts running up to $11,000,000 were deposited in a certain bank, and the officers of the bank testified they did not know any of the parties so depositing. Witnesses have presented to us evidence showing that breweries have been operated in the heart of a great city with the knowledge of prohibition agents, in some of which as much as $200,000 was invested in the plant. In one large city three breweries were openly operated, and at least up to April 1, 1930, were making real beer and delivering it around the city. Every one of the vicinity except the prohibition agents seemed to know of the breweries. Truck loads of liquors have been transported under the protection of police. In one state prohibition agents sent to a great university to look into the situation at a "Home Coming" were found drinking with some of the students in a hotel room. In many of the cities there was developed under prohibition an entirely new underworld, due to the large amounts of money involved in the bootlegging business. The gangster and his crew have taken an important part in politics, and in connection with politicians and under their protection control the liquor business in many of the cities. In one of them gangs have entered into agreements dividing the city for plunder, and providing that the beer privilege shall belong in certain parts of the city to certain particular gangs, and criminal syndicates take care through politics of those who buy from the gangs.

There are thousands of speakeasies operating in the large cities--the number is appalling. Speakeasies cannot operate openly unless protected from prosecution. One who can operate a speakeasy in a block where policemen are constantly passing is enabled to do so only because of one thing, and that is protective graft. In some cities there is complete protection by ward politicians who must have back of them the influential political bosses. The speakeasies could not run a day if the authorities would act. The combination of liquor and politics has been almost fatal to law enforcement, but surely the government is not powerless to strike, and strike hard at such a situation. Surely enough honest men can be found to act as prohibition agents and as police. If not, there is no use in any further efforts to enforce these laws or any other laws.

I have referred to only a part of the evidence before us showing the mess of corruption. It is difficult in view of the secret policy of the Commission to prepare any report doing justice to the subject that may not do injustice to the many able and honest men in the service. Some of the evidence is so startling that it is difficult to believe it. Of course, there was corruption prior to prohibition. The saloon was the center of political activity, but I think the corruption was not so widespread and flagrant as it now is. The amounts involved were not so large. Corruption had not become such an established art and racketeering was unknown. It has now developed to a high degree of efficiency. Nothing but a Congressional investigation could give to the public the whole story.

This situation has developed a type of politician-lawyer unknown to the federal courts in earlier days, who sells his supposed influence with the district attorney's office and acquires the bootlegger's legal business in many instances by virtue of his political connections and influence.

Certain abuses in some of the cities in the permit system of handling alcohol have added to the difficulty. Political influence has been exerted to secure permits and the reinstatement of revoked permits. Quite a business along that line has been carried on by some political lawyers. One witness who knows the situation in one of the larger cities states that permits are sometimes secured by getting men with decent reputations to appear as the real applicants, when in fact behind it are gangsters and underworld men. Some legitimate permittees have been blackmailed by threats to revoke permits. In some cases where administrators have denied applications the applicants have gone to the federal district court, and that court in some instances has directed issuance of the permit. Today the courts are more inclined to sustain the administrator where he refuses a permit than they formerly were. In some instances the cases were not properly presented to the court on behalf of the administrator.

How in view of all these things, can it be reasonably claimed that prohibition laws have had any real honest test as to enforceability? It seems to me they have never had a chance. Laws against murder and arson under similar conditions, could not have been enforced. If a different beginning had been made in the enforcement of these laws, there might have been a very different story.

No law can be enforced without reasonable public sentiment behind it. Public sentiment against the prohibition laws has been stimulated by irritating methods of enforcement, such as the abuse of search and seizure processes, invasion of homes and violation of the Fourth Amendment to the Constitution, entrapment of witnesses, killings by prohibition agents, poisonous denaturants resulting in sickness and sometimes blindness and death, United States attorneys defending in the federal courts prohibition agents charged with homicides, the padlocking of small places, and the lack of any real attempt to padlock clubs or prominent hotels where the law is notoriously violated, the arrest of small offenders and comparatively few cases brought against the larger ones. The limitation of the amount of liquor that physicians may prescribe for medicinal purposes, restraint in the use of alcohol for scientific purposes, the fruit juice proviso of the National Prohibition Act (Section 29, Title II) which practically permits the making of wines in the homes when there is no similar provision as to the making of beer, have contributed to the dissatisfaction.

That there have been abuses of search and seizure processes is without question; likewise as to entrapment of witnesses. We have studied the numerous cases of killings by prohibition agents in the attempt to enforce the laws. There have been few convictions. Some of the shootings were apparently careless and unjustifiable, and evidence the reckless use of firearms and disregard of human life. There has been a too free and easy use of firearms by some of the prohibition agents. This is now being restrained.

On the other hand, many prohibition agents have lost their lives in attempting to perform their duties, concerning which little reference is made by the press.

The defense by United States district attorneys of prohibition agents charged with killing has made difficult the conviction of such agents.

The Supreme Court of the United States holds that agents of the government engaged in enforcement of the prohibition laws have the right of removal of a case against them from the state to the federal court where they are charged with homicide while engaged in their duties. Maryland v. Soper, 270 U.S.9. The present Attorney General has announced a very wise doctrine on this subject, which may be summed up, I think, by the statement that while the United States attorneys will defend in these cases after removal to the federal courts, they will not attempt to procure the acquittal of guilty men or attempt to justify unlawful or illegal acts by federal officers. This question of defense by district attorneys of the United States raises very difficult questions of policy and of justice. The Federal Government might be seriously impaired if its officers were to be tried in state courts for conduct in carrying out their legitimate official duties. On the other hand, it is apparent that with the United States attorney defending a man in the federal court there is little possibility of conviction. It seems to me the policy of Attorney General Mitchell will alleviate to some extent this particular irritation.

The present book of instructions to agents issued by the Prohibition Bureau stresses the idea that enforcement must be by lawful methods. Government lawlessness in law enforcement is an abhorrent proposition. The Fourth and Fifth Amendments to the Constitution safeguarding the rights of citizens are fully as important as the Eighteenth Amendment. "Let the homes alone," should be the policy of enforcing officials, unless there is a clear showing that the home is being used as a place for the sale of liquors or the manufacture for sale. (Such is apparently the present policy of the new Administrator.) The doctrine that a man's home is his castle still applies so long as it is used as a bona fide home. Nothing can tend to create public sentiment against these laws more than the invasion of the home.

The use of poisonous denaturants in alcohol cannot be justified. Death or blindness is too heavy a punishment to administer to one who may indulge in a drink of liquor. We are advised that arrangements have now been made for the use of non-poisonous denaturants which make the liquor nauseating but not fatal. Congressman Sirovich of New York clearly pointed out in a speech in the House of Representatives on January 17, 1930, how this can be done.

Some of the physicians who have appeared before us make no objection to the restrictions upon physicians in the use of liquors as medicines. They differ as to the necessity for such use, but the majority of them resent these limitations as to the maximum amount of alcohol that may be permitted to a patient within a given period placed upon them by laymen who have no knowledge of the needs therefor, and take them as a reflection on the medical profession. Physicians should be permitted, under reasonable regulations, to prescribe whatever liquor in their judgment is necessary for a patient. If a physician can be trusted to prescribe dangerous drugs he can be trusted to prescribe liquors as medicines.

The forfeiture of automobiles of innocent persons in which liquor may be found adds to the irritation.

These things have not helped to create a friendly attitude toward the prohibition laws by those who might be considered as neutrals, and undoubtedly have interfered with their enforcement by creating public sentiment against them. Public sentiment changes quickly in the United States and a fair and honest trial of prohibition laws with less of the irritating methods of enforcement might change much of public sentiment on the question.

It is impossible to obtain satisfactory statistics to show whether or not more intoxicating liquor is being consumed today than during pre-prohibition days. I am satisfied there is not. The liquor bill of the nation before prohibition was staggering. It required a tremendous outpouring of liquor to support 178,000 saloons openly selling and soliciting business. Most of the witnesses agree that there is less drunkenness under prohibition than before. Statistics generally can be secured to prove almost any proposition, and we have a mass of them in our files on various phases of the subject. Figures uninterpreted may be very misleading. The years 1920 and 1921 seem to have shown the best results under prohibition. The low mark in arrests for drunkenness was reached in those years. In many parts of the United States it appears that arrests for drunkenness have increased since 1920.

Arrests for drunkenness are not an infallible index, but do have significance. The attitude of the police of one city toward prohibition laws may be entirely different from that of another. Some do not regard violations of such laws as serious, and leave the entire matter to the United States Government, making few arrests. Others regard drunkenness as more serious than in the pre-prohibition days.

Alcoholics in detention institutions have apparently increased, and the figures given out by the Metropolitan Life Insurance Company tend to show there have been more deaths from alcoholism in the last few years than heretofore. The company in a report on the subject says:

"The rising alcoholism death rate in this country since 1920 cannot, in our judgment, be explained by increased consumption of 'hard' liquor as compared with war-time and pre-war-time years. The reason must lie, we think, in the greater toxicity of the alcoholic liquors which are now used so generally throughout the country. The only encouraging feature in this picture is that officials of various states, responsible for the public health, are now stirred by the situation and are preparing measures for its more adequate control."

This upward trend in the death rate from alcoholism is accounted for by some on the theory that the liquor available today is more injurious to life than that available before prohibition.

That there is an abundance of intoxicating liquor is evident. It is idle to close one's eyes to that fact. It is supplied by smuggling, illicit distilling and diversion of industrial alcohol.

In the report made to the President on January 13, 1930, we have spoken of the tremendous border line of this country which makes the control of smuggling difficult. While some of the reports that have been given out by the Prohibition Bureau would indicate that smuggling has decreased, the figures before us tend to show it has not, except in spots. At some particular point, such as Windsor, smuggling may have lessened, only to break out at other places, such as Amherstburg. The situation at Detroit is one of the worst in the United States, and the few boats, the small force of the customs and prohibition agents of the government, are totally inadequate to cope with the problem in that vicinity. Bank statements at Detroit would show the tremendous business of some smugglers.

The Canadian Parliament has recently passed a law forbidding exportation of liquor to this country, which it was supposed would be helpful in meeting the problem as far as the Canadian boundary line is concerned, but it appears that since this change there has been more smuggling than before the passage of the act.

That it will require a tremendous force in the nature of a border patrol to prevent smuggling from Canada and Mexico is apparent. It should be a unified border patrol. To prevent all smuggling along our extended water fronts is impossible. It requires constant vigilance to hold it within any reasonable bounds.

The Prohibition Bureau makes reports as to the seizure of stills, illicit distilleries and paraphernalia used in the manufacture of whisky. These figures show an enormous increase in the number of stills seized by agents of the Bureau since 1920, in which year there were approximately 32,000 stills seized. In 1928, there were about 261,000. These still are sold by mail order houses and department stores in sections and easily set up. General Lincoln C. Andrews, formerly Prohibition Administrator, before the Senate Committee investigating this subject in 1926, testified that the department in twelve months had seized 172,600 stills and had not captured, he thought, more than one in ten. That testimony would indicate a tremendous number of stills. The evidence before us tends to show a great increase in the number of stills and a universality of operation extending all over the country. The amount of moonshine liquor made in this country per year cannot be estimated within any reasonable bounds.

It is asserted there has been a great increase in the manufacture of flasks and corks. We have been unable to obtain any evidence as to this.

The question of diversion of industrial alcohol as a source of the liquor supply is discussed in the report. That there have been serious and unconscionable diversions of industrial alcohol in the past is without question. The specially denatured alcohol permittee is the chief diverter of industrial alcohol into beverage channels. Major Mills estimated a diversion of fifteen million gallons of industrial alcohol in New York per year when he became Prohibition Director for that state. At Buffalo in one three-month period ninety carloads of such diverted alcohol were seized. We have before us reports of special agents made to their superior officers in the year 1930 with relation to the legitimate consumption of industrial alcohol in one district in a large western state to be used by 2,300 drug stores, 200 hospitals, 25 Turkish baths, and miscellaneous consumers. The report shows that 60,000 gallons would cover the actual needs for these purposes, but the amount imported in 1929 to that district as four times the quantity legitimately used. In this particular district it was estimated that industrial alcohol products constitute approximately thirty per cent of the total contraband liquor seized. In this same state it was estimated by those who should know that in the northern part of the state ten to fifteen per cent of seized liquor is diverted alcohol, while in the southern portion it is thirty per cent. Others estimate it at seventy per cent. Two important cases were brought by the government last year, one at Baltimore and one at Chicago, involving the question of a conspiracy in diversion of industrial alcohol. It is charged in the Chicago case that during a period of seven years a million gallons a year of alcohol have been diverted to illicit distilleries. The ramifications of this conspiracy reach from New York to Los Angeles. Large quantities of industrial alcohol are seized in carload lots that never reach a still. In the Chicago case over three carloads had been seized and the railroad records showed that approximately 138 carloads of the same product had been shipped into Chicago in six months. Carloads of pure grain alcohol have been seized where the consignor and the consignee were both fictitious. The diversion of industrial alcohol in the New England district was forty-four per cent of the total in the district a year and a half ago. It ahas been, according to the prohibition officers, reduced to twelve per cent. One administrator captured within two or three months last year on carload on insecticide. Forty per cent of it was alcohol. It came from New Jersey, and was ordered destroyed by the Federal Court. Another car of the same stuff was captured at Cleveland. >From January 1, 1927, to March 4, 1927, the same administrator captured nineteen carloads of straight alcohol. It came from the Federal Chemical Company of Nitro, West Virginia. Figuring 78,000 gallons of straight alcohol to the car would be 1,482,000 gallons. It was all billed to firms that did not exist (otherwise known as corer houses). It was not certain that any denaturants whatever had been placed in this alcohol. A Chemical and Products Company in the same district, which was a fake concern operating under a permit, had a capacity of 80,000 gallons of alcohol per month. This would make three times the amount of bootleg whisky, or 240,000 gallons, which would sell at $30.00 a gallon. In one district alone millions of gallons have been diverted, and enough withdrawn in a few months for perfume manufacturers to perfume the South Sea Islanders. There has been enough specially denatured alcohol withdrawn in one year by one corporation for hair tonics "to supply the world with hair tonic," as one witness puts it. There have been diversions of medicinal and sacramental alcohol, but they are minor compared with the diversion of industrial alcohol.

The legitimate uses of alcohol throughout the nation in industry have tremendously increased. There were some 38,000,000 gallons withdrawn in 1921 for denaturing purposes, while in 1929 there were 182,000,000 gallons withdrawn, an increase of nearly five hundred per cent. The Department of Commerce has been unable to furnish us the figures as to the amount of alcohol needed per year for legitimate industry. The permittee has not been required to follow through to ultimate destination the alcohol he sells, and through the instrumentality of cover houses the system of fraudulent diversion has been built up in this country by crooked permit-holders Corporations and partnerships have been created merely for the purpose of using diverted industrial alcohol. The independent denaturing plant is a fraud, and should not be permitted to exist apart from the manufacturing plant. Undoubtedly the Bureau is strenuously endeavoring to remedy this leak. Such things as supposed manufacture under permits and formulas for hair tonics, perfumeries, deodorants, barber supplies, tobacco sprays, lacquers, paints and varnishes, furnish opportunity for diversions. In many instances where permits have been taken away new companies representing the same parties have been organized and new permits secured. Fly-by-night concerns, dignified by titles of chemical companies and drug associations have been acting as cover houses and denaturing plants. It is possible the situation could be remedied by requiring accounting by concerns which purchase from the permittee, or by the adoption of regulations urged by Mrs. Willebrandt when Assistant Attorney General, requiring permittees to follow the liquor through to ultimate destination, although there is some legal difficulty in the matter.

It is impossible to estimate with any degree of accuracy the amount of industrial alcohol diverted into bootleg channels. Any estimate is a mere guess. The Bureau announced some time ago that it had cut down on permits some fifteen million gallons of industrial alcohol per year in the future.

How the Bureau arrives at his arbitrary figure we are not advised. If the Bureau can arbitrarily cut the amount allowed to permittees fifteen million gallons, it is some evidence that at least that much diversion has been taking place. The Director of Prohibition estimates the diversion for the year ending June 30, 1930, as nine million proof gallons. One estimate is probably as good as another. My own would be from the evidence before us that tem million gallons per year over a period of years was the minimum average of diversion, at least up to the present time: and while under the efforts of Dr. Doran such diversion has been materially lessened, it has not stopped. The problem is a most difficult one.

The production of corn sugar, which it is claimed is used largely in the manufacture of whisky, has increased from 157,000,000 pounds in 1919 to 894,985,794 pounds in 1929. What percentage of the increased production of corn sugar is used for the production of illicit whisky is problematic. Of the unrefined product from which alcohol can be made, approximately one hundred million pounds are used per year for the manufacture of rayon. It is also used in other textiles as starch: is used in tanning leather, vinegar manufacture: by caramel makers, for candy fondant, ice cream and condensed milk. The legitimate uses of corn sugar, however, do not account for the enormous increase, and it must be assumed that a considerable proportion of the corn sugar goes into the bootleg trade, and is one of the chief sources in the manufacture of illicit liquor. Corn sugar is preferred by the moonshiner because of the price, though cane and beet sugar contain more fermentable material and hence offer a larger return of alcohol.

The blame for the supply of illegitimate liquor should not be placed entirely on corn sugar, which has enough to answer for without putting on it all the responsibility for the prevalence of illicit alcohol. It is undoubtedly contributing its part. While alcohol can probably be produced more cheaply form corn sugar, it is not so safely done as to obtain it by diversion.

The beer situation has changed vary materially under prohibition.

The increase in the production of hops in the United States has been quite marked, viz., 27,744,000 pounds in 1922, 33,220,000 pounds in 1929. some hops are used for medicinal and commercial purposes. Probably 10,000,000 pounds go into the manufacture of beer. There has been a large increase in the production of yeast. In recent years considerable beer has been shipped from New Jersey to other states. Breweries are openly operating in New York City. In some of the leading cities large plants have been engaged in manufacturing beer. No man is buying a brewery since prohibition except for bootlegging purposes. Some great breweries such as the Anheuser Busch Company at St. Louis have obeyed the law and upon the enactment of the prohibition laws ceased to make real beer.

What is known as wort, a product of barley, is now being used in the production of beer, and in the industry known as "alley brewing" which has developed in the large cities. It seems impossible to secure any information as to wort. We took up the question with the secretary of the National Malt Products Association, but he could furnish us no information as to the amount of its production or use in this country. It is interesting, however, to note in this connection that the state of Michigan in 1929 imposed a privilege tax upon the sale of malt syrup, malt extract and wort. The question of wort being subject to this tax is now in the courts. From August 28,

1929 to Mar4ch 20, 1930, there was collected form the tax approximately $600,000.00.

The general report has covered rather fully the question of increased drinking of liquor among college students. These students know that a large number of American citizens are daily helping those who are violating the prohibition laws by patronizing the bootlegger and smuggler. They see the laws ridiculed in many of the motion pictures of today and in the newspaper cartoons. It is little wonder that their respect for the law has been lessened. There was drinking in colleges before prohibition. It is not clear how any system that might make liquor easier to procure would remedy this situation. Efforts to teach the bad effects of drinking intoxicating liquor upon the health and efficiency of the individual seems to have lessened if not entirely stopped since the adoption of prohibition, and the growing youth of today has not had any advantage from such teachings as in the pre-prohibition days. Hence to a considerable extent he does not understand the reason for having prohibition laws and rebels against what is considered restraint on liberty.

The government could well afford to appropriate money for an educational campaign throughout the Nation to educate the youth of the land in respect for law. It is fully as important as to appropriate money for many of the governmental purposes of today. Nothing is more fundamental to the stability of the Republic than a deep seated respect for law among the youth thereof. Education is not so important as to the older citizens, for they will soon pass off the stage. Any plan of education as to respect for law should be limited to the youth of the country. It would be a useless performance as to those who consider themselves so completely educated as to be above law.

There is much to be placed on the credit side of prohibition, even under the inauspicious circumstances surrounding its supposed enforcement, that should incline public sentiment favorably toward a further test of enforceability of the law. Approximately 178,000 legal saloons have been closed under prohibition. Only one or two witnesses before us have favored the return of the saloon. They were driven to that position by their theories as to local option and the leaving of the matter entirely with the states. While there are thousands of speakeasies today in the great cities, where people may sneak in side doors or down an alley and in some back way and get liquor, or may go to other speakeasies more openly operated, yet it must be that the abolition of the saloon has been a mighty movement of the betterment of the Nation. The saloon was in partnership with crime. It was the greatest aid in political corruption. It never did a good thing or omitted to do a bad one. Nothing good could be said of it, and it is notable that very few people advocate its return. The open saloon in this country is dead beyond any resurrection. People are prone to forget the picture of conditions before prohibition. Speakeasies, so prevalent in the large cities, are not entirely a product of prohibition – they existed prior thereto. Interesting is the following account from a Pittsburgh paper of November 15, 1900: "At the meeting of the retail liquor dealers yesterday the statement was made that there are in Allegheny County 2,300 unlicensed dealers who sell liquor, in violation of the law, every day in the year, Sundays and election days included. This is a decidedly startling assertion, for while it is notorious that speakeasies exist and, are to some extent tolerated by the authorities, there has been no visible reason to suppose that illicit traffic was being conducted on so large a scale. The district attorney of the county and the public safety directors of the city ought to be heard from on this head. If the law is being violated so extensively as the licensed dealers claim, it is manifest that there must be a wholesome neglect of duty in official quarters."

Some witnesses before us have strongly challenged the claim that prohibition has benefited industry. At the Hose of Representatives hearings and before us, representatives of great industries spoke against prohibition. These same representatives take strong ground against their employees drinking. It is an irritating circumstance to labor that great captains of industry favor prohibition to prevent the laboring men securing a glass of beer on the ground that they can get more work out of them if they do not have liquor, while they reserve to themselves the right to have all they want in their cellars and their club lockers. We asked many of the leaders of industry to express themselves on the question of whether conditions in industry were better than before the passage of the prohibition laws. Some appeared and some filed statements. I quote from a few. From the president of a great coal company: "I know the business men of my acquaintance, quite generally, have something wet around their homes, if they want it, but the spirit of it is more that of the mischievous school boy who rather shuns the 'goody-goody' path but is not positively bad. When some of our best people are evading taxes, concealing dutiable goods, violating the Sunday laws, divorcing, swapping mates, speeding, gambling etc., I do not quite understand the agitation about liquor violations. Law enforcement has always been one of the chief functions of government, and one would think the Eighteenth Amendment was expected to enforce itself.

The old liquor laws aimed to control the public nuisance feature of drinking and failed. The present law, in our mining towns at least has largely corrected that failure. There is some moonshine liquor, some home-brew, and some bootleg, but the old days of the pay-day whoopee are gone. What drinking there is, is under cover, the practice of drinking up a whole month's pay, and challenging the world to mortal combat has passed. A drunken miner in public is so rare a sight that when it happens one would think a dancing bear had come to town, and even his chance acquaintances rally to get hem out of sight.

... I have seen pay days when it was not safe to ride on the branch-line trains going to and from mining towns. I have seen at Christmas season the station platforms jammed with a swearing, fighting, vomiting mod, with cheap Christmas toys thrown away, tramped on and lost. I have lain awake listening to the crack of revolvers as miners staggered up and down the railroad tracks. I have fought with crazy drunks at the pay window. I have seen Christmas-tree entertainments broken up, religious worship interrupted, and Sunday School picnics turned into a stampede of terror.

Wages have not increased enough to provide for any great amount of liquor at prevailing prices and at the same time to buy automobiles, radios, electrical appliances, and better food and clothing. The drink bill must be much less than before.

It is only fair to state that whatever success prohibition has had in the mining fields may be somewhat attributed to the mine operators. No matter how much they may talk wet and drink wet in the great convention sites, they do not want any 'modification' at their mines.

I believe I have noticed some increase in drinking during the past year, and it may be due to the publicity given the matter by the wets and drys.

* * * * * * * *

... Prohibition may be an utter failure other places, but is not so here nor with the industrial people with whom I make contract. They are spending more money for things the whole family enjoy, are better fit for work, better fed, and they constitute a majority of our population."

From the head of a great industrial company: "Improvement in the economic condition of employees' families is evidenced by the fewer cases of distress among employees reported from time to time. Visiting nurses, whom we employ to visit and administer to families of employees in case of sickness, report that the economic condition of such families is much better now than prior to prohibition."

From another: "The working people are better off under prohibition, they make more money and have more time. I do not dread Monday morning like I used to before prohibition. There is less of the effects of liquor on the job today than there was four of five years ago."

There are many other statements of similar import, and only a few of different view. Mr. Samuel Crowther in articles in The Ladies Home Journal last year sets forth many statements on the subject from industrial leaders. We find from a check-up that these statements are substantially correct and can be relied on.

My conclusion on this subject from the evidence before us is, that while there is some drinking now creeping into certain of the large industrial establishments, and the bootlegger is endeavoring to ply his trade there, on the whole industry has vastly benefited by prohibition. Accidents have been fewer and efficiency greater. The working men and their families are more prosperous than before prohibition. The contest for the Saturday night pay check between the wife and the saloon keeper is no more.

Some of those in favor of prohibition are wont to claim that increased life insurance, homebuilding, bank deposits, automobiles, radios are to a large extents the result of prohibition. The marvelous progress of this Nation can not of course be entirely attributed to prohibition. There are many factors, apparent to any thinking person, which have been at work to build up what we like to call prosperity. There has been an industrial revolution in the United States, and industrial development has contributed materially to prosperity. Certainly, however, much of the money formerly spent on the saloon has gone into the purchase of automobiles, radios, better furniture in the homes, That prohibition has been a factor contributing to our prosperity can not well be denied. Savings deposits have increased from $11,534,850,000.00 in 1918, $28,538,533,000.00 in 1930. High wages during and since the war and steady work in industry have of course been a contributing cause. It is impossible to determine approximately what per cent of the increase of savings deposits is due to prohibition, but some undoubtedly is.

As to the question of the effect of prohibition upon social welfare: we have had statements before us from Miss Evangeline Booth and Miss Mary McDowell, head of the University of Chicago

Settlement House, and others who are familiar with conditions among the poor and working people in industry, to the effect that prohibition has resulted in a better condition of affairs. Miss McDowell states that in the packing house district of Chicago the homes of the working men are better; their children better fed and clothed; there is less rioting and shooting up alleys; more observance of law and order; that there were hundreds of saloons in that neighborhood prior to prohibition, and while now there may be some speakeasies, there are no open places to entice the workingman and relieve him of his pay check. In a remarkable statement to the Commission by Miss Evangeline Booth, she says in part: "To sum up the conclusion of the Salvation Army in a sentence or two, I desire to state in unmistakable terms that the benefits derived from prohibition far outweigh any difficulties that may have been raised against its enforcement, that the wettest of wet areas is less wet today than it was when the saloon, usually accompanied by the speakeasy, were wide open, and that much of the outcry against the Volstead Act, so far from undergoing a failure of enforcement, arises from persons who in fact cannot obtain all the liquor that they desire. As Commander-in Chief of the Salvation Army in the United States, and with full support of my officers, I warn the Commission that any surrender to the forces of crime and indulgence at this time will be followed inevitably by a heavy toll in human life and by a loss of the prosperity which has been an untold blessing to millions of our homes. The hope that crime will be diminished by concessions to crime is preposterous on the face of it.

"The Salvation Army knows the underworld. Tens of thousands of its victims have been rescued by our efforts, and a victory of the wets over the law of the land, if permitted, will be a signal for an orgie of exultation and renewed excesses, by those whose entire life is a rebellion against orderly citizenship."

Other words of Miss Booth that challenge attention are: "You can hush every other voice of national and individual entreaty and complaint! You may silence every other tongue – even those of mothers of destroyed sons and daughters, of wives of profligate husbands – but let the children speak! The little children, the wronged children, the crippled children, the abused children, the blind children, the imbecile children, the dead children. This army of little children! Let their weak voices, faint with oppression, cold and hungry, be heard! Let their little faces, pinched by want of gladness, be heeded! Let their challenge – though made by small forms, too mighty for estimate – be reckoned with. Let their writing upon the wall of the nation – although traced by tiny fingers, as stupendous as eternity – be correctly interpreted and read, that the awful robbery of the lawful heritage of their little bodies, minds and souls is laid at the brazen gates of Alcohol!"

If anyone is entitled to speak with authority on the subject, it is Miss Booth, and what she says is not paid propaganda.

It has been charged by some who have appeared before us that the criminal elements in the United States now engaged in violating this law, as well as every other law, find encouragement from the attitude of those who have been termed by witnesses "the upper crust" of society, meaning that portion of the very rich people of the Nation constituting so-called fashionable society. It is not fair to indict all the so-called "upper crust" of the Nation as law-breakers, but it has been frankly stated before our Commission that many of these people of great wealth and prominence will not obey the prohibition laws, do not intend to, and boast of the fact that they will not because they do not believe in them and consider them an encroachment on personal liberty. In other words, that they will obey the laws in which they believe, and refuse to obey the laws in which they do not believe. If that is to be the standard of law observance, our government will fail. The forger and the back robber; the highwayman and the embezzler, do not believe in laws that restrain them. There is no more reason why what is termed the "upper crust" of society should choose the laws they will obey than that the same privilege should extend to the "under crust."

Clubs in some of the cities, officered by distinguished men, leaders in finance and in the life of the community, are maintaining bars where liquor is freely dispensed to the members. People who by bootleg liquor are assisting in violating the law and are contributing money for purposes of bribery and corruption, for they know that the system of illicit sale of liquors cannot be carried on to the extent that it is without bribery and graft. They are moral accessories to the illegal business of the bootlegger. They are assisting in breaking down law in the Nation.

One of the greatest of American manufacturers is reported by the newspapers to have recently said: "That portion of 'high society' that buys bootleg liquor is just a part of our underworld." A truth well stated.

Honorable Herbert Hoover, in his address accepting the Republican nomination for President, said in part: "Modification of the enforcement laws which would permit that which the Constitution forbids is nullification. This the American people will not countenance. Change in the Constitution can and must be brought about only by the straightforward methods provided in the Constitution itself. There are those who do not believe in the purposes of several provisions of the Constitution. No one denies their right to seek to amend it. They are not subject to criticism for asserting that right. But the Republican Party does deny the right of anyone to seek to destroy the purposes of the Constitution by indirection."

In his inaugural address of March 4, 1929, he said: "But a large responsibility rests directly upon our citizens. There would be little traffic in illegal liquor if only criminals patronized it. We must awake to the fact that this patronage from large numbers of law-abiding citizens is supplying the rewards and stimulating crime."

"... The duty of citizens to support the laws of the land is coequal with the duty of their government to enforce the laws which exist. No greater national service can be given by men and women of good will – who, I know, are not unmindful of the responsibilities of citizenship – than that they should, by their example, assist in stamping out crime and outlawry by refusing participation in and condemning all transactions with illegal liquor. Our whole system of self-government will crumble either if officials elect what laws they will enforce or citizens elect what laws they will support. The worst evil of disregard for some law is that it destroys respect for all law. For our citizens to patronize the violation of a particular law on the ground that they are opposed to it is destructive of the vary basis of all that protection of life, of homes and property which they rightly claim under other laws. If citizens do not like a law, their duty as honest men and women is to discourage its violation; their right is openly to work for its repeal."

127

In his address at the annual luncheon of the Associated Press in New York City, April 22, 1929, he said in part:

"What we are facing today is something far larger and more fundamental-- the possibility that respect for law as law is fading from the sensibilities of our people. Whatever the value of any law may be, in the enforcement of that law written in plain terms upon our statute books is not, in my mind, a debatable question. Law should be observed and must be enforced until it is repealed by the proper processes of our democracy. The duty to enforce the laws rests upon every public official and the duty to obey it rests upon every citizen."

"No individual has the right to determine what law shall be obeyed and what law shall not be enforced. If a law is wrong, its rigid enforcement is the surest guaranty of its repeal. If it is right, its enforcement is the quickest method of compelling respect for it. I have seen statements published within a few days encouraging citizens to defy a law because that particular journal did not approve of the law itself. I leave comment on such an attitude to any citizen with a sense of responsibility to his country."

* * * * * * * *

"...Respect for law and obedience to law does not distinguish between federal and state laws – it is a common conscience."

General Pershing, at a dinner to ex-service men is reported to have said:

"Ex-service men must stand up courageously and fearlessly for everything sacred in our institutions. No man or woman can fulfill the obligations of citizenship who remains passive regarding the enforcement of the law."

These statements at this time are entitled to the thoughtful consideration of the American people. This government will continue to be a government of law or it will cease to be a government at all. The representatives of great property interests who are well within their rights in seeking repeal of the laws go far beyond such rights when they defy the laws' enforcement. The day may come in this country when representatives of great property interests will realize that they need the protection of the law for the properties they represent more than other people may need it.

Everything in the way of breaking down of law, prison riots, hard times, increase in crime, is charged to prohibition by its enemies. That there is an increase of crime in this country is evident to all practical thinking citizens. The whole age in which we live has changed. Crime is more sensational, is featured all too much by the newspapers, and has become nauseating. The great was affected the thought and habits of people, and resulted in a national letdown in our moral fibre. All this has borne on the question of criminality. Surely the terrorizing of the people of some large cities by gangs of murderers who seek to create an American Mafia in this country cannot be laid at the door of prohibition. The revenue of these gangsters comes from gambling establishments, dance halls, houses of prostitution and other vice dens and not entirely from beer and other liquors.

The calm judgment of the American people must face the situation as it now exists. It is probable that the Eighteenth Amendment cannot be repealed. The other alternatives are enforcement, modification, or nullification. Nullification is an odious word in this republic and yet the Fifteenth and parts of the Fourteenth Amendment to the Constitution have been nullified and such nullification accepted by the people. The situation now as to use wine concentrates, which seems to be backed by governmental appropriations, amounts to a nullification in part of the Eighteenth Amendment. That the Eighteenth Amendment is now nullified in many of the large cities of the country cannot be denied by anyone willing to face the facts, and this very nullification is producing public sentiment against the prohibition laws and affecting the judgement of those who earnestly believe that it is a dangerous proposition for a country to permit its laws to be nullified. It would be better to modify the Eighteenth Amendment than to nullify it. I have pointed out the reasons why, in my judgement, the prohibition laws have never had a fair chance of enforcement. The effort to enforce the same is now quickened, due I think somewhat to the statements made by the President in his various addresses, from which I have quoted, and due to the transfer of enforcement to the Department of Justice.

It has been admitted by some of the strongest prohibition leaders of the country whom we have had before us that the prohibition laws cannot be enforced without the cooperation of the states, that the cost would be almost prohibitive, and it is doubtful if the people of the Nation would countenance a system of federal policing of our cities. Certainly that is a duty that should not rest on the federal government. Dr. Doran and General Andrews, testifying in 1926 before a Senate Committee, stated it would require $300,000,000 a year to administer the prohibition laws if state cooperation could not be secured. It is idle under our form of government to talk of enforcing these laws by the military and naval forces. In large cities in the states which have no enforcement laws the National Prohibition Laws are bound to become more or less of a dead letter, unless public sentiment therein changes. The government can go ahead and prosecute some of the larger cases, but every little violation cannot be taken care of by the federal government at least without creating a system of courts and police that would be staggering.

I do not like to admit that the Federal Government cannot enforce its laws without the help of the states, but I am satisfied it cannot enforce completely the prohibition laws without such aid. Certainly it cannot enforce them in a state where there is active opposition on the part of the officials of the state, and while there is no legal duty on the states that could in any way be enforced to assist in carrying out the federal statutes, it is apparent that Congress in providing for concurrent jurisdiction expected the states to assist. There is a moral obligation on the states to assist in enforcing the Eighteenth Amendment and laws passed in pursuance thereof. They should take care of the violations coming peculiarly within the province of the state, such as intrastate violations of the law. States are a part of the federal government. surely there is a solemn moral duty on the states to support the Constitution. The Constitution and amendments and laws to carry them into effect are still the supreme law of the land. What kind of a Union of States is this if there is no obligation on the part of the states to assist in preserving the government which makes possible the existence of the states and guarantees to every state a republican form of government and protects it against invasion. It is a dangerous doctrine that the states of the Union have no interest in preserving the Federal Government. The words of Senator Borah in an article in the New York Times of January 28, 1929, hit the nail squarely on the head. He said:

"The most inconsistent and indefensible thing in all government is for a state to be a part of a government, to belong, as it were, to a government, to enjoy the interstate trade and commerce, the prosperity and the dignity of such government, but whose will and policy and authority it rejects. It is a part of the government for its supposed burdens. That is a false and mistaken position to take and no argument, no plea will be able to justify such a position or give it a place of dignity and honor."

Officials of states swear to support the Constitution of the United States. If they give aid and comfort to the attempts to nullify laws passed by Congress to carry out Constitutional provisions, they are not supporting the Constitution of the United States and are violating their oaths of office. There are moral obligations in government binding on those representatives of the people. True, Congress is not compelled to appropriate money to carry on the government. It can paralyze the administrative and judicial branches of government by refusing to provide necessary funds by taxation and to make appropriations for carrying them on and thus cause the Federal Government to perish. The honest patriotism of the legislators is the safeguard against such course.

The present situation as to prohibition in the large cities is intolerable and presents a serious question to the thinking people of the Nation, vis., are they willing to have a few states, through the influence of large cities, and that influence affected by thousands who have come to our shores from foreign countries and who have been naturalized, but insist that their customs and habits shall not be interfered with, nullify the Constitution of the United States, and if they are not willing what are they going to do about it? The seriousness of these questions cannot be underestimated. The seeds of national trouble are implanted therein, and thoughtful citizens may well give pause and meditate thereon.

Inasmuch as the amendment was ratified by all of the states of the Union except two it would seem that opponents of the prohibition laws ought to be willing to have them given a fair trial. After such fair trial if they cannot be enforced any better than in the past, the proponents of these laws should be willing to have the Eighteenth Amendment modified or repealed and abandon the effort for national prohibition. The general report states: "There has been more sustained pressure to enforce this law than on the whole has been true of any other federal statute. No other federal law has had such elaborate state and federal enforcing machinery put behind it." That is true, but no law has had as much propaganda against it as these laws, and while the pressure was not of the nature applied to enforce other laws.

Much has been said about the Eighteenth Amendment having been adopted while the boys were overseas and that the people have had no chance to express themselves upon it. In view of growing opposition to the prohibition laws and the prevalence of this sentiment, it seems to me there should be if possible a referendum which would settle the proposition of whether the majority of the American people favor prohibition as a national policy. There is no provision of the Constitution for a referendum and a mere straw vote referendum by states or magazines is unsatisfactory. There could be an expression by the people under Article 5 of the Constitution. An amendment could be proposed to the Constitution to repeal the Eighteenth Amendment, and the Congress could provide that the ratification should be by conventions in the various states, delegates to be elected by the people. That would present as clear cut an issue on the subject as is possible under the Constitution.

The people are the source of power, and on a question of this character, where the discussion has become nation-wide and excludes consideration of other great questions involved in our national political life, the people should have a right to speak and to register their desires. Such an amendment as I have suggested, if submitted to conventions in the states, delegates to be chosen by the people, would find the nation soon engaged throughout its length and breadth in an educational campaign, and such campaign would be beneficial. After ten years of trial, such as it has been, why should the people not have an opportunity to register their feeling on this subject? If the great majority of the American people are against prohibition and say so in the selection of delegates to constitutional conventions in the states, it will be apparent that such laws cannot be nationally enforced. If a large majority of the people declare against repeal of the Eighteenth Amendment, many who are opposed to it will see that the policy of the Eighteenth Amendment is to be the national policy and will adjust themselves to the situation. My firm judgment is that the referendum herein suggested would be the best thing that could happen to assist in settling this troublesome situation. A limit of time should be fixed as to the meetings of the conventions, so that the matter may not be stretched over a period of years and so that the will of the people may be expressed at substantially the same time. This can be done under the authority of Dillon v. Gloss, 256 U.S. 368.

If it were possible to repeal the Eighteenth Amendment what in the way of a regulatory measure is to take its place? Those who advocate its repeal offer no program. The answers to this question propounded to practically all of those who appeared before us advocating a change or repeal of the prohibition laws brought little help. Some advocated the substitution of the Canadian system. There are as many different systems in Canada as there are provinces, and there is no Canadian system, as such.

Honorable E.C. Drury, former Premier of the Province of Ontario, was before us, and stated that bootlegging is carried on in the Province of Ontario to as great an extent now as during prohibition days; that there is much drunkenness, and that arrests for drunkenness have not diminished. He stated that the present system in Ontario is not satisfactory; that liquor consumption and crimes have increased under governmental liquor control. Other prominent Canadians are quoted to the contrary in the papers. Throughout Canada it will be found that there are complaints as to violations of their laws. It must be remembered that under prohibition in Canada licenses upon the payment of one dollar were issued for home-brewing, and citizens were permitted to make wines in their homes out of native fruit juices. This practically amounted to permitting the manufacture in the homes of light wines and beers. Undoubtedly there has been increased sale and consumption of intoxicating beverages in Canadian provinces that have given up prohibition.

The Bratt system of Sweden which bears some similarity to the Quebec system has been explained before us as an ideal system. The Commission has had the benefit of the testimony of our Minister to Sweden and has been fortunate in that Honorable Henry W. Anderson, one of the members of the Commission, visited Sweden during the summer and gave a careful study to the situation. They have presented very fully to the Commission the operation of the Bratt system. It is based on a paternalism which would be rather odious to citizens of this republic. It should be carefully studied, however, if any change is to be made.

Many of the witnesses before us representing organizations opposed to prohibition insist that state local option is a proper method of control; that inasmuch as the government trusts the state to punish murderers it can trust them to handle the liquor traffic. Others point to the fact that under such local option all of the difficulties that arise as to prohibition are found.

There is no doubt from the experiences of this Nation and others that there are tremendous difficulties involved in any control or regulation of the liquor traffic and always will be. No system of control anywhere is satisfactory. Even Soviet Russia is having all kinds of trouble with it. Any restraint of the liquor traffic is regarded by many as infringing on personal liberty, and probably that idea will always prevail. The traffic never can be entirely eliminated as long as the appetite for drink remains. A repeal of the prohibition laws and the Eighteenth Amendment, without some satisfactory plan to take their place, is unthinkable. The result would be chaos. In this high-powered age of universal rapid traveling by automobiles on the interstate highways of the Nation, an awakened public would not long submit to the situation that would be brought about by an uncontrolled or state sporadic control of the liquor traffic. Public roads and drunken automobile drivers are not a good combination.

If prohibition cannot be successfully enforced, I should favor a trial of the system proposed by Commissioner Anderson in his report--which could only be after some modification of the Eighteenth Amendment putting the matter in the hands of Congress. Professor Chafee of Harvard University interestingly discusses in the January Forum of 1931 a somewhat similar proposal.

It seems to me, in fairness to a great social and economic experiment, that the enforceability of the prohibition laws should have further trial under the new organization in the Department of Justice; that if, after such reasonable trial it is demonstrated they cannot be enforced any better than they have been in the past, the modification of the Eighteenth Amendment suggested by the Commission should be brought about and the power placed in Congress to deal fully with the subject; that in the meantime, the feeling of the people on the subject should be registered by a referendum on repeal of the Eighteenth Amendment in the manner suggested herein.

WILLIAM S. KENYON
Washington, D.C., January 7, 1931

STATEMENT BY FRANK J. LOESCH

On the evidence before the Commission, together with my experience as a prosecuting officer, and from personal observation, I have come to the conclusion that effective national enforcement of the Eighteenth Amendment in its present form is unattainable; therefore, steps should be taken immediately to revise the Amendment.

The revision should give to Congress the power to legislate upon the entire subject of the liquor traffic.

The traffic has transcended state lines and has become a matter of national concern. Even if it were a possibility of accomplishment in the near futures it would be unwise to repeal the Eighteenth Amendment.

Such repeal would cause the instant return of the open saloon in all states not having statewide prohibition.

The public opinion as voiced in the testimony before us appears to be unanimous against the return of the legalized saloon.

A strong reason, among others, why I favor immediate steps being taken to revise the Amendment is in order to destroy the power of the murderous, criminal organizations flourishing all over the country upon the enormous profits made in bootleg liquor traffic. Those profits are the main source of the corruption funds which cement the alliance between crime and politics and corrupt the law enforcing agencies in every populous city.

Those criminal octopus organizations have now grown so audacious owing to their long immunity from prosecutions for their crimes that they seek to make bargains with law enforcing officers and even with judges of our courts to be allowed for a price to continue their criminal activities unmolested by the law.

Those organizations of murderers and arch criminals can only be destroyed when their bootleg liquor profits are taken from them. So long as the Eighteenth Amendment remains in its present rigid form the nation, the states, the municipalities, the individual citizen, are helpless to get out of reach of their poisonous breaths and slimy tentacles.

If not soon crushed those criminal organizations may become as they are now seeking to become supergovernments and so beyond the reach of the ordinary processes of the law.

It is asked, supposing the Amendment is revised, what legislation is to follow? What plan is there to take the place of a national prohibition act? Of the suggestions put before us the most carefully thought out is that proposed in the memorandum of Mr. Anderson. He has made a thorough study of what seems to be the most satisfactory system of liquor control thus far devised and his plan based on that study and on consideration of our experience in federal control of other important subjects seems to me to afford the best solution.

FRANK J. LOESCH
Washington, D.C., January 7, 1931

133

STATEMENT BY PAUL J. McCORMICK

From the evidence before the Commission I have reached the conclusion that the outstanding achievement of the Eighteenth Amendment has been the abolition of the legalized open saloon in the United States. Social and economic benefits to the people have resulted and it is this proven gain in our social organization that has justified the experiment of national prohibition. I am unable to find that there has been any further general moral improvement shown. It has been so clearly established that contemporaneously with national prohibition there has been developed such a wide-spread spirit of lawlessness, hypocrisy and unprecedented disrespect for authority that in fairness and candor it must be stated that in the final analysis of conditions now, no other national moral improvement can be credited to prohibition. Nevertheless, the gain should not be jeopardized until it has been demonstrated after the fairest possible trial that the experiment is completed and has proven to be a failure.

The evidence has raised the doubt in my mind as to whether the enforceability of this law has been conclusively determined. I am not entirely convinced that complete and irreparable failure has been shown, neither am I satisfied in the light of the evidence before us as to a bad enforcement machinery that the law has had that fair trial that a solemn constitutional provision should be given. Until quite recently the federal enforcement organization, agencies and methods, were very unsatisfactory. They are still inadequate. More improvement is needed before they can be said to be sufficient and before any indubious conclusion can be reached as to whether the Amendment can be nationally enforced.

I believe it is well within the established facts to conclude that fanatical, illegal and corrupt methods of enforcement throughout a long period in the decade of national prohibition, have been proximate causes of an extensive public sentiment against the enforceability of this law that is generally prevalent at this time. It has been proven to my entire satisfaction that there is today neither proper observance nor adequate enforcement of prohibition throughout the country. I am not entirely convinced, however, that the situation is utterly hopeless. I feel that much can be done to mollify and to change public opinion by intelligent, dispassionate and reasonable legislation and administrative effort. If improvements that appear to have been brought about by Civil Service requirements and by the Prohibition Reorganization Act of 1930, did not hold out some degree of hope for the law, I would favor abandonment of the experiment now and the immediate invocation of constitutional processes by state conventions to revise the Amendment in the form suggested in the report of the Commission. This report, however, makes recommendations which, if followed and made effective at once, will, I believe strengthen the law and may operate to reclaim public opinion in many important localities where indifference and even hostility is pronounced. If sincere public sympathy can be nationally developed for this law it can be intelligently enforced as adequately as other police regulations.

It is evident, however, that national prohibition cannot be properly enforced by the federal government alone. State cooperation, supported by wholehearted favorable local public opinion is absolutely necessary. It is not unreasonable from the facts before the Commission to believe that an improved enforcing policy, organization, personnel and equipment can restore to a sufficient degree state cooperation and public favor so as to make national prohibition reasonably

134

and adequately enforceable except in a few metropolitan localities. At least the possibility of bringing this about within a reasonable time is sufficient to warrant further trial of the experiment.

There is another reason that has dissuaded me from the conclusion that the Amendment be modified immediately without further trail. It is my inability to suggest or find any other satisfactory remedial substitute for the existing law. My study of the systems of liquor control in other countries and of plans that have been submitted to the Commission to supplant present conditions in the United States leaves me in doubt as to whether any of them would be adaptable to our diversified, populous and extensive nation or to the heterogeneous aspect of its people. The plan developed by Mr. Anderson and presented in his statement seems to me to be the best, and if after further trial prohibition is not enforceable I should favor serious consideration of this system. I believe that the experience in one of the states of the dispensary system has demonstrated the insufficiency of such a solution as a national institution.

Absolute repeal is unwise. It would in my opinion reopen the saloon. This would be a backward step that I hope will never be taken by the United States. The open saloon is the greatest enemy of temperance and has been a chief cause of much political corruption throughout the country in the past. These conditions should never be revived.

The states favoring prohibition should be protected against wet commonwealths. This right would be defeated by remitting the entire subject of liquor control and regulation to the several states exclusively. Federal power incident to taxation and interstate commerce was insufficient in pre-prohibition days to protect dry states from encroachment from without their boundaries. There should be retained in the Constitution an express grant of federal power to preserve prohibition in those states which locally adopted it.

It is my belief that a solution of this vexatious problem would be accelerated by ascertaining the majority sentiment of our citizenry upon the desirability of prohibition as a national policy. This public attitude has never been directly expressed through legal processes. It could be learned by direct submission of the repeal of the Eighteenth Amendment through state conventions and under Article V of the Constitution. I favor and recommend such action. I think it should be undertaken immediately. The submission processes should be arranged and timed so as to avoid confusing the prohibition question with party or other issues or campaigns.

I have signed the report of the Commission. I believe it to be an impartial and dispassionate composite expression from all of the material that has come before the Commission. I concur in the findings of fact stated therein. I do not concur in all of the reasons, observations and statistics stated in the report. I am in accord with all of the Conclusions and Recommendations except that in which a revision of the Eighteenth Amendment is suggested immediately. I am not convinced by the evidence that the experiment has had a fair trial under the most auspicious conditions, and I believe an opportunity should now be given to the Congress and the administrative agencies to immediately give it such trial. If within a reasonable time observance and enforcement conditions are not clearly proven to be nationally better than they are now, then the Amendment should be revised as recommended in the Commission's report. I believe there is credible evidence before us that justifies the opinion that if the Congress enacts the recommended changes at the present session, one year would be a reasonable time to indubitably conclude whether or not the Eighteenth Amendment can be properly enforced as a national mandate.

To hopefully look forward to any satisfactory settlement of this momentous question it is not sufficient that National Prohibition have a fair trial, it is essential that its fair-minded proponents and the general public believe it has had a fair trial.

PAUL J. McCORMICK
Washington, D.C., January 7, 1931

STATEMENT BY ROSCOE POUND

As I interpret the evidence before us, it establishes certain definite economic and social gains following national prohibition. But it establishes quite as clearly that these gains have come from closing saloons rather than from the more ambitious program of complete and immediate universal total abstinence to be enforced concurrently by nation and state. Thus the task is to conserve the gains while finding out how to eliminate the abuses and bad results which have developed in the past decade. Those results are due chiefly to: (1) the enormous margin between the cost of producing or importing illicit liquor and the prices it commands; (2) the hostility or at best lukewarmness of public opinion in important localities and of a significant part of the public everywhere; and (3) the tendency of many states to leave the matter to the Federal Government and of the Federal Government to seek to confine itself to certain larger aspects of enforcement. Instead of the two governments each pressing vigorously toward a common end, as contemplated in the Amendment, they allow enforcement in large part to fall down between them.

Americans have had a perennial faith in political mechanics; and, in the spirit of that faith, it is urged that the organization and machinery of enforcement and the legislative provisions may be so far improved as to bring about an adequate observance and enforcement which admittedly do not exist. But there is no reason to suppose that machinery and organization and equipment will change public opinion in the places and among the classes of the community where public opinion has proved an obstacle, nor that they will succeed in the teeth of public opinion any more than they have in the past. Hence, while making enforcement as effective as we may, so long as the Amendment as it is remains the supreme law of the land, we should be at work to enable the fundamental difficulties to be reached. This, it seems clear, can only be done by a revision of the Amendment. It can be done only by so redrawing the Amendment as, on the one hand, to preserve Federal control and a check upon bringing back of the saloon anywhere, and, on the other hand, allow of an effective control adapted to local conditions in places where, as things are at least, it is futile to seek a nationally enforced general total abstinence.

Objection is made to immediate steps toward revision on the ground that they will hamper and discourage enforcement; that there has been no fair test of enforceability; and that no assuredly workable systems of control are at hand if revision of the Amendment were to make them possible. As to the first, the conditions which call for revision are recognized by the Bureau of

Prohibition in its program for an enforcement abdicating a large part of the task which the Amendment imposes on the Federal Government. I do not understand how a frank endeavor to deal adequately with the parts of the task which it is giving over, while seeking to enable it to do more thoroughly what it is attempting to do, should discourage its performance of the restricted task. As to the second objection, the Amendment and the National Prohibition Act, enacted in an era of enthusiasm, enforced in a decade of prosperity, backed by an exceptional machinery for special enforcement both Federal and Sate, and guarded by strong organizations urging action and jealously watching for lack of zeal or want of efficiency seem to me to have had the best chance they are likely to have of showing what they can achieve. My fear is that obstinate attempt to maintain them at all hazards as they are will give impetus to a reaction in which the gains will be lost.

Federal control of what had become a nation-wide traffic, and abolition of the saloon are great steps forward which should be maintained.

As to what might be done if the Amendment were revised, it would be possible to retain or come back to complete prohibition throughout the land, or to retain it where it is effective, protecting such areas in their policy, and yet to establish some form of control for localities where complete prohibition has proved or may prove ineffective. It requires an unwarranted lack of faith in American political ingenuity to assume that no such forms of control may be worked out. Mr. Anderson has proposed a well thought out plan, based on study of systems of liquor control and their operation. His plan deserves careful consideration as the best and most complete which has been brought to our attention. This or some like plan for adapting national control to local conditions may well be the next forward step.

ROSCOE POUND
Washington, D.C., January 7, 1931

Franklin P. Adams, a columnist for the *New York World*, summarized his opinion of the Commission's report with this poem:

> Prohibition is an awful flop.
> We like it.
> It can't stop what it's meant to stop.
> We like it.
> It's left a trail of graft and slime,
> It don't prohibit worth a dime,
> It's filled our land with vice and crime.
> Nevertheless, we're for it.

SOME DEMOCRATIC ISSUES IN 1932

BY

GOVERNOR ALBERT C. RITCHIE

OF MARYLAND

ADDRESS

BEFORE THE DEMOCRATIC
WOMEN'S LUNCHEON CLUB
OF PHILADELPHIA

JANUARY TWENTY-FIVE, NINETEEN THIRTY-TWO

138

Now, a word to apply some of these principles to one subject that I have been asked to say something about,—national prohibition.

In the first place, we ought to start out by remembering that this subject should not involve any question of "wet" or "dry". Those are catchy phrases, "wets" being applied to those who are against this national prohibition system, and "drys" being applied to those who are for it. But the question we have got to meet, as American citizens and as voters, does not involve those words; they are inept and inappropriate.

National prohibition raises a question of government, whether or not, under our governmental system, it is sound or safe to endeavor by one hard, fast, unbending rule, applying everywhere throughout the country, to regulate the personal conduct of all the citizens in accordance to the terms of the Eighteenth Amendment.

We must remember that the true goal of everybody, whether wets or drys, ought to be the same; it ought to be temperance. Prohibition is not the goal for free thinking and free acting and self respecting American people. Temperance is the goal that all of us ought to seek, that all of us ought to try to attain. There are two roads which we can follow, and two different schools of thought as to which road we ought to take. One road is the State road, and the other road is the Federal or national road. Now, we tried the State road for a good many years, and it was working pretty well. I do not believe there is anybody who would not agree that during the fifty years preceding the adoption of the Eighteenth Amendment, temperance made wonderful and stirring strides. (Applause.) And it did this by the State road, each State handling the question for itself in accordance with the needs of its own people. Then, not satisfied with that, we tried the Federal road, and the progress towards temperance stopped. This was because our country is too diversified for a Constitutional provision like that applying everywhere. We have our great cities and we have our little cities, we have our agricultural areas and our urban areas, we have our rural communities, and our thickly settled industrial centers. We have a population drawn from all the climes on the face of the globe. You can not take out a Federal yardstick and make it apply exactly in all the diversified conditions of all those diversified communities. The result is that the Federal road has clogged our courts, filled our jails to overflowing, has almost overwhelmed us with the cost of its attempted enforcement, and what is worse than anything else, it has impaired the temperate habits of the boys and girls of today, when they are compared with the habits of the youth in the other days of State regulation. (Applause.)

Our great progress toward temperance was made before we tried to mix up politics, legislation and morals, all in the same crucible, and produced out of it the Eighteenth Amendment and the Volstead Act. Our great progress towards temperance was made before we put prohibition in the Constitution, where it ought not be, and while we were leaving it to the States, where it ought to be, with the Federal government fulfilling its true function of protecting a dry State against interstate shipments which would be in contravention of its laws.

So it seems to me that the solution of this thing is by the kind of liberalism I mentioned before—not going ahead when experience shows we are going ahead with a failure, but going back to what has been tried and tested, and found to be true, safe and right. Turn the subject back to the States from which it never ought to have been taken. Let the States pass such provisions as they wish in order to see that the saloon never comes back into the country again. Let the Federal Government see that its interstate powers are used to the limit to see that a State remains in whatever character of dryness its people vote it to be. But in the last analysis, turn back to the people of each State this question which never ought to have been taken from them, so that the people of each State can settle it in accordance with the desires and needs of their own people, thus promoting law observance, temperance and morality. Do not have a settlement forced on any State from the outside, which is in accordance, not with the wishes of its people, but with the wishes of people of other States who know nothing about it in the first State, acting through the Congress or the Federal Government. (Applause.)

Personally, I would feel from a Democratic point of view,—those of us who think that way, and certainly a great many do, and those Republicans who share that view also,—it ought to be up to us to try to see that the platforms of our respective parties contain our convictions upon this subject of prohibition. We do not straddle the affairs of our private lives, we do not sidestep the duties of our personal lives, we do not quibble about those things in which we daily have and exchange communications. Well, why sidestep, why quibble, why straddle when it comes to political convictions and political beliefs? That is why I would like our party's platform to contain a clear enunciation of our party's stand upon that question.

My friends:

Once upon a time an orator who was describing the scenery of his State remarked that in the North it was "mountaineous" and that in the South it was "moisterious."

That classic description reminds me of the Republican national ticket this year — "high and dry" at one end and at the other end "increasing moisture."

But before I come to further elucidation on that point let me make another clear.

However we may differ as to method, we all agree that temperance is one of the cardinal virtues. In dealing with the great social problems in my own State, such as the care of the wards of the States, and in combating crime, I have had to consider most earnestly this question of temperance. It is bound up with crime, with insanity and, only too often, with poverty. It is increasingly apparent that the intemperate use of intoxicants has no place in this new mechanized civilization of ours. In our industry, in our recreation, on our highways, a drunken man is more than an objectionable companion, he is a peril to the rest of us. The hand that controls the machinery of our factories, that holds the steering wheel of our automobiles, and the brains that guide the course of finance and industry, should alike be free from the effects of over-indulgence in alcohol.

But the methods adopted since the World War with the purpose of achieving a greater temperance by the forcing of Prohibition have been accompanied in most parts of the country by complete and tragic failure. I need not point out to you that general encouragement of lawlessness has resulted; that corruption, hypocrisy, crime and disorder have emerged, and that instead of restricting, we have extended the spread of intemperance. This failure has come for this very good reason: we have depended too largely upon the power of governmental action instead of recognizing that the authority of the home and that of the churches in these matters is the fundamental force on which we must build. The recent recognition of this fact by the present Administration is an amazing piece of hindsight. There are others who have had foresight. A friend showed me recently an unpublished letter of Henry Clay, written a hundred years ago. In this letter Clay said that the movement for temperance "has done great good and will continue to do more" but "it will destroy itself whenever it resorts to coercion or mixes in the politics of the country."

Another statesman, given to the Nation by this State of New Jersey, pointed out this necessary course when Federal Prohibition first became a great issue. President Wilson foresaw the economic and social results of such an attempt. It was not necessary for him to live through the disastrous experience in order to come to the conclusion now confessed by our present

142

President. In statesmanship an ounce of foresight is better than a pound of hindsight.

The experience of nearly one hundred and fifty years under the Constitution has shown us that the proper means of regulation is through the States, with control by the Federal Government limited to that which is necessary to protect the States in the exercise of their legitimate powers. This I submit is the principle embodied in our Democratic platform; and I state further that it is not the principle stated in the Republican platform or in the speeches of acceptance of the two candidates of the Republican Party.

This time of depression has caused us to see even more plainly than before not only the political and moral consequences of our action but its economic results as well.

We threw on the table as spoils to be gambled for by the enemies of society the revenue that our Government had theretofore received, and the underworld acquired unparalleled resources thereby. The multiplication of enforcement agencies created resentment and a cynical and complacent attitude toward lax enforcement resulting from connivance between such agencies and the law breakers. The general disregard for and defiance of such law of nationwide application bred disrespect for other law. The attempt to impose the practice of virtue by mandate of the fundamental law produced an attitude of intolerance to other forms of restraint and a denial even of the basis of authority. The violation of fundamental principles set in motion a chain of consequences that no one not politically blind could fail to see; and all the time a steady flow of profits, resulting from the exactions of a newly created industry, was running into the pockets of racketeers. The only business of the country that was not helping to support the Government was in a real sense being supported by the Government. This was the business that was the direct product of the 18th Amendment and the Volstead Law — a business which is lucrative, vicious and corrupting in its influence on the enforcement agencies of Government.

Unquestionably our tax burden would not be so heavy nor the forms that it takes so objectionable if some reasonable proportion of the uncounted millions now paid to those whose business has been reared upon this stupendous blunder could be made available for the expenses of Government.

On this subject the two parties offer the voters a genuine choice this year. On the one hand a definite method of relief in the true American tradition, with the States authorized to carry out their part of the responsibility, and the Nation doing what it is practically and constitutionally able to do; on the other side, evasion and indirection.

I should be something less than candid — in fact I should be dishonest — if I did not in this campaign continue to speak very plainly of these evasions, insincerities and deceptions. As I have repeatedly pointed out. Republican leaders are attempting to fight this battle with words. And in fighting with words we may use them either as a flaming sword, frankly, honestly and with courage, to press home the cause of truth, or we may use them as shields, to turn aside, evade and obstruct the attack of an adversary. It is in this latter sense that the Republicans have been fighting a battle of words. Now a shield is a bigger thing than a sword and so when they would use words as a defense, they must use more of them. Witness the Republican platform —

long, indirect, ambiguous, insincere, false, compared with the concise sincerity of our own platform. And this is especially true of what they say about Prohibition. We first have a long, rambling party pronouncement in the Republican platform. And then we have long, rambling explanations of its meaning. Words upon words. Evasions upon evasions. Insincerity upon insincerity. A dense cloud of words. We rush into the cloud to find whether there is meaning and substance at the bottom of it all, and we find nothing. When we emerge from the cloud, we see another in the distance and we rush over to that. And again we find nothing. And so we rush from cloud to cloud and find at the bottom of each, nothing but dust, meaningless, worthless dust, at the bottom of a cloud of words.

One of the stories that we learned in our youth was that of the famous Oracle of Delphi. In ancient Greece, it is told, there was a place where volcanic gas came forth from a crevice in the earth. Over this crevice the pagans built a temple, and directly above the fumes arising from the earth, they set the throne of the Oracle. When the Oracle was partially stupefied by the poisons in the gas, she uttered strange and incoherent words. The high priests of the temple were supposed to tell the people the meaning of these incoherent words. The people never suspected that the priests were not possessed of a real understanding of these words and that they interpreted them to suit their own convenience. But great issues were decided by this method. Pagan kings came to the Oracle and on its incoherent mumblings the fate of Nations was sometimes staked.

In June, the Republican Oracle sat in Chicago. There was a fume of heated oratory; clouds of Prohibition proposals were emitted; the Resolutions Committee and the Convention itself succumbed to the stupefying influence. It uttered words in the party platform — words and more words, till meaning was lost and reason slumbered. And then when the Convention ended and the people asked the high priests of the party what it all meant, the answers were so diverse that one was tempted to suspect the worst — that it meant nothing at all. The Secretary of State explained in the choicest phrases of Republican diplomacy; Senator Borah spoke out in his forthright fashion and said it sounded wet to him; President Butler said the words were dry.

I suspect that those who wrote that plank thought that it would sound dry to the drys and wet to the wets. But to the consternation of the high priests it sounded dry to the wets and wet to the drys. This was very serious indeed. Something had to be done about it.

Well, something was done about it. The Democratic Party fairly and squarely met the issue. It adopted, by an overwhelming vote, a plank so plain and clear and honest that no one could doubt its meaning and the candidates accepted this statement one hundred percent.

And then public opinion, moved by a true American admiration for brave and honest statement, expressed itself in no uncertain terms. It liked the Democratic platform. It liked people who spoke their minds. It liked courage and candor. This must have been disturbing to the high priests of the Republican Party, but, as always, they hesitated and temporized. And then in the six weeks following the Democratic Convention, a vast air of expectancy surrounded the White House. Rumors came forth that the high priests were to speak. People were to be told at last the meaning of what the June Oracle had said.

There were difficulties in the way, because the high priests had often spoken of this subject before. In 1928 the Republican candidate for the Presidency said: "I do not favor the repeal of the Eighteenth Amendment," and, amplifying his meaning at that time, he added that it was "a great social and economic experiment noble in motive and far-reaching in purpose."

He brought about the creation of the Commission on Law Enforcement and Obedience composed of "an able group of distinguished citizens of character and independence of thought, representative of different sections of the country." When, after eighteen months of sincere and painstaking work, this Commission reported its findings to him, he submitted the report to the Congress commending all of the minor findings of the Commission but not approving of the Commission's proposed revision of the Eighteenth Amendment.

He condemned the report with faint praise, thus: "It should stimulate the clarification of the public mind and the advancement of public thought." It did stimulate and clarify the public mind to the extent that it showed it what it had long suspected was true, that national Prohibition had not been and could not be enforced. But it apparently did not stimulate and clarify the Presidential mind because the White House, so far as Prohibition was concerned, fell into a deep silence. As the Republican Convention approached, according to the newspapers of the time, appeal after appeal was made to him and innumerable drafts of a Prohibition plank were submitted to him. Out of it all came the incoherent utterance of the Chicago Oracle to which I have alluded.

At last, on the eleventh day of August, the President spoke to the people. To anyone who will read the Prohibition plank in the Republican platform and the remarks of the President on this question in his acceptance speech, the difficulty under which the President labors will become obvious and the reason for his use of meaningless words will become clear. It is the difficulty that always attends sacrificing principles for votes, and attempting to conceal that fact by the use of pussy-cat words. That statement can be no better substantiated than by the President's own statement that "I have always sympathized with the high purpose of the Eighteenth Amendment." Does that spell out a prohibitionist attempting to retain the support of the drys?

But the President has at last learned what the facts have shown these many years—that laws opposed by majority sentiments "create resentment which undermines enforcement and in the end produces degeneration and crime."

This seems to mean State Home Rule. But apparently the President does not really believe in State Home Rule, if by the use of force there can be effective Federal control. He is willing to believe in the principle of State control only when the Federal Government cannot get away with the destruction of State control.

His statement proceeds deliberately to misrepresent the position of the Democratic Party. He says: "Our opponents pledge the members of their party to destroy every vestige of constitutional and effective Federal control of the traffic."

I have the right to assume that the President read the Democratic platform and on that assumption I charge that this statement was made to mislead the people of this country and I assert that a mere reading of the plain, unequivocal provisions of the Democratic platform will sustain that charge. So that there can be no possible misunderstanding, let me read the provisions of the Democratic platform on this point. It begins:

"We advocate the repeal of the Eighteenth Amendment. To effect such repeal we demand that the Congress immediately propose a Constitutional Amendment to truly representative conventions in the States called to act solely on that proposal."

So much for repeal. Now what does it tell the States to do:

"We urge the enactment of such measures by the several States as will actually promote temperance, effectively prevent the return of the saloon and bring the liquor traffic into the open under complete supervision and control by the States."

It then clearly states what the President either accidentally overlooked or deliberately misrepresented:

"We demand that the Federal Government effectively exercise its power to enable the States to protect themselves against importation of intoxicating liquors in violation of their laws." It then goes on to speak of the Volstead Law:

"Pending repeal, we favor immediate modification of the Volstead Act to legalize the manufacture and sale of beer and other beverages of such alcoholic content as is permissible under the Constitution and to provide therefrom a proper and needed revenue."

Thus the Democratic platform expressly and unequivocally opposes the return of the saloon and with equal emphasis it demands that there be Federal control of the liquor traffic to protect dry States. Only on the theory of seeking to return to power by the mere use of words can such statements of the President of these United States be explained.

But, meanwhile, another high priest has been heard from. In the period following August eleventh, the anti-repealists of the Republican Party raised their voices in lamentation, like Jeremiah of old.

The Republican candidate for Vice-President heard this wailing. He hastened to avow his devotion to the Republican platform, but he found in the words of the Oracle full justification for the belief that the Eighteenth Amendment should not be repealed. And so, in the true spirit of those who in ancient times controlled the Oracle for their own ends, provision is made for all possible contingencies. It is said that an ancient King when he consulted the Oracle as to the probability of his success in a war that he was about to undertake, was told that if he went to war a great army would be destroyed. But he did not realize that the Oracle had not made it clear that it might be his own army that would be destroyed. My friends, the high priests have failed to inquire of the Oracle the answer to the question that the King of old forgot. A great army is to be destroyed. But they do not realize which army it is to be.

In New York State in 1930 there was a party which tried to ride two horses at the same time. The Republican Party had one foot, its candidate for Governor, on the wet horse, and the other foot, its candidate for Lieutenant Governor, on the dry horse. The voters of New York State saw that it was a circus stunt. Honest wets and honest drys — Democratic, Republican and Independent — were disgusted. They threw the ticket into the discard.

This year the Republican national leaders have tried the same circus stunt. The answer of the voters throughout the Nation will be precisely the same.

In the last analysis, my friends, the Prohibition issue comes down to a question of faith and confidence in leadership and in the words of leaders.

However people may differ as to the principle of Prohibition, national or State, they all will agree that a temporizing and insincere policy is disastrous not only to the cause of Prohibition, but to that of temperance as well. The present leadership stands convicted of attempting to evade and confuse this issue. The honest dry will, I know, honor more the honest wet than the shifty dry; and the anti-prohibitionist prefers, I know, the four-square dry to the uncertain wet. All will join in condemning a fearful and timid practice of evasion.

Here, as before, I emphasize that the deep question in this campaign is one of confidence in leadership — in leaders. The measure of the truth of what they say is what they have said; the measure of what they will do is what they have done.

Citation: John T. Woolley and Gerhard Peters, The American Presidency Project [online]. Santa Barbara, CA. Available from World Wide Web: ttp://www.presidency.ucsb.edu/ws/?pid=88395.

[CHAPTER 4.]

AN ACT

To provide revenue by the taxation of certain nonintoxicating liquor, and for other purposes.

Be it enacted by the Senate and House of Representatives of the United States of America in Congress assembled, That **(a)** there shall be levied and collected on all beer, lager beer, ale, porter, wine, similar fermented malt or vinous liquor, and fruit juice, containing one-half of 1 per centum or more of alcohol by volume, and not more than 3.2 per centum of alcohol by weight, brewed or manufactured and, on or after the effective date of this Act, sold, or removed for consumption or sale, within the United States, by whatever name such liquors or fruit juices may be called, a tax of $5 for every barrel containing not more than thirty-one gallons, and at a like rate for any other quantity or for the fractional parts of a barrel authorized and defined by law, to be collected under the provisions of existing law. The tax imposed by this section upon any beverage shall, if any tax is now imposed thereon by law, be in lieu of such tax from the time the tax imposed by this section takes effect. Nothing in this section shall in any manner affect the internal-revenue tax on beer, lager beer, ale, porter, wine, similar fermented malt or vinous liquor, or fruit juice, containing more than 3.2 per centum of alcohol by weight, or less than one-half of 1 per centum of alcohol by volume. As used in this section the term "United States" includes only the States, the Territories of Alaska and Hawaii, and the District of Columbia.

(b) Paragraph "First" of section 3244 of the Revised Statutes (U. S. C., title 26, sec. 202) is amended to read as follows:

"First. Brewers shall pay $1,000 in respect of each brewery. Every person who manufactures fermented liquors of any name or description for sale, from malt, wholly or in part, or from any substitute therefor, containing one-half of 1 per centum or more of alcohol by volume, shall be deemed a brewer."

(c) Nothing in this Act shall be construed as repealing any special tax or administrative provision of the internal revenue laws applicable in respect of any of the following containing one-half of 1 per centum or more of alcohol by volume and not more than 3.2

March 22, 1923.
[H.R. 3341.]
[Public, No. 3.]

Revenue tax provisions on certain nonintoxicating liquors.
Post, pp. 315, 467.
Alcoholic content.

Vol. 41, p. 308, amended.
U.S.C., p. 853.

Tax rate.

To be in lieu of present tax.

Higher or lower alcoholic strength.

Terms defined.

R.S. sec. 3244, p. 622.
U.S.C., p. 740.

Brewer's tax on each brewery.
Post, p. 315.
Brewer defined.

Laws not repealed.
Vol. 40, p. 1105; Vol. 45, p. 868.

148

per centum of alcohol by weight: Beer, ale, porter, wine, similar fermented malt or vinous liquor, or fruit juice.

SEC. 2. The second, third, and fourth paragraphs of section 37 of Title II of the National Prohibition Act, as amended and supplemented (U. S. C., title 27, secs. 58, 59, and 60), are hereby repealed. National Prohibition Act. Certain provisions repealed. Vol. 41, p. 318. U.S.C., p. 860. Acts not affected by. Post, p. 430.

SEC. 3. (a) Nothing in the National Prohibition Act, as amended and supplemented, shall apply to any of the following, or to any act or failure to act in respect of any of the following, containing not more than 3.2 per centum of alcohol by weight: Beer, ale, porter, wine, similar fermented malt or vinous liquor, or fruit juice; but the National Prohibition Act, as amended and supplemented, shall apply to any of the foregoing, or to any act or failure to act in respect of any of the foregoing, contained in bottles, casks, barrels, kegs, or other containers, not labeled and sealed as may be prescribed by regulations. Application to containers, not labeled, etc.

(b) The following Acts and parts of Acts shall be subject to a like limitation as to their application: Limitation of application further extended.

(1) The Act entitled "An Act to prohibit the sale, manufacture, and importation of intoxicating liquors in the Territory of Hawaii during the period of the war, except as hereinafter provided," approved May 23, 1918 (U. S. C., title 48, sec. 520); Hawaii. Vol. 40, p. 560. U.S.C., p. 1601. Post, p. 467.

(2) Section 2 of the Act entitled "An Act to provide a civil government for Porto Rico, and for other purposes," approved March 2, 1917; Puerto Rico. Vol. 39, p. 951. U.S.C., p. 1616.

(3) The Act entitled "An Act to prohibit the manufacture or sale of alcoholic liquors in the Territory of Alaska, and for other purposes," approved February 14, 1917 (U. S. C., title 48, secs. 261 to 291, both inclusive). Alaska. Vol. 39, p. 903. U.S.C., p. 1580. Post, p. 583.

(c) Nothing in section 5 of the Act entitled "An Act making appropriations for the service of the Post Office Department for the fiscal year ending June 30, 1918, and for other purposes," approved March 3, 1917, as amended and supplemented (U. S. C., title 18, sec. 341; Supp. VI, title 18, sec. 341), shall prohibit the deposit in or carriage by the mails of the United States, or the delivery by any postmaster or letter carrier, of any mail matter containing any advertisement of, or any solicitation of an order or orders for, any of the following containing not more than 3.2 per centum of alcohol by weight: Beer, ale, porter, wine, similar fermented malt or vinous liquor, or fruit juice. Advertisement, etc., by mail. Vol. 39, p. 1069; Vol. 41, p. 313. U.S.C., p. 483; Supp. VI, p. 242. Post, p. 316.

SEC. 4. (a) The manufacturer for sale of beer, ale, porter, wine, similar fermented malt or vinous liquor, or fruit juice, containing one-half of 1 per centum of alcohol by volume and not more than 3.2 per centum of alcohol by weight, shall, before engaging in business, secure a permit authorizing him to engage in such manufacture, which permit shall be obtained in the same manner as a permit under the National Prohibition Act, as amended and supplemented, to manufacture intoxicating liquor, and be subject to all the provisions of law relating to such a permit. Such permit may be issued to a manufacturer for sale of any such fermented malt or vinous liquor or fruit juice, containing less than one-half of 1 per centum of alcohol by volume, if he desires to take advantage of the provisions of paragraph (2) of subsection (b) of this section. No permit shall be issued under this section for the manufacture of fermented malt or vinous liquor or fruit juice in any State, Territory, or the District of Columbia, or political subdivision of any State or Territory, if such manufacture is prohibited by the law thereof. Permits to manufacture, etc. If containing less than one half of 1 per cent. Issue forbidden if local laws prohibit.

(b) (1) Such permit shall specify a maximum alcoholic content permissible for such fermented malt or vinous liquor or fruit juice at the time of withdrawal from the factory or other disposition, Specifications of permit.

which shall not be greater than 3.2 per centum of alcohol by weight, nor greater than the maximum alcoholic content permissible under the law of the State, Territory, or the District of Columbia, or the political subdivision of a State or Territory, in which such liquor or fruit juice is manufactured.

Reduction of excess alcoholic content.

(2) In such permit may be included permission to develop in the manufacture of such fermented malt or vinous liquor or fruit juice by the usual methods of fermentation and fortification or otherwise a liquid such as beer, ale, porter, wine, or fruit juice, of an alcoholic content in excess of the maximum specified in the permit; but before any such liquid is withdrawn from the factory or otherwise disposed of the alcoholic content shall, if in excess of the maximum specified in the permit, be reduced, under such regulations as may be pre-

Removal for reduction, under bond.

scribed, to or below such maximum; but such liquid may be removed and transported, under bond and under such regulations as may be prescribed, from one bonded plant or warehouse to another for the purpose of having the percentage of alcohol reduced to the maximum specified in the permit by dilution or extraction. Such liquids may be developed, under permit under the National Prohibition Act, as amended and supplemented, by persons other than manufacturers of beverages containing not more than 3.2 per centum of alcohol by weight, and sold to such manufacturers for conversion into such

Tax.

beverages. The alcohol removed from such liquid, if evaporated, and not condensed and saved, shall not be subject to tax; if saved, it

Credit allowed.

shall be subject to the same law as other alcoholic liquors. Credit shall be allowed on the tax due on any alcohol so saved to the amount of any tax paid upon distilled spirits or brandy used in the fortification of the liquor from which the same is saved.

Fortified wines.

(3) When fortified wines are made and used for the production of nonbeverage alcohol, and dealcoholized wines containing not more than 3.2 per centum of alcohol by weight, no tax shall be assessed or paid on the spirits used in such fortification, and such dealcoholized wines produced under the provisions of this section, whether carbonated or not, shall be subject to the tax imposed by section 1.

Burden of proof.

(4) In any case where the manufacturer is charged with manufacturing or selling for beverage purposes any beer, ale, porter, wine, similar fermented malt or vinous liquor, or fruit juice, containing more than 3.2 per centum of alcohol by weight, the burden of proof shall be on such manufacturer to show that the liquid so manufactured or sold contained no more than 3.2 per centum of alcohol by weight. In any case where a manufacturer, who has been permitted to develop a liquid such as beer, ale, porter, wine, or fruit juice, containing more than the maximum alcoholic content specified in the permit, is charged with failure to reduce the alcoholic content to or below such maximum before such liquid was withdrawn from the factory or otherwise disposed of, then the burden of proof shall be on such manufacturer to show that the alcoholic content of such liquid so manufactured, sold, withdrawn, or otherwise disposed

Expense of analysis.

of did not exceed the maximum specified in the permit. In any suit or proceeding involving the alcoholic content of any beverage, the reasonable expense of analysis of such beverage shall be taxed as costs in the case.

Penalty provisions.

(c) Whoever engages in the manufacture for sale of beer, ale, porter, wine, similar fermented malt or vinous liquor, or fruit juice, without such permit if such permit is required, or violates any permit issued to him, shall be subject to the penalties and proceedings provided by law in the case of similar violations of the National Prohibition Act, as amended and supplemented.

(d) This section shall have the same geographical application as the National Prohibition Act, as amended and supplemented. Geographical application.

SEC. 5. Except to the extent provided in section 4 (b) (2), nothing in section 1 or 4 of this Act shall be construed as in any manner authorizing or making lawful the manufacture of any beer, ale, porter, wine, similar fermented malt or vinous liquor, or fruit juice, which at the time of sale or removal for consumption or sale contains more than 3.2 per centum of alcohol by weight. Excessive alcoholic content prohibited.

SEC. 6. In order that beer, ale, porter, wine, similar fermented malt or vinous liquor, and fruit juice, containing 3.2 per centum or less of alcohol by weight, may be divested of their interstate character in certain cases, the shipment or transportation thereof in any manner or by any means whatsoever, from one State, Territory, or District of the United States, or place noncontiguous to but subject to the jurisdiction thereof, or from any foreign country, into any State, Territory, or District of the United States, or place noncontiguous to but subject to the jurisdiction thereof, which fermented malt or vinous liquor or fruit juice, is intended, by any person interested therein, to be received, possessed, sold, or in any manner used, either in the original package or otherwise, in violation of any law of such State, Territory, or District of the United States, or place noncontiguous to but subject to the jurisdiction thereof, is hereby prohibited. Nothing in this section shall be construed as making lawful the shipment or transportation of any liquor or fruit juice the shipment or transportation of which is prohibited by the Act of March 1, 1913, entitled "An Act divesting intoxicating liquors of their interstate character in certain cases" (U. S. C., Supp. VI, title 27, sec. 122). Interstate shipment.

Transportation into State contrary to its laws.
Vol. 37, p. 699.
U.S.C. Supp. VI, p. 598.

SEC. 7. Whoever orders, purchases, or causes beer, ale, porter, wine, similar fermented malt or vinous liquor, or fruit juice, containing 3.2 per centum or less of alcohol by weight, to be transported in interstate commerce, except for scientific, sacramental, medicinal, or mechanical purposes, into any State, Territory, or the District of Columbia, the laws of which State, Territory, or District prohibit the manufacture or sale therein of such fermented malt or vinous liquor or fruit juice for beverage purposes, shall be fined not more than $1,000 or imprisoned not more than six months, or both; and for any subsequent offense shall be imprisoned for not more than one year. If any person is convicted under this section any permit issued to him shall be revoked. Nothing in this section shall be construed as making lawful the shipment or transportation of any liquor or fruit juice the shipment or transportation of which is prohibited by section 5 of the Act entitled "An Act making appropriations for the service of the Post Office Department for the fiscal year ending June 30, 1918, and for other purposes," approved March 3, 1917, as amended and supplemented (U. S. C., Supp. VI, title 27, sec. 123). Penalty for violation.

Revocation of permit.
Advertisements, etc.

Vol. 39, p. 1069.
U.S.C. Supp. VI, p. 598.

SEC. 8. Any offense committed, or any right accrued, or any penalty or obligation incurred, or any seizure or forfeiture made, prior to the effective date of this Act, under the provisions of the National Prohibition Act, as amended and supplemented, or under any permit or regulation issued thereunder, may be prosecuted or enforced in the same manner and with the same effect as if this Act had not been enacted. Preexisting offenses, rights, etc.

SEC. 9. This Act shall take effect on the expiration of fifteen days after the date of its enactment, except that permits referred to under section 4 may be issued at any time after the date of enactment, and except that liquor taxable under section 1 may be removed prior to the effective date of this Act for bottling and storage on the permit premises until such date and when so removed shall be subject to tax at the rate provided by section 1. Effective date.

SEC. 10. If any provision of this Act, or the application thereof to any person or circumstances, is held invalid, the remainder of the Act, and the application of such provision to other persons or circumstances, shall not be affected thereby. Separability clause.

Approved, March 22, 1933.

Governor Ritchie's Message

TO THE

Extraordinary Session of the General Assembly of Maryland

CONVENED NOVEMBER 23, 1933.

Members of the General Assembly of Maryland:

It becomes my duty under the authority imposed upon me by the Constitution to call your Honorable body into special or extraordinary session in order to consider and act upon the following subjects:

1. The regulation and control of intoxicating liquors and beverages within this State, and all questions incident thereto, after the repeal of the Eighteenth Amendment to the Constitution of the United States.

2. Legislation necessary to enable the political units of the State to accept or receive the benefit of any laws or decrees of the Federal Government, now or hereafter enacted or promulgated, on the subject of Public Works and Construction, or Relief of the people from Unemployment, or any subject connected with or related to the Recovery program of the Federal Government.

3. Legislation necessary to enable any political unit of the State to provide for the relief and aid of its people from Unemployment.

4. Legislation to promote and expedite the administration of criminal justice and procedure in the State of Maryland, including all related matters.

5. Legislation on the subject of Banks and Banking made necessary or appropriate by Federal legislation on the same subject.

6. Legislation pertaining to the fiscal affairs and public revenues of the State.

BEER, WINE AND LIQUOR CONTROL
IN MARYLAND

Preliminary Remarks

Recently I prepared and distributed certain recommendations relating to the control and supervision of beer, wine and liquor in the State, in the hope that this might be helpful to the members of the Legislature, and furnish the basis of discussion by them and others interested in the preparation of a sound and effective law for Maryland on this very difficult and debatable subject.

Since then I have had the benefit of a good many viewpoints in regard to this plan, and there are respects in which it seems to me that the plan can be improved.

The principal changes I would suggest relate to the subject of wines. I think that the light or natural wines should be excluded from the proposed excise tax. This tax should apply to distilled spirits and to the sparkling and fortified wines, but it should not apply to the light and natural wines or to beer.

I think also that provision should be made for retailing light wines along with beer for on-premise consumption, in those political units which wish to have the right to do this, instead of requiring light wines to be retailed with liquor.

Further consideration has also indicated certain changes which should be made in the several license classifications, in order to make more complete and effective the local option privileges which are the basis of the plan.

I am reproducing in this Message my previous recommendations on the subject, with the above and perhaps some other changes embodied.

Even as now submitted, however, the plan and its details are intended to be subjected to thorough scrutiny and con-

153

sideration at your hands, and to revision where that seems desirable.

I recognize fully that any control plan to be effective must conform to the wants and must receive the sanction of the people of the political unit to which it applies. This is vital, and such merit as the plan here recommended may have, lies largely in the fact that it does away with the innumerable, diverse and often confusing local laws which have hitherto always been resorted to on this subject, and at the same time the plan does enable each political unit of the State to have whatever class or classes of license its people want, under administrative and regulatory provisions which will be uniform with respect to the particular class or classes of license any political unit sees fit to adopt.

THE PROBLEM OF LIQUOR CONTROL

National Prohibition was given a full and fair trial. It failed, and the task now is to work for Temperance, and devise a method of liquor control which will do away with the evils National Prohibition brought about without re-establishing the evils which brought about National Prohibition.

This is no easy task. The liquor problem has been with us through the centuries. There is no magic solution of it. No matter what is done now, there will be many people who will think something else should have been done. On more than one vital point the decision will necessarily be not the ideal one, but the selection of the better of two alternatives. The problem is real, and our approach to it must be realistic.

It may take long to regain the ground lost during the Prohibition era. In that era new conditions arose,—new habits, new temptations, new crimes, new social perils,— which now make the task much more difficult.

Whatever plan of control is adopted, it must of necessity be in some measure experimental in nature. Experience will suggest faults and improvements, and for this reason I recommend that between the close of the forthcoming special session of the Legislature and the regular session which will convene in January 1935 a thorough study be made of the administration and practical operation of the systems adopted in other States.

One vital lesson to be drawn from National Prohibition is that prohibitions of what people do not consider inherently wrong will not work. The life of law is its enforcement, and law without sanction cannot be enforced. The lack of popular sanction was one of the reasons why National Prohibition failed. The new system should not repeat that defect. It should contain no requirements which do not conform to the standards and social convictions of the people to whom it applies.

The repeal of the Eighteenth Amendment returns the liquor question to the States for each State to decide as it deems best for its own people. The State, however, is not homogeneous enough for one uniform law on this subject. At least, Maryland is not. Half our population lives in the great industrial center of Baltimore City. The other half lives in smaller cities, in towns, villages, rural and county districts, and in the environment of our great expanse of bay and rivers. Throughout these localities conditions differ and popular opinions and sanctions differ. It is not possible to reconcile them.

LOCAL OPTION THE ONLY SOLUTION

I see no possible solution of the liquor question in this State except on the principle of local option. This is in accord with Maryland traditions and practices. In that way only can we adapt the new plan to the needs and conditions of the various localities of the State, and put behind it that sanction of popular approval in each locality which is necessary for its enforcement.

I have considered asking the legislative representatives of Baltimore City and each county to come to the Special Session with their own control plans for their respective political units. I am advised that some of them will do this, but that others may not, and it has seemed to me on the whole best that the Governor should submit to the Legislature a plan for liquor and beer control,—as was done in the case of beer control alone,—which the political units

155

of the State may, if their representatives so desire, accept in whole or accept in part, rather than adopt a large number of separate, different and unrelated local laws for their own.

EACH POLITICAL UNIT TO HAVE ONLY WHAT ITS PEOPLE WANT

Accordingly, I am suggesting consideration of a plan which will classify separately each of the various kinds of licenses for the sale of beer, wines or liquors, and give the right to Baltimore City and to each one of the counties to adopt all of these forms of license if they so desire, or to reject them all if they desire to do that, or to reject some and adopt others.

The proposed bill will be elastic enough to enable each political unit to select the particular kind of license or licenses which will be permitted within its limits, and the administrative machinery, the license fees, and the provisions for supervision and regulation will all, if acceptable, be on a uniform basis.

To be more specific, the legislation I am proposing will submit the following general forms of license:

1. Manufacturers and Wholesalers.

2. Beer.
   Off Premise consumption only.
   Consumption on the Premises.

3. Beer and Light Wines.
   Off Premise consumption only.
   Consumption on the Premises.

4. Liquor, Wines and Beer.
   Off Premise consumption only.
   Consumption on the Premises.

Assuming the conditions and regulations of the bill to be satisfactory, then its passage will enable Baltimore City and any county of the State to permit all of the above forms of license. Any political unit, however, which is not satisfied with any one or more of these forms of license, can through

156

at all that the practice would prevail. Legal beer has proven a great boon to the people. It has supplanted liquor and eliminated drunkenness and near-beer speakeasies to an amazing degree. It satisfies without harming, and it is quite probable that under liberal conditions such as surround it now the sale of beer alone may prove increasingly popular and profitable. At all events the experience we have had with legal beer has been so healthy and beneficial, that I believe the great majority of people all over the State want the sale of beer to continue on the present basis, and do not want it sold only where liquor is sold. At least a real effort to preserve the benefits which come from the sale of beer alone should be made.

WINES

The natural or light wines are the home drink of a great many of our people, particularly those of foreign origin or extraction. As commonly used they are not harmful, or at least very rarely so, and they should be encouraged.

At first I was concerned whether a workable distinction could be made, particularly from the law enforcement angle, between the natural wines, on the one hand, and the sparkling and the fortified wines, on the other. I was also concerned as to the desirability of permitting the consumption of wine in an establishment which is not licensed to sell liquor, but is licensed to sell beer for on premise consumption. It seemed to me that it might be inadvisable to permit an "On Sale" beer licensee to have the right to sell wines also for on premise consumption, in view of the fact that even the natural wines have a higher alcoholic content than beer.

On reflection, however, I think that both these objections can and should be met.

The distinction between natural and fortified wines is well understood and recognized in law, and need give, I believe, no actual difficulty in practice, with regard to the enforcement provisions of the State law.

The second objection can be met by providing for what may be known as a Beer and Light Wine "On Sale" license, that is, a license which will permit the holder to sell both its representatives in the Legislature add a proviso to the bill that such licenses shall not be applicable in such political unit, or in some locality thereof, and in that case only the other licenses not excepted would apply. And any political unit desiring none of the specified licenses, can in the same way exempt itself from all of them.

In this way, any political unit, such as Baltimore City, which wishes to do so, can permit licenses for beer, wine, and liquor, for consumption both on and off the premises, subject to the prescribed regulations. Any county which wants to permit beer alone, can do so by exempting itself from the other license provisions. Any county which wishes to permit the sale of beer and light wines, but no liquor, can do so in the same way. Any county which wants to permit the consumption of beer on the premises, and also the sale of liquor in bottles for consumption off the premises only, can do that by simply exempting itself from the other license provisions. And so on. Each political unit can then have exactly what it wants and discard what it does not want, and the law will be uniform throughout the State with respect to every form of license permitted.

Before submitting the details of the plan herein suggested, certain fundamental questions must be settled.

SEPARATION OF BEER AND LIQUOR

The obvious difference between beer and liquor is recognized in every State control law which has so far been passed, or which is under consideration. It seems to me that it should be recognized in Maryland by providing a low license fee and liberal conditions for the retail sale of beer and a much higher license fee and stricter conditions for the retail sale of liquor.

To this the objection is made that the sale of beer alone is not generally profitable, and that an establishment where beer alone is sold cannot compete with an establishment where liquor is sold, and the former would resort to the illicit selling of liquor.

Strict supervision should reduce any such unlawful practice to a minimum, but aside from that there is no certainty beer and light or natural wines for consumption on the premises. Any political unit which does not want this to be permitted, but does want to permit the on-premise consumption of beer alone, can do so by simply exempting itself from the Beer and Light Wine "On Sale" license, and accepting only the Beer "On Sale" license.

The fortified wines and the sparkling wines I would still classify with liquors for "On Sale" purposes.

It seems to me also that not only beer, but the natural wines as well, should be excepted from the payment of the excise tax, so that the excise tax would apply only to distilled spirits, fortified wines and sparkling wines.

RIGHT TO DRINK ON THE PREMISES

This problem is not presented by beer but by liquor. It involves greater differences of opinion than any other problem in the whole subject.

There is no doubt that what are called the "evils of the old saloon" did much to bring about National Prohibition. No one should want to bring those "evils" back again. At the same time we must realize that human nature cannot be changed, and that if the man who can afford to belong to a club or frequent a hotel or restaurant is to get his drink and his sociable and congenial company there,—as he undoubtedly will,—then the man who cannot afford those facilities is going to get his drink and his sociable and congenial company somewhere else and under some other conditions. He will not, moreover, want to be told that he must buy a whole bottle and take it home. I am by no means sure that this would promote temperance, but aside from that a man may want a drink and not a bottle, and he may not have the price of a bottle.

It is vital that this question be approached realistically. To my mind it presents two alternatives. I believe that in certain industrial environments the choice is going to be between a place where the law permits you to drink your drink where you buy it, under suitable and strict regulations and supervision and under decent and proper surroundings, or an unlawful, illicit and unregulated speakeasy or blind

159

In this situation the answer, I think, is clear. The option to permit consumption on the premises should be allowed in any political unit of the State where the conditions are such that the people desire it. This should only be under regulations which will not revive the evils of the old time saloon, but which will permit the individual to drink his drink where he buys it under legal limitations and conditions, capable of enforcement and actually enforced.

I think the provisions in the proposed bill for "On Sale" licenses in communities which want them, fully meet the above requirements, and I may add that I can see no practical difference between taking a drink sitting down and taking one standing up, and no particular efficacy in requiring one to eat a meal because he wants a drink.

MANUFACTURE

Impressive arguments for State dispensaries and State breweries can be made. The principal ones seem to be that State manufacture would "take the profit out of liquor", so that dealers and retailers could not exploit the public, and the State would get more revenue, and that the quality of beverages would be improved.

I do not discount the force of these arguments, but it would be a very radical thing for this State to undertake the business of manufacturing beer, wines and liquor, or to assume the wholesale distribution of them. Personally I am not disposed to recommend the venture, at least until more conservative methods which give promise of success receive a full and fair trial.

DATE OF REPEAL OF THE EIGHTEENTH AMENDMENT

BY THE PRESIDENT OF THE UNITED STATES OF AMERICA

A PROCLAMATION

Eighteenth Amend-
ment to the Constitu-
tion, repeal.
Preamble.
Statutory citation.
Vol. 47, p. 1625.

WHEREAS the Congress of the United States in second session of the Seventy-second Congress, begun at Washington on the fifth day of December in the year one thousand nine hundred and thirty-two, adopted a resolution in the words and figures following, to wit:

"JOINT RESOLUTION

Proposing an amendment to the Constitution of the United States.

"*Resolved by the Senate and House of Representatives of the United States of America in Congress assembled (two-thirds of each House concurring therein)*, That the following article is hereby proposed as an amendment to the Constitution of the United States, which shall be valid to all intents and purposes as part of the Constitution when ratified by conventions in three-fourths of the several States:

"'Article—

"'Section 1. The eighteenth article of amendment to the Constitution of the United States is hereby repealed.

"'Sec. 2. The transportation or importation into any State, Territory, or possession of the United States for delivery or use therein of intoxicating liquors, in violation of the laws thereof, is hereby prohibited.

"'Sec. 3. This article shall be inoperative unless it shall have been ratified as an amendment to the Constitution by conventions in the several States, as provided in the Constitution, within seven years from the date of the submission hereof to the States by the Congress.'"

National Industrial
Recovery Act.
Ante, p. 208.

WHEREAS section 217 (a) of the act of Congress entitled "AN ACT To encourage national industrial recovery, to foster competition, and to provide for the construction of certain useful public works, and for other purposes", approved June 16, 1933, provides as follows:

"Sec. 217. (a) The President shall proclaim the date of—

(1) the close of the first fiscal year ending June 30 of any year after the year 1933, during which the total receipts of the United States (excluding public-debt receipts) exceed its total expenditures (excluding public-debt expenditures other than those chargeable against such receipts), or

(2) the repeal of the eighteenth amendment to the Constitution,

whichever is the earlier."

PROCLAMATIONS, 1933.

WHEREAS it appears from a certificate issued December 5, 1933, by the Acting Secretary of State that official notices have been received in the Department of State that on the fifth day of December 1933 conventions in 36 States of the United States, constituting three fourths of the whole number of the States had ratified the said repeal amendment;

NOW, THEREFORE, I, FRANKLIN D. ROOSEVELT, President of the United States of America, pursuant to the provisions of section 217 (a) of the said act of June 16, 1933, do hereby proclaim that the eighteenth amendment to the Constitution of the United States was repealed on the fifth day of December 1933.

December 5, 1933, proclaimed repeal date.

FURTHERMORE, I enjoin upon all citizens of the United States and upon others resident within the jurisdiction thereof to cooperate with the Government in its endeavor to restore greater respect for law and order, by confining such purchases of alcoholic beverages as they may make solely to those dealers or agencies which have been duly licensed by State or Federal license.

Cooperation for greater respect for law and order enjoined.

Observance of this request, which I make personally to every individual and every family in our Nation, will result in the consumption of alcoholic beverages which have passed Federal inspection, in the break-up and eventual destruction of the notoriously evil illicit liquor traffic, and in the payment of reasonable taxes for the support of Government and thereby in the superseding of other forms of taxation.

I call specific attention to the authority given by the twenty-first amendment to the Government to prohibit transportation or importation of intoxicating liquors into any State in violation of the laws of such State.

I ask the whole-hearted cooperation of all our citizens to the end that this return of individual freedom shall not be accompanied by the repugnant conditions that obtained prior to the adoption of the eighteenth amendment and those that have existed since its adoption. Failure to do this honestly and courageously will be a living reproach to us all.

I ask especially that no State shall by law or otherwise authorize the return of the saloon either in its old form or in some modern guise.

The policy of the Government will be to see to it that the social and political evils that have existed in the pre-prohibition era shall not be revived nor permitted again to exist. We must remove forever from our midst the menace of the bootlegger and such others as would profit at the expense of good government, law, and order.

I trust in the good sense of the American people that they will not bring upon themselves the curse of excessive use of intoxicating liquors, to the detriment of health, morals, and social integrity.

The objective we seek through a national policy is the education of every citizen towards a greater temperance throughout the Nation.

IN WITNESS WHEREOF, I have hereunto set my hand and caused the seal of the United States to be affixed.

DONE at the City of Washington this fifth day of December, in the year of our Lord nineteen hundred and thirty-three, and of [SEAL] the Independence of the United States of America the one hundred and fifty-eighth.

FRANKLIN D ROOSEVELT

By the President:
WILLIAM PHILLIPS
Acting Secretary of State.

[No. 2065]

162

FEDERAL ALCOHOL ADMINISTRATION ACT OF 1935 [EXCERPTS]

§ 203. Unlawful businesses without permit; application to State agency

In order effectively to regulate interstate and foreign commerce in distilled spirits, wine, and malt beverages, to enforce the twenty-first amendment, and to protect the revenue and enforce the postal laws with respect tc distilled spirits, wine, and malt beverages:

(a) It shall be unlawful, except pursuant to a basic permit issued under this subchapter by the Secretary of the Treasury—

(1) to engage in the business of importing into the United States distilled spirits, wine, or malt beverages; or

(2) for any person so engaged to sell, offer or deliver for sale, contract to sell, or ship, in interstate or foreign commerce, directly or indirectly or through an affiliate, distilled spirits, wine, or malt beverages so imported.

(b) It shall be unlawful, except pursuant to a basic permit issued under this subchapter by the Secretary of the Treasury—

(1) to engage in the business of distilling distilled spirits, producing wine, rectifying or blending distilled spirits or wine, or bottling, or warehousing and bottling, distilled spirits; or

(2) for any person so engaged to sell, offer or deliver for sale, contract to sell, or ship, in interstate or foreign commerce, directly or indirectly or through an affiliate, distilled spirits or wine so distilled, produced, rectified, blended, or bottled, or warehoused and bottled.

(c) It shall be unlawful, except pursuant to a basic permit issued under this subchapter by the Secretary of the Treasury—

(1) to engage in the business of purchasing for resale at wholesale distilled spirits, wine, or malt beverages; or

(2) for any person so engaged to receive or to sell, offer or deliver for sale, contract to sell, or ship, in interstate or foreign commerce, directly or indirectly or through an affiliate, distilled spirits, wine, or malt beverages so purchased.

This subsection shall take effect July 1, 1936.

This section shall not apply to any agency of a State or political subdivision thereof or any officer or employee of any such agency, and no such agency or officer or employee shall be required to obtain a basic permit under this subchapter.

§ 204. Permits

(a) Who entitled thereto

The following persons shall, on application therefor, be entitled to a basic permit:

(1) Any person who, on May 25, 1935, held a basic permit as distiller, rectifier, wine producer, or importer issued by an agency of the Federal Government.

(2) Any other person unless the Secretary of the Treasury finds

(A) that such person (or in case of a corporation, any of its officers, directors, or principal stockholders) has, within five years prior to the date of application, been convicted of a felony under Federal or State law or has, within three years prior to date of application, been convicted of a misdemeanor under any Federal law relating to liquor, including the taxation thereof; or

(B) that such person is, by reason of his business experience, financial standing, or trade connections, not likely to commence operations within a reasonable period or to maintain such operations in conformity with Federal law; or

(C) that the operations proposed to be conducted by such person are in violation of the law of the State in which they are to be conducted.

(b) Refusal of permit; hearing

If upon examination of any application for a basic permit the Secretary of the Treasury has reason to believe that the applicant is not entitled to such permit, he shall notify the applicant thereof and, upon request by the applicant, afford him due notice and opportunity for hearing on the application. If the Secretary of the Treasury, after affording such notice and opportunity for hearing, finds that the applicant is not entitled to a basic permit hereunder, he shall by order deny the application stating the findings which are the basis for his order.

(c) Form of application

The Secretary of the Treasury shall prescribe the manner and form of all applications for basic permits (including the facts to be set forth therein) and the form of all basic permits, and shall specify in any basic permit the authority conferred by the permit and the conditions thereof in accordance with the provisions of this subchapter. To the extent deemed necessary by the Secretary of the Treasury for the efficient administration of this subchapter, separate applications and permits shall be required by the Secretary of the Treasury with respect to distilled spirits, wine, and malt beverages, and the various classes thereof, and with respect to the various classes of persons entitled to permits hereunder. The issuance of a basic permit under this subchapter shall not operate to deprive the United States of any remedy for any violation of law.

(d) Conditions

A basic permit shall be conditioned upon compliance with the requirements of section 205 of this title (relating to unfair competition and unlawful practices) and of section 206 of this title (relating to bulk sales and bottling), with the twenty-first amendment and laws relating to the enforcement thereof, and with all other Federal laws relating to distilled spirits, wine, and malt beverages, including taxes with respect thereto.

(e) Revocation, suspension, and annulment

A basic permit shall by order of the Secretary of the Treasury, after due notice and opportunity for hearing to the permittee,

(1) be revoked, or suspended for such period as the Secretary of the Treasury deems appropriate, if the Secretary finds that the permittee has wilfully violated any of the conditions thereof, provided that for a first violation of the conditions thereof the permit shall be subject to suspension only; or

(2) be revoked if the Secretary finds that the permittee has not engaged in the operations authorized by the permit for a period of more than two years; or

(3) be annulled if the Secretary finds that the permit was procured through fraud, or misrepresentation, or concealment of material fact. The order shall state the findings which are the basis for the order.

(f) Service of orders

Orders of the Secretary with respect to any denial of application, suspension, revocation, annulment, or other proceedings, shall be served

(1) in person by any officer or employee of the Secretary designated by him or any internal revenue or customs officer authorized by the Secretary for the purpose, or

(2) by mailing the order by registered mail, addressed to the applicant or respondent at his last known address in the records of the Secretary.

(g) Duration

A basic permit shall continue in effect until suspended, revoked, or annulled as provided herein, or voluntarily surrendered; except that

(1) if leased, sold, or otherwise voluntarily transferred, the permit shall be automatically terminated thereupon, and

(2) if transferred by operation of law or if actual or legal control of the permittee is acquired, directly or indirectly, whether by stock-ownership or in any other manner, by any person, then such permit shall be automatically terminated at the expiration of thirty days thereafter: Provided, That if within such thirty-day period application for a new basic permit is made by the transferee or permittee, respectively, then the outstanding basic permit shall continue in effect until such application is finally acted on by the Secretary of the Treasury.

(h) Appeal; procedure

An appeal may be taken by the permittee or applicant for a permit from any order of the Secretary of the Treasury denying an application for, or suspending, revoking, or annulling, a basic permit. Such appeal shall be taken by filing, in the court of appeals of the United States within any circuit wherein such person resides or has his principal place of business, or in the United States Court of Appeals for the District of Columbia, within sixty days after the entry of such order, a written petition praying that the order of the Secretary be modified or set aside in whole or in part. A copy of such petition shall be forthwith transmitted by the clerk of the court to the Secretary, or any officer designated by him for that purpose, and thereupon the Secretary shall file in the court the record upon which the order complained of was entered, as provided in section 2112 of title 28. Upon the filing of such petition such court shall have exclusive jurisdiction to affirm, modify, or set aside such order, in whole or in part. No objection to the order of the Secretary shall be considered by the court unless such objection shall have been urged before the Secretary or unless there were reasonable grounds for failure so to do. The finding of the Secretary as to the facts, if supported by substantial evidence, shall be conclusive. If any party shall apply to the court for leave to adduce additional evidence, and shall show to the satisfaction of the court that such additional evidence is material and that there were reasonable grounds for failure to adduce such evidence in the proceeding before the Secretary, the court may order such additional evidence to be taken before the Secretary and to be adduced upon the hearing in such manner and upon such terms and conditions as to the court may seem proper. The Secretary may modify his findings as to the facts by reason of the additional evidence so taken, and he shall file with the court such modified or new findings, which, if supported by substantial evidence, shall be conclusive, and his recommendation, if any, for the modification or setting aside of the original order. The judgment and decree of the court affirming, modifying, or setting aside, in whole or in part, any such order of the Secretary shall be final, subject to review by the Supreme Court of the United States upon certiorari or certification as provided in section 1254 of title 28. The commencement of proceedings under this subsection shall, unless specifically ordered by the court to the contrary, operate as a stay of the Secretary's order.

(i) Limitation

No proceeding for the suspension or revocation of a basic permit for violation of any condition thereof relating to compliance with Federal law shall be instituted by the Secretary more than eighteen months after conviction of the violation of Federal law, or, if no conviction has been had, more than three years after the violation occurred; and no basic permit shall be suspended or revoked for a violation of any such condition thereof if the alleged violation of Federal law has been compromised by any officer of the Government authorized to compromise such violation.

206. Bulk sales and bottling

(a) Offenses

It shall be unlawful for any person—

(1) To sell or offer to sell, contract to sell, or otherwise dispose of distilled spirits in bulk except, under regulations of the Secretary of the Treasury, for export or to the following, or to import distilled spirits in bulk except, under such regulations, for sale to or for use by the following: A distiller, rectifier of distilled spirits, person operating a bonded warehouse qualified under the internal -revenue laws or a class 8 bonded warehouse qualified under the customs laws, a winemaker for the fortification of wines, a proprietor of an industrial alcohol plant, or an agency of the United States or any State or political subdivision thereof.

(2) To sell or offer to sell, contract to sell, or otherwise dispose of warehouse receipts for distilled spirits in bulk unless such warehouse receipts require that the warehouseman shall package such distilled spirits, before delivery, in bottles labeled and marked in accordance with law, or deliver such distilled spirits in bulk only to persons to whom it is lawful to sell or otherwise dispose of distilled spirits in bulk.

(3) To bottle distilled spirits unless the bottler is a person to whom it is lawful to sell or otherwise dispose of distilled spirits in bulk.

(b) Penalty

Any person who violates the requirements of this section shall, upon conviction thereof, be fined not more than $5,000 or imprisoned for not more than one year or both, and shall forfeit to the United States all distilled spirits with respect to which the violation occurs and the containers thereof.

(c) "In bulk" defined

The term "in bulk" mean in containers having a capacity in excess of one wine gallon.

MENCKEN, RITCHIE AND PROHIBITION

Speech given before the Library Company of the Baltimore Bar, Feb. 8, 2011

by Marion Elizabeth Rodgers

Thank you for inviting me to be here this evening, in this beautiful and historic Courthouse. Mencken wrote about this building in 1899, when he was just starting out as a young reporter.

During those days, Mencken worked directly across the street, at the Baltimore Herald, a structure that held its own during the Great Baltimore Fire of 1904, and which Mencken said may have helped save this Courthouse from the flames. As a very young reporter, Mencken roamed the halls of this building, and, as one judge recalled, "pestered me with unanswerable questions."

So, it gives me great pleasure to be here in this building with all of you tonight. I note that, after this talk, you will also be having a wine reception. On such occasions of happy conviviality, I am reminded of one of Mencken's favorite doctrines, that "the whole world would be better if the human race was kept gently stewed" – which now brings me to the topic of this evening.

Throughout its history, Maryland has always taken pride in being an independent state. But at no other time was Maryland's independence better emphasized than during Prohibition. No one fought harder against Prohibition than H. L. Mencken, the colorful author and legendary journalist for the Baltimore Sunpapers, and Governor Albert Ritchie, Maryland's popular governor. Their stand against it made front page news.

Mencken saw Prohibition as a violation of a man's civil rights. In his arguments against it, Mencken cited the Bill of Rights. During the thirteen years that Prohibition remained in force, Mencken devoted at least 42 newspaper columns in the Baltimore Sunpapers to the subject; he wrote about it in his magazines, "The Smart Set" and "The

American Mercury." Prohibition is mentioned throughout his books, notably in his six volume collection of "Prejudices."

Governor Albert Ritchie took issue with Prohibition on legal grounds. Ritchie had been a lawyer, then served as Attorney General of Maryland. As Governor, he had improved the school system, balanced the budget and reduced taxes. His stand against the Ku Klux Klan made him popular among immigrants and African-Americans. Ritchie's stand against Prohibition was potentially a politically disastrous step. But it was one of the most dramatic things he had ever done. It raised him overnight from being a local celebrity to a national figure, and almost made him a nominee for President of the United States.

The story of how Mencken and Ritchie together turned the tide against Prohibition is what I will be speaking to all of you tonight.

You will be able to see the full story of Prohibition when Ken Burns comes out with his new documentary on the subject. There is a lot of Mencken in it. Because you should know that for Mencken, Prohibition was a ghastly torture. As Mencken described himself, " I am ombibulous. I drink every known alcoholic drink, and I enjoy them all."

Prohibition, said Mencken, was responsible for ruining classical Maryland dinners. As he put it, you just couldn't eat wild duck without having the proper wines or sherries. Served with water, he said, those meals were "as preposterous as beer without foam."

Another thing. He could hardly relax whenever he took a date to a restaurant – not only because liquor had become so expensive – but because of federal agents. His date was constantly in a state of nerves, thinking that at any moment, there was going to be a raid. As Mencken said, "The first effect of Prohibition will be to raise up impediments to marriage. Absolutely sober men will be harder to snare."

As for dining out at other people's homes – even this was no longer charming. You had to always be worried about the liquor supply of your host. Mencken said, "If drinks are served, one hesitates to gullet them freely." Then again, if drinks were not served, "one wishes one's host were in hell."

Many of the bottles in Mencken's own cellar were bought from his bootlegger in New York, who regularly made his grand entrance into Mencken's New York office and was greeted "like a visiting ambassador."

Bootleggers, wrote Mencken, were now taking on the dignity of well-to-do businessmen. The young men of Harvard, who formerly became stockbrokers, were now casting their eyes at the profession. "If I had a son," said Mencken, "I'd be tempted to let him try his gifts. A life of learning has got me nowhere."

Later, Mencken could be seen walking the streets of New York, toward the train headed for Baltimore, lugging a heavy suitcase of liquor, his body leaning to the side, looking like a boat in full sail, keeling against the wind.

This had its risks, as Mencken well knew. Bags could be searched on trains, people seized. A man might risk losing precious bottles of Scotch – and pay up to $500 on bail. All because, as Mencken said, "a vast horde of Prohibition spies" had been set loose upon the community – "spies whose livelihood consisted of making themselves a nuisance to their fellow citizens." "I make it a point," said Mencken, "to get up a bottle of 1902 Beaujolais every time I hear that another such slimy fellow has been murdered."

Back in Baltimore, Mencken hid his own bottles of booze in a small room, located in the basement of his home at Hollins Street. You can still see that room today – decked out with rows and rows of shelves.

He built in 1919, right before the onset of Prohibition. On the door he hung up a sign that read:

THIS VAULT IS PROTECTED
BY A DEVICE RELEASING CHLORINE GAS
UNDER 200 POUNDS PRESSURE.
ENTER IT AT YOUR OWN RISK.

In 1919, Mencken advised his readers to do the same. "See to your locks and chain bolts, and get a smallpox sign to hang on the door. Hire a confirmed diabetic to mount guard. Fill every third bottle with nitroglycerine, that heaven may swiftly welcome any righteous scoundrel who horns in." As Mencken wrote to Sinclair Lewis, he had enough bottles to keep him stewed for fifteen years.

Now, one should keep in mind, when Ritchie had been first elected governor in 1919, he had never mentioned Prohibition or the matter of states rights. During those years Ritchie's focus was on statistics, as he devoted himself to balancing the state budget.

Meanwhile, a new era had dawned for the Baltimore Sunpapers. Mencken had rejoined the staff. He, along with the publisher, hammered out a memorandum about the new direction the paper would go. One section of their memo dealt with "American Ideas" – in it they said how federal bureaucracies had interfered with the common rights of man. They also decided the editorial page would be less cautious from now on.

On January 16, 1920, when Prohibition officially began, Mencken, along with the rest of the staff, decided that every day they would have at least one editorial denouncing the new law. This was unique for that time. Most newspapers had abandoned the fight, thinking opposing Prohibition was a lost cause.

But not the Sun, especially the Evening Sun, which kept up a drumbeat against Prohibition. So did Mencken. His regular Monday column for the Evening Sun achieved national fame, making him, as one critic said, "one of the most volcanic newspapermen this country has ever known." Thanks to Mencken, and the new editorial policy, during the 1920s the Sunpapers had the reputation and cachet that the Washington Post acquired after Watergate. It was one of the first newspapers that the President read each morning. It was the out of town newspaper New Yorkers bought each day.

By this time, Ritchie had become a regular visitor to the Baltimore Sun offices. Mencken, along with his colleagues, spoke with Ritchie about the extent to which the federal government was destroying the concept of liberty. As one editor recalled, "Ritchie began to seize on these ideas."

Now something really wonderful happened.

Shortly after this, Ritchie attended the Governor's Conference in Washington, D.C. President Harding demanded that, when it came to Prohibition, all the states must enforce the law. All the governors sat silent. Except for Ritchie.

To the surprise of everyone in the room, Ritchie rose from his chair, and directly addressed the President. Prohibition, he said, was a drastic federal infringement on Maryland's state and personal rights. Liquor control was a matter for each state. It had to be settled by the will of its own people.

For this, Ritchie was accused of being un-American, an anarchist, and a traitor. But it brought Ritchie cheers in Maryland.

Behind the scenes, Ritchie used pressure to make Maryland the first state not to give in to the Anti-Saloon League. As a result, Maryland did not have a state enforcement act. Mencken celebrated the governor in his newspaper column, calling Ritchie "the first independent statesman that Maryland had seen since the Civil War," an opinion which, Governor Ritchie, had truly pleased his mother.

From now on, of the thousands of speeches Ritchie gave, almost 85% of them concentrated on States Rights. One of Ritchie's most famous speeches was one he gave

172

at the Jefferson Day banquet at the National Democratic Club. It attracted national attention and was reproduced in the Congressional Record.

Now you should know that Ritchie had already began sharing his speeches with Mencken and other editors of the Baltimore Sunpapers. One of the sentences of his most famous speech, describing the "incompetent, extravagant control radiating from Washington" sounds almost Menckenesque, especially the use of the word "radiating." Though we have no proof that Mencken helped Ritchie write his speeches, he certainly promoted them. "The fame of Maryland has got about the country," he said. "Governor Ritchie's speeches, at first sneered at and unattended, have gradually made their way into [various] newspapers. [As I travel across the country] I am asked about him almost as often as I am asked to have a drink."

Privately, Mencken wrote in his memoirs that much of Ritchie's success over Prohibition was thanks to the Baltimore Sunappers, which had supplied Ritchie with his ideas.

Well, it is true that the Ritchie's use of the term, the Maryland Free State, still proudly used to this day, was actually the invention of the editor Hamilton Owens, at the Baltimore Sunpapers.

At the height of the debate over Prohibition, a Republican congressman had denounced Maryland as a traitor to the union because it had refused to pass a State Enforcement Act. Owens wrote a mock-serious reply called "The Maryland Free State." Owens later decided not to print it, but the phrase, "Maryland Free State" was used in other editorials. Mencken took up the phrase. So did Governor Ritchie, who repeated it in all of his speeches and in his reelection campaign as governor, and won by an overwhelming majority – the first Maryland governor up until that time to return to a second term. Other newspapers and politicians also picked up the phrase, until the Maryland Free State became common usage.

But is not true, as Mencken said, that all of Ritchie's ideas came from the Sun. States Rights had always been a key factor in Ritchie's life. In fact, until he died, Ritchie had in his possession a speech defending States Rights that his father had delivered to the University of Virginia Law School in 1856. Ritchie had underlined key passages.

When it came to Constitutional development, Ritchie thought the United States fell into three periods. In the first period, lasting until the Civil War, Ritchie thought the nation had leaned too far to States Rights. The second, from the Civil War to World War I, was a balanced period. Now, said Ritchie, the growth of federal bureaus and commissions had been a burden on the taxpayer. It threatened to destroy individual rights.

As Ritchie confessed to a reporter during this time, he concentrated on states rights not only because he believed in them; he thought Prohibition was an issue that could unite Democrats and Republicans alike. As Ritchie well knew, polls showed a majority of voters were for Prohibition's repeal.

With the support of the Sunpapers and the people of Maryland, Ritchie continued to defy the federal government, so much so that in Baltimore, the years 1920 and 1933 had a character all of its own. Maryland was now one of the wettest states in the Union.

According to Sun reporter R. P. Harriss, Governor Ritchie had announced that places selling alcoholic beverages would not be bothered by state troopers – though they would have pay state tax. But because speakeasies didn't legally exist, they were declared to be cigar stores. Each speakeasy had a front room, with a glass counter, filled with cheap cigars. There would be a door with a window. When you knocked on the door, all you had to say was, "Joe sent me."

U. S. 1 was full of speakeasies. There were also many between Calvert and Broadway. None of them apparently served good wine. Many did provide soda to accompany any whiskey or gin you might have in your hip flask.

Baltimore 42-mile shoreline along the Chesapeake Bay was a perfect port for bootleggers, making it convenient for smuggling Cuban and Canadian liquor. Whiskey in Baltimore was plentiful. It came from illegal distillers from Western Maryland.

Even so, hard liquor was expensive for the average working stiff. There were ways to get around it. They say that if you had a friendly doctor, you could tell him you were feeling really run down. He would give you a prescription for some whiskey, which the druggist would fill out. If you look back at the ledgers of the old pharmacies, you will see that almost everybody during those days was apparently suffering from the same infirmity. But since you had to pay $2 for the prescription, and another $2 for the whiskey, well, the average person could not indulge in this remedy too often. You only did it if you were getting tired of bathtub gin. And since only the affluent could afford to drink hard liquor without risking blindness or death, most people stuck to beer.

Mencken began making his own, with the best German ingredients he could obtain, including dried yeast from the Lowenbrau brewery in Munich. On Sunday afternoons in West Baltimore, the German neighborhood where Mencken lived, you could smell malt and hops in the air as neighbors began brewing their beer. Each Sunday, Mencken would shoo his mother from the kitchen and begin cooking away. His very first attempt was bottled too soon, with the result that every single bottle he put out into the garden to cool suddenly exploded like a burst of gunfire, greatly alarming his neighbors.

Mencken and his friends shared their beer-making recipes. They were precise about what type of spring water they used, how much corn sugar to put in. Mencken's careful notes about his beer making still exist. In one entry he describes "a curious flocculent growth" – in other words, *a fungus* – growing on top of his ale. The guinea pigs for Mencken's experiments were his musical friends from the Saturday Night Club, who often met at Mencken's house to play music, eat crabs – and drink his beer. Sometimes they got sick to their stomachs and other times they got cheerfully boiled. But they drank it all the same.

175

Ah, life in Maryland was good in those days! As Mencken said, it was a place of sound and comfortable living. And all of this was thanks to Governor Ritchie. Alone among larger cities, Baltimore had little organized crime. Instead, it was quiet and orderly. The police went about their own business. The courts were not jammed with liquor cases. Federal agents were left to enforce Federal enactments on their own. And since the Feds found that they had no police protection in Baltimore, raids gradually became more infrequent.

Maryland, wrote Mencken, was one of the few states in which in the state's courts, the constitutional guarantees of the citizen were jealousy guarded. According to the Sun, Marylanders had achieved an ethnic unity. "The people of the Free State asked only to be let alone."

Mencken believed Ritchie's stand against Prohibition had been an influential contribution to the general political thought in the country. It had also encouraged none other than Governor Roosevelt of New York, who, by 1931, was beginning to toy with the idea of running for President.

During this period Mencken and Ritchie began meeting more regularly. They would sit up late, sometimes until 1:30 or 3:30 in the morning, eating pretzels and drinking, discussing Ritchie's possible presidential campaign for 1932. At that time, no one was sure that Roosevelt had the nomination in hand. Mencken advised Ritchie the way seemed clear.

To help Ritchie out, Mencken renewed his praise for him in the Sunpapers. "He has done as much as any man to make Prohibition disreputable, and he has done so sincerely," wrote Mencken. "It is a grand chance. He would make an excellent President....He is so intelligent as to make a sort of miracle in American public life." Mencken later said that if Ritchie had been elected President in 1932, the nation's problems would have been tackled with more common sense.

The 1932 Democratic convention proved to be a turning point for Ritchie. More than 100 thousand people greeted him when he arrived in Chicago – so many that Ritchie lost one of his shoes in the crush. Fans showered him with confetti. Delegates carried signs: "WIN WITH RITCHIE." In the hall, people cheered his name. Roosevelt's manager, James Farley, was so impressed that he offered Ritchie the place of Vice-President on the Roosevelt ticket. Ritchie refused.

Instead, he concentrated on his big speech against Prohibition. As Mencken advised, this was the issue on which he would win. The ovation lasted forty minutes. Although Ritchie's successful anti-Prohibition plank probably helped grease the way for Repeal, after a lot of politicking in the back rooms, as you know the nomination went to Roosevelt. After the general election, Mencken thought Ritchie might win a spot in Roosevelt's cabinet. Roosevelt never even considered it.

Disappointed, Ritchie later admitted how unwise he had been to reject the role of Vice President. He had been given a golden opportunity. His role in national affairs would not come again.

Meanwhile, in Maryland, the Depression grew worse. Ritchie complained to Mencken that the Federal government was handing out so much money, and so many states were accepting, that he could not see how Maryland could keep resisting federal aid and still be able to balance the state budget – though God knows, Maryland was practically the only state which had done so.

Although Mencken and Ritchie considered themselves lifelong Democrats, as the 1930s wore on, so did their dislike for the New Deal. To the end of their lives, they both believed balanced budgets and frugality were the way to solve economic problems.

As Social Darwinists, both Mencken and Ritchie believed the way to solve the economy was not to interfere. They continued to subscribe to the Jeffersonian idea that the best government was the one that governed least. Neither man ever questioned the

177

harmful effects of too little government intervention. Mencken and Ritchie were of the generation that had lived through the Depression of 1892 and 1893. No one at that time believed that the unemployment was the responsibility of the government.

But their resistance to Roosevelt came at a cost. During the Depression, the popularity of both men suffered. When Ritchie ran for his fifth term as governor, Mencken publicly supported him, for which Ritchie was grateful. "If all the world falls from you," Ritchie wrote to Mencken, "I will still be with you."

After Ritchie's defeat, he returned to practicing law, but not for long; he died a year later. He was mourned in the editorial pages of newspapers across the country. "If Maryland today is seen as a place of freedom and tolerance," they said, it was because of Ritchie's fight against Prohibition, and his championing of what many now regarded as "the lost cause" of States Rights.

As for Prohibition?

Well, it officially came to an end while Ritchie was still governor, on December 5, 1933. The legalization of beer came even sooner, almost immediately after Roosevelt was inaugurated. The "return to sanity" was set for midnight, April 7, 1933.

In gratitude, a local brewer sent Governor Ritchie several cases of beer, tied in bright ribbons. In arrived in Annapolis by motorcade. Ritchie did not join in the festivities. He remained in the Statehouse, working late.

In Baltimore, the manager of the Rennert Hotel invited Mencken to have the honor of being served the very first glass of legal beer. Across the country, H. L. Mencken was being hailed as the reporter who had worked hardest to bring about Prohibition's end.

That evening, the Rennert was packed. In the crowd was a young student from Johns Hopkins. He told me he went just because he wanted to see history being made. As the clock struck twelve, the bartender handed over the very first glass of beer over to Mencken.

"Here it goes!" said Mencken.

Everyone leaned forward, waiting to hear the verdict. Mencken tilted back his head, and drank it in one gulp.

"Not bad at all," he said. "Fill it again."

Not one arrest for drunkenness was made that night. For those who were there, no New Year's Eve celebration ever equaled that glorious evening. The photograph of Mencken drinking the first legal beer in the Maryland Free State was sent to millions around the world.

It was, as Mencken said, "an epochal event in the onward march of humanity. It is perhaps the first time in history that any of the essential liberties of man has been gained without the wholesale emission of blood."

Marion Elizabeth Rodgers is the author of <u>Mencken: The American Iconoclast</u> (Oxford, 2005, 2007). (C) Copyright 2011 Marion E. Rodgers

Pg 11 - 27 K -

180